To Become a Sage

NEO-CONFUCIAN STUDIES

TO BECOME A SAGE

The Ten Diagrams on Sage Learning
by Yi T'oegye

Translated, Edited, and with Commentaries by
Michael C. Kalton

Calligraphy for diagrams by Margaret C. Kalton

New York
Columbia University Press
1988

A grant from the Korea Research Foundation and matching funds from The Wichita State University have supported the publication expenses of this book.

Library of Congress Cataloging-in-Publication

Yi, Hwang, 1501–1570.
To become a sage.

(Neo-Confucian studies)
Translation of: Sŏnghak sipto.
Bibliography: p.
Includes index.
1. Yi, Hwang, 1501–1570. Sŏnghak sipto.
2. Neo-Confucianism—Korea. I. Kalton, Michael C.
II. Title. III. Series.
B5254.Y483S663813 1988 181′.09512 87-22413
ISBN 0-231-06410-1

Columbia University Press
New York Guildford, Surrey

Printed in the United States of America
c 9 8 7 6 5 4 3 2

Hardbound editions of Columbia University Press are Smyth-sewn and printed on permanent and durable acid-free paper

Book design by J.S. Roberts

To
Margaret, Max, and Annaka
Always my wellspring

NEO-CONFUCIAN STUDIES

Contents

Illustrations

Translator's Preface

Works in the Korean Neo-Confucian tradition are unrepresented in western language translations. As a work generally considered to be the masterpiece of Korea's leading philosopher, Yi Hwang (T'oegye), the *Ten Diagrams on Sage Learning* is an obvious choice to begin the process of making the original works of this tradition more accessible to a western audience. Although it is a relatively short work, it is a full and systematic presentation of both the philosophical framework and the practical application to spiritual self-cultivation of the orthodox Ch'eng-Chu school which predominated in China, Korea, and Japan. Thus it may well serve to introduce serious students to Neo-Confucianism as such, as well as present valuable material for specialists interested in learning more about the particular Korean development of this rich tradition.

Each chapter of translation is followed by a commentary that contains both my remarks and considerable additional material translated from T'oegye's other works. Each commentary supplies a background of basic Neo-Confucian ideas that T'oegye could presume his audience to understand, and also expands certain ideas and topics related to the text so that the reader can see their particular shape or role in the overall context of T'oegye's thought and the Korean milieu. These commentaries have been divided by topic to facilitate consultation.

Neo-Confucian thought employs a number of terms that bear a denotation or connotation that cannot be adequately rendered by any single English term. A brief discussion of the most important of these is presented in the Appendix on Terminology. Readers unfamiliar with Neo-Confucian thought would benefit by beginning with this appendix.

For this translation I have used the text of the *Ten Diagrams* found in the standard edition of T'oegye's writings, the *T'oegye chŏnsŏ* (T'oegye's Complete Works), published by the Taedong Munhwa Yŏnguwŏn of Sŏnggyun'gwan University, Seoul, 1958. The additional translations contained in the commentary are also from this source. *T'oegye chŏnsŏ* is a two-volume photo-reprint compilation of the best available ancient editions of T'oegye's various writings. References to the first volume ("A") all refer to *T'oegye sŏnsaeng munjip naejip*;[1] in references to the second volume ("B"), which contains a disparate collection of materials, the title of the work will appear before the fascicle (*kwŏn, chüan*) and page number. References give both the pagination of the original works had the consecutive page numbers of these volumes. In the commentary, passages translated from *T'oegye chŏnsŏ* are followed by the volume, fascicle, and page numbers in parentheses.

Frequent references are made to the *T'oegye sŏnsaeng ŏnhaengnok* (*OHN*) (The Record of Master T'oegye's Sayings and Conduct), compiled by his disciples. This is a corrected edition of an earlier, somewhat hastily compiled version, the *T'oegye sŏnsaeng ŏnhaeng t'ongnok* (The Comprehensive Record of Master T'oegye's Sayings and Conduct). Both appear in the second volume of the *chŏnsŏ* with the marginal title, "*Ŏnhaengnok*," which can easily give rise to confusion.

Each chapter of the *Ten Diagrams* is a compilation of materials from various sources, concluded by T'oegye's own comments. I have added subtitles to clarify the transition between the several sections of material. In some chapters T'oegye includes a section of brief remarks by authorities other than Chu Hsi or the Ch'eng brothers. The combination of authors and passages selected in these cases points to the *Hsing-li ta-ch'üan* rather than the original works as T'oegye's source, and it is to that compilation that I have referred these passages in the notes. The inaccessibility of many of the original works also made this the expedient course. Chu Hsi and the Ch'eng brothers are T'oegye's major authorities, and every effort has been made to trace passages attributed to them back to the original sources.

In premodern Korea, writings intended for an educated audience were written in literary Chinese, but Korean pronunciation of the characters differs from the Chinese. Names of persons, titles of works, etc., which are Chinese are rendered according to their Chinese pronunciation following the modified Wade-Giles system of romanization. Korean names and titles are rendered according to the Korean pronunciation, following the simplified McCune-Reischauer system developed by Prof. Gari Ledyard of Columbia University. But where modern Koreans use a different convention in romanizing their names it will be respected. When technical terms are romanized in the text both the Korean (first) and Chinese (second) pronunciations will be given initially, and the Korean alone in subsequent appearances in the same passage, unless the provenance is clearly Chinese. An exception, however, is the term "principle" (Kor. *i*, Chin. *li*). The Chinese pronunciation is appropriate to the general discussion of Ch'eng-Chu thought woven throughout this book and is familiar to the scholarly community, so for simplicity the Chinese *li* will be used throughout. The Chinese characters for all romanized names, titles, and terms will be found in the glossary.

The following abbreviations will be used for these standard works:

CTTC	*Chu Tzu ta-ch'üan*
HLTC	*Hsing-li ta-ch'üan*
TGCS	*T'oegye chŏnsŏ*
YL	*Chu Tzu yü-lei*

Acknowledgments

Confucians are vividly aware of interdependence, and I would be indeed lacking if I did not recognize that this book is in the deepest sense the product of the many persons who have befriended, taught, and inspired me over a span of many years. With deep gratitude to all of these, I will mention here only a few persons and organizations that have been directly involved with this project.

A translation of the *Ten Diagrams* was first suggested to me in 1978 by Professor Wm. Theodore deBary. He not only suggested it, but found financial support for its initiation and reviewed the manuscript through several stages of preparation. His criticism and advice have greatly enhanced this book. Special thanks is also due to Professor Wing-tsit Chan, whose advice at a critical juncture committed me to the difficult but rewarding task of writing a commentary based largely on T'oegye's Collected Works.

My wife Margaret has been a source of continual encouragement and support throughout this long project. The book has been greatly improved by the hours she spent editing the manuscript for style and clarity, and her trained hand is responsible for the styling and calligraphy of the diagrams that are the backbone of the book.

I would also like to express my appreciation to the editors at Columbia University Press, especially Jennifer Crewe and David Diefendorf, for an unfailingly pleasant and helpful association throughout the publication process and for their special cooperation in helping this manuscript meet an early deadline for the T'oegye Study Prize competition.

The preparation of this volume was made possible in part by a grant from the Division of Research Programs of the National Endowment for the Humanities, an independent federal agency. An American Council of Learned Societies Grant for Recent Recipients of the Ph.D. helped me complete the initial translation. Basic research for the commentary was accomplished while I was a Visiting Scholar at the Korea Institute of Harvard University's Fairbank Center for East Asian Studies; I owe them thanks not only for providing office space and research facilities, but also for the personal interest and friendship which supported my work. The Wichita State University has been a continuous support in this research, first with summer research grants and finally with subvention assistance for publication costs. A generous grant from the Korea Research Foundation completed the funds needed to make publication of this book possible.

Introduction

The Sung Dynasty Neo-Confucian Revival

There were two interrelated facets in the tradition founded by Confucius (551–479 B.C.): government and proper social order were a major concern on the one hand, and on the other it presented a profound vision of the qualities and modes of conduct necessary to be a full and worthy human being. These were intimately linked, for in the Confucian view morality or humanity consisted primarily in the cultivation and conduct of proper social relationships, and the essence of government was morality. Confucius was China's first private educator. His role was to train young men for service in government and his most fundamental conviction was that the essential preparation for such service must be character formation: true learning was moral learning, and society should be ruled (ordered) by a meritocracy based on such learning.

During the Han dynasty (206 B.C.–220 A.D.) this classical Confucian core was effectively synthesized with elements of what had originally been competing schools of thought, most notably the cosmological speculations of the Yin-Yang and Five Agents philosophies.[1] Man, society, and government were woven together with the cosmos in a complex system of correspondences that described an all-encompassing underlying order, a fitting reflection of the unity of the great Chinese empire.

But the vision that reflected the success of the Han dynasty became less plausible when Chinese society again slid toward chaos as the dynasty declined. In the minds of many the malfunction and disorder of the last decades of the Han discredited not only the government, but the ideology that had been sponsored by the government and legitimated it.

China was ready for something new. In the centuries of disorder and division that followed the collapse of the Han, Indian Buddhism competed with a resurgent religious Taoism for predominance. The foreign tradition brought with it a metaphysical and ascetical sophistication hitherto unknown in China, and as the Chinese came to understand and appreciate these doctrines Buddhism became a magnet for the best minds and most profound spirits. Confucianism as a conventional social morality or a form of learning associated with government service was commonly regarded as a complement to the more profound philosophy and spirituality of Buddhism. But its approach to self-cultivation through good habits and self-discipline seemed mundane and banal in comparison with an enlightenment to be achieved through the inner discipline of meditation; its cosmology looked like naive commonsense in comparison with the metaphysics of emptiness, one mind, all-in-one-one-in-all, and the like with which the various Buddhist schools supported their meditative disciplines.

Buddhism reached a creative and flourishing peak during the T'ang dynasty (618–907); but the Sung dynasty (979–1279) saw a reaction to the "foreign" religion and a creative revitalization of the stagnant Confucian tradition. In the political world this took the form of a reform movement which attempted to address the pressing socioeconomic problems of the day by a creative reinterpretation of ancient ideal Confucian institutions. But of more lasting importance was the intellectual and spiritual reshaping of the tradition. In a milieu long shaped by Buddhist predominance, men again began to take the Confucian classics seriously. Not surprisingly, they found what they were looking for: a long "lost" ascetical doctrine dealing with the cultivation of the inner life of the mind, and a metaphysics that could frame this with a philosophical account of sagehood, self-cultivation, and, ultimately, the universe.

The morphology of this renewed or "neo" Confucian vision equals the compass and scope of Buddhism. It was effected, however, not by borrowing, but by a creative reinterpretation of the traditional Confucian core to meet new intellectual and spiritual expectations. It answers the Buddhist transcendence of the mundane by transcendentally grounding the mundane: human interpersonal relationships and concern for society and government are inseparably united with deepened ascetical practice as the path to ultimate personal fulfillment. There are Neo-Confucian retreats, but no Neo-Confucian monasteries.

The four main architects of this new vision during the early years were Chou Tun-i (1017–1073), Chang Tsai (1020–1077), and his nephews, the brothers Ch'eng Hao (1032–1083) and Ch'eng I (1033–1108). Chou's *Diagram of the Supreme Ultimate* appears in chapter 1 of the *Ten Diagrams;* it became the cornerstone of Neo-Confucian metaphysics. Chang Tsai elaborated a monistic metaphysics based, like Chou's Diagram, on the *Book of Changes.* Although his metaphysical system was largely supplanted by that developed by his nephews, his work was of seminal importance for Neo-Confucian psychological theory.[2] Confucian ethics was reestablished on a metaphysical foundation by his famous essay, *The Western Inscription,* which appears in chapter 2. The Ch'eng brothers were responsible for the introduction of the concept *li,* "principle," which became the pivot point of Neo-Confucian metaphysics, psychology, and ascetical doctrine.

The central figure in this Confucian revival, however, was Chu Hsi (1130–1200). He creatively synthesized the rather disparate contributions of these earlier thinkers into a coherent, powerful vision. His commentaries on the Four Books[3] wove a classical foundation for this vision so persuasively that in 1313 his interpretation was made normative for the civil service examinations. The Ch'eng-Chu school, so called because of the centrality of the Ch'engs' contribution to Chu Hsi's system, thus achieved the status of an officially sanctioned orthodoxy.

Though it maintained this central position down to the modern era, the Ch'eng-Chu school was not the only school of Neo-Confucian thought. The most notable alternative was the school of Wang Yang-ming (1472–1529), often referred to as the "Lu-Wang school" because

Wang's thought bore a marked similarity to the ideas of Chu Hsi's contemporary and rival, Lu Chiu-yüan (Hsiang-shan, 1139–1193).

The "Lu-Wang school" equated mind with *li* or principle and so followed an approach to self-cultivation that was based on the mind's direct intuitive grasp of the proper way, as opposed to the Ch'eng-Chu emphasis on the need for diligent study or "the investigation of things." Chu Hsi's school vehemently rejected this as a form of Ch'an (Zen) Buddhism decked out in Confucian garb, but the Lu-Wang school became a strong movement, overshadowing the orthodox tradition throughout the remainder of the Ming period. That it found no equal acceptance or popularity in Korea constitutes one of the most obvious of the important differences between the subsequent Chinese and Korean traditions.

The Neo-Confucian movement developed metaphysical and ascetical dimensions essential to revitalizing the Confucian tradition. In the course of this, it also reshaped the classical canon as attention focused particularly on works which spoke to these new concerns. The *Great Learning* was extricated from its obscure position in the voluminous *Book of Rites* to become the most authoritative description of the process of self-cultivation. Another section of the *Book of Rites,* the *Doctrine of the Mean,* likewise attained new prominence as an independent classic; it furnished vital elements of a metaphysically grounded psychological theory and a depiction of sagehood. The *Mencius,* long well known but ancillary to the classical corpus, now became one of the most important classical authorities; more than any other ancient source, it spoke to Neo-Confucian concerns regarding the mind, human nature, and cultivation of the inner life. The *Analects,* the classic containing the words of Confucius himself recorded by his direct disciples, remained, as always, fundamental: the Sung Confucians understood themselves as finally recovering the full meaning of the ancient deposit of sage wisdom, and it was necessary that the words of the Master himself inform and sanction their vision. These four texts, collectively referred to as "the Four Books," became the new core of the Confucian canon; intensively studied, analyzed, and debated, they furnished much of the substance and vocabulary of Neo-Confucian discourse.

Neo-Confucian Development in Korea

THE LATE KORYŎ–EARLY YI TRANSITION PERIOD

When the rising tide of Mongol power finally engulfed China and founded the Yüan dynasty (1279–1368), the Koryŏ dynasty (918–1392) on the Korean Peninsula had already been under Mongol domination for two decades. To solidify their control of Korea, the Mongols now began a policy by which Koryŏ crown princes were raised at the Yüan capital and married to Mongol princesses. Diplomatic missions constantly traveled between the capitals, and this period of enforced internationalism provided the context for the introduction of Neo-Confucianism to Korea. Both of the men associated with the introduction of the new learning, An Hyang (1243–1306) and Paek Ijŏng (?), studied it first while in residence at the Yüan capital. An Hyang is remembered for establishing a government-supported school and scholarship fund for students of the new teaching, while Paek in 1314 first brought essential Neo-Confucian texts to Korea.

Both Buddhism and Confucianism had been introduced to the peninsula in the late fourth century. The first national Confucian Academy was founded in 682, followed a century later by a civil service examination which tested candidates' ability in reading the Chinese classics. But Confucianism was largely limited to the narrow world of government functionaries, and its vital institutions such as the schools and examination system functioned only sporadically, often lapsing for centuries. The development of Buddhism, by contrast, was continuous and widespread. Buddhism became the cornerstone of government and society, while Confucianism coexisted as a useful discipline in literary skills and mores for public officials.

By the middle of the fourteenth century, there was still only a very limited group of Neo-Confucian scholars in Korea. The government school system was in a state of decay, and the private schools of the aristocracy mainly provided the scions of noble families with the kind of literary education which was still the focus of the civil service examinations. The ongoing close connection with Yüan China introduced the conditions for change, however. It was not uncommon for young Korean scholars to complete their education with a period of residence in China where Neo-Confucianism was already the officially sanctioned learning. They competed successfully in the Yüan civil service exams, and some served an apprenticeship in government posts in China before returning to Korea.

By the latter half of the fourteenth century, this process had generated enough momentum to establish indigenous roots in Korea. In 1367 the Confucian Academy was reestablished with a leading scholar-official, Yi Saek[4] (1328–1396) as headmaster. Under his leadership the curriculum was revised, and literature was supplanted by the Four Books and Five Classics as the core. Young scholars such as Chŏng Mongju[5] (1337–1392), Yi Sungin (1349–1392), Kim Kuyong (1338–1384), and Pak Sangch'ung (1332–1375), most of whom had studied Neo-Confucianism in China, lectured a growing student body attracted to the new learning. Yi Saek not only lectured, but also led enthusiastic extracurricular discussions investigating the meaning of the new texts.

Koryŏ government and society were at this point in need of drastic reform. The central government was in a state of severe economic crisis, its fiscal base eroded by the extensive land-holdings of the aristocratic families who dominated the higher levels of officialdom and thwarted any attempt at land reform. Buddhism, long the object of government favor, was now also inextricably bound up in the problem. Numerous Buddhist temples were supported by large endowments of land and slaves which further eroded the government's tax base. The large body of monks sapped the manpower needed for labor and military, and scarce state resources continued to flow into extravagent temple building projects and lavish Buddhist rituals.

Land reform, then, would have to await the advent of some new power on the scene. The Buddhist establishment, however, was more vulnerable to criticism. The new learning offered an alternative base from which critical voices began to be heard. Early Korean Neo-Confucians such as Yi Saek criticized Buddhist corruption and strongly opposed expensive building projects and rituals; they stopped short of an outright rejection of Buddhism as such, however, for the tradition of Buddhist and Confucian complementarity was deeply rooted. But younger Neo-Confucians became more vehement, and the tone of the attack changed: it was no longer just that expenditure on things Buddhist was excessive or that monasteries harbored many unworthy monks, but rather that Buddhist teachings were false and the Buddhist way of life fundamentally wrong. Where earlier critics had called for a strict limitation and restriction of the Buddhist establishment, later extremists endorsed measures that would amount to wholesale repression.

The Koryŏ dynasty had been founded under expressly Buddhist auspices; the symbolic connection was so close that an all-out attack on Buddhism implied a radical alternative: founding a new dynasty on Neo-Confucian principles. Not all Neo-Confucians of the time wished to draw such a conclusion, however. Outstanding Neo-Confucians of aristocratic families, such as Yi Saek, Chŏng Mongju, and Kwŏn Kŭn[6] (1352–1409), served in high office and remained loyal to the dynasty even as they desperately sought reform. But a younger and less established group of graduates of the Confucian Academy now filled the lower ranks of officialdom; these men, whose stipends could not be paid by the bankrupt government, were not so hesitant. In 1388 when Yi Sŏnggye, a general who had attained eminence in repulsing the Red Turbans, effected a coup d'etat, this group formed his principle political base. The long needed land reform was set in place, and in 1392 he finally ascended the throne as the founder of the Yi dynasty.

The strategist and architect of Yi's takeover was Chŏng Tojŏn[7] (? – 1398). Chŏng, a brilliant political and military tactician as well as an outstanding Neo-Confucian scholar, was the leader of the extremist group of young Neo-Confucians. As teacher and headmaster of the Confucian Academy, his fulminations against Buddhism and expositions of the True Way left a deep impression on many of the young students, contributing much to the radicalization of opinion that made dynastic change a palatable alternative.

The coup Chŏng engineered was history's only Neo-Confucian revolution. It mattered not that the man who became ruler, Yi Sŏnggye, was a devout Buddhist; time would solve the problem of Buddhism within the royal family. What counted was that the institutions at the foundation of government and society be shaped in terms of Confucian norms and values.

Chŏng and his group, now at the helm of power, set about the immense task of Confucianizing a non-Confucian society. This could not be accomplished in a few years, or even a few decades; it was the main occupation of Confucian minds and talents for much of the next century. During this period the focus of attention was much more on the public than the personal face of Confucianism, on institutions, ritual, and paradigmatic values rather than metaphysics and inner self-cultivation.[8] Classical authorities on government and ritual such as the *Chou li* and *Book of Rites* were ransacked for guidance and precedents. Both Chu Hsi's *Chia li* (Family Rituals) and *Hsiao hsüeh* (Elementary Learning) were recognized as fundamental reference points, the former as a guide to adapting ancient ritual to changed circumstances, the latter as a presentation of essential moral values and conduct. Oral exams in these two works became mandatory preliminaries for the civil service examinations.

Because of this preoccupation with social concerns the record of fifteenth-century Korean Neo-Confucianism offers little regarding more technical philosophical or ascetical thought. The Ming court sent to Korea its officially sanctioned compendia of Neo-Confucian thought, the *Hsing-li ta-ch'üan* (Great Compendium of Neo-Confucianism) and the *Ssu-shu wu-ching ta-ch 'üan* (Great Compendium on the Four Books and Five Classics), and other works containing Yüan and late Sung interpretations of Ch'eng-Chu thought also gradually found their way to the peninsula. But political relations with the new Ming dynasty were not smooth, and the Chinese consistently denied Korean scholars permission to study in China. The pattern of direct contact that characterized the early years of Korean Neo-Confucianism was now reversed, and Koreans were left on their own to analyze and assimilate this vast and complex material. The groping character evident in the intellectual discussion that emerged in the early sixteenth century reflects men finding their own way with no preestablished "orthodox" interpretation.

As a result the Yi dynasty established a pattern of relative independence from the Ming intellectual world. Later Korean thinkers might appeal to Yüan and Sung authorities, but they tended rather to sit in critical judgment on Ming developments. Once in mature intellectual command of the Ch'eng-Chu heritage they looked askance at the deviant current of Wang Yang-ming thought sweeping China and saw themselves as defenders of true orthodoxy.

RISE OF THE SARIM MENTALITY AND THE LITERATI PURGES

The term *sarim (shih-lin)* came into prominence after the first two bloody political clashes (1498, 1504) known, along with two later ones (1519, 1545) as the *sahwa* or "literati purges."[9] *Sarim,* literally "forest of literati," in early sixteenth-century Korea became a term to designate the righteous oppressed, those who were purged and their spiritual forebears and heirs. The oppressors were for the most part the entrenched political establishment, particularly the most senior officials, the High State Councillors who were the king's immediate advisors. Termed the *kwanhakp'a* or "bureaucratic learning faction" by modern historians, most of these men came from families that attained wealth and power as the result of "merit subject" status awarded for service to the throne at the begining of a dynasty, at subsequent enthronements, or at times of crisis. Common human tensions were involved in the *sarim-kwanhak* clash: younger vs. elder, newcomers vs. established, idealists vs. pragmatists. One could also add a particular Confucian tension: the power of remonstrance vs. the executive authority of the throne and high policy makers.

The purges that ensued had the short term-effect of debilitating the Neo-Confucian scholarly community, but in their heat the "*sarim* mentality" crystallized. The *sarim* mentality, a rigorous and idealistic moralism that focused on the absolute centrality of moral self-cultivation and exclusive commitment to the true Way, was the self-conscious ambience which prevailed among the men who brought the Ch'eng-Chu school to full maturity in Korea. There was nothing particularly idiosyncratic about these qualities as such; they were deeply embedded in the Ch'eng-Chu heritage, and it was precisely this aspect that earned for the school the appellation, *tao hsüeh* (Kor. *tohak*), "the school of the Way." But the bloody history that attended the emergence of Korean *tohak* highlighted these qualities in a way that left a distinctive imprint upon subsequent Korean Neo-Confucianism, particularly the thought of T'oegye.

Throughout most of the first century, as we have mentioned, Neo-Confucian energies in Korea were devoted mainly to the transformation of government and social institutions. Understandably, men involved in the world of officialdom had little time or attention to give to the ascetical, meditative, and self-cultivation-oriented aspects of the Ch'eng-Chu tradition. But although this dimension was not much in evidence in the public Neo-Confucian world of the capital, it was being cultivated by a parallel "dropout" tradition evolving in the countryside.

The symbolic ancestor of this movement was Chŏng Mongju, a Koryŏ loyalist who was assassinated in 1392 because of his staunch opposition to the dynastic change. It was continued by Kil Chae (1353–1419); having served Koryŏ, he refused service under the new dynasty and remained in retirement, studying and teaching a large group of disciples. Students moved from the quiet scholarly retreats of the countryside to the busy turmoil of public life, and periodic political crises such as the Sejo Usurpation (1455) renewed the ranks of idealistic dropouts. There was no self-conscious movement involved, but this process was gradually forming the moral idealism inherent in Neo-Confucianism into a political force.

The means by which this current found voice and emerged as a distinctive political force were the three government offices that shared the power of remonstrance: the Office of the Inspector General, the Office of the Censor General, and the Office of Special Counselors.[10] The lower ranks of these offices were commonly filled with young men at an early stage of their careers. They functioned as overseers of all aspects of royal, official, and popular conduct and had a limited veto power over official appointments below the fourth rank.

Remonstrance, intended for the corrective guidance and restraint of both rulers and officialdom, thus had an exceptionally strong institutional foundation in three offices which could act in concert. In the aristocratic society of Korea the tradition of kingship was not despotic, but rather that of first among equals, and this also added to the possibility of remonstrative powers gaining a disproportionate role in government.

King Sŏngjong (r. 1469–1494) was strongly committed to the doctrine of remonstrance and unusually tolerant of its practice. In this permissive atmosphere the power of the remonstrating organs waxed, and use became abuse. Speaking with the voice of unimpeachable moral authority, they became increasingly dogmatic and inflexible when opposed to appointments or policies and increasingly vehement in their criticism of senior officials. They were unwilling to take no for an answer, continuing remonstrance on an issue for months on end and vilifying their opponents as amoral and vicious men. Power tactics such as mass resignations and even strikes by the politicized student body of the Confucian Academy became increasingly common. Replacing one roster of officials with another did little, for their replacements felt honor-bound to maintain the same line.

Unfortunately, Sŏngjong's successor, Yŏnsan'gun (1495–1506) was not only less tolerant, but also of delicate mental balance. After three years of running battles with the censoring organs, in 1498 he learned that a scholar preparing the draft of the official dynastic history had written in a vein critical of his grandfather's usurpation of the throne. He lashed out, executing or exiling over thirty men connected with the school of Kim Chongjik (1431–1492), whose disciple had written the offensive draft. The purge of 1495 was a symbolic warning shot: there was to be no questioning or challenging of established authority.

The message, if understood, went unheeded. Remonstrance continued as Yŏnsan'gun slipped further and further into extravagance, sensuality, and paranoia. In 1504 the dam finally burst: the official world was plunged into a bloodbath. For over a year a series of investigations visited death or beatings and exile upon anyone high or low who had been connected with "improper" remonstrance or comment; gossip was a crime worthy of death. Government personnel were forbidden to visit with one another; finally the paranoid king forbid officials to visit anyone at all but their parents.

Such madness could not continue indefinitely; finally, toward the end of 1506, high officials organized the almost bloodless coup that put King Chungjong (1507–1544) on the throne. For this deed they became Chungjong's merit subjects, and so stood to continue in powerful positions; at the same time they were vulnerable, tainted by having served in high office under Yŏnsan'gun. Further, because of the insane excess of his predecessor's attempt to repress all criticism, Chungjong had to legitimize himself by strongly supporting Confucian moralism and remonstrance. In effect, a new clash was all but inevitable.

The atmosphere of a Neo-Confucian revival or restoration that prevailed in the first decade of Chungjong's reign fueled the fires of moralistic idealism; the *sarim* now became a fully self-conscious movement. At its head was the charismatic and brilliant young Cho Kwangjo (1482–1519). He entered office first in 1515; his learning and force of character completely won Chungjong's confidence and in four years he advanced from senior sixth rank to junior second, an unprecedented rise that brought him to the pinnacle of political influence and power. He used this influence to advance like-minded idealistic young officials, and together they set about a thorough program of renovation and reform.

Momentum was now completely with the *sarim.* Cho and his group firmly believed that Korea was on the verge of attaining once more the legendary perfection of the age of China's sage rulers, Yao and Shun. The Village Contract[11] system was set up to regulate and moralize the populace, and austere regulations restrained officialdom: no more wearing of silk robes, no more female entertainers. Earnest young Neo-Confucians prolonged the Royal Lectures into the wee small hours with endless moral preachments to the king. For a brief period the morally serious, self-cultivation-oriented form of Neo-Confucianism became a popular movement. The official historian captures the mood of the time in a passage in the *Sillok* (Veritable Records):[12]

At this time many men of learning attached themselves to the Cho Kwangjo group. They esteemed Chu Hsi-ism and did not hold in high regard the literary arts. Beginning students too, fell under Cho's spell; they did not study texts but all day long sat rigidly as if in Zen-like meditation. Their teachers all deplored this, but yet did not have the courage to rectify this harmful practice.[13]

The perfection was not to be. The somewhat jaundiced tone of the passage reflects the suspicion under which this kind of Neo-Confucianism fell in the period following the 1519 purge of Cho and his group.

Cho Kwangjo, and even more, his enthusiastic and uncompromising young followers, pushed too far too fast, alienating conservative opinion and making enemies of powerful figures who feared their criticism. Chungjong became surfeited with moralizing, and Cho's enemies skillfully planted in his mind fears that a movement was afoot to put Cho on the throne. Worse, Cho's group again began using the unyielding power tactics of remonstrance that threatened to hamstring royal authority. Their final mistake was to force a bitterly opposed Chungjong to delete almost three-quarters of the names on the merit roster of those responsible for his enthronement.

A few days later the purge began: denounced for cliquism, Cho and his closest associates were condemned to death. A wave of protest from all levels of officialdom resulted in temporary mitigation to beating and banishment, but the plotters of Cho's downfall now had the king's full support. The censoring organs were soon filled with opponents of the Cho group, and as the atmosphere became more hostile Chungjong repented his leniency and had Cho commit suicide. In the course of the next two years virtually all those associated with Cho's group were purged from the government and their reforms and innovations were rescinded. The kind of Neo-Confucian learning they represented was under a cloud, and a more pragmatic and conventional group of senior officials resumed control.

Cho Kwangjo failed politically, but his martyrdom made him a permanent symbol of *sarim* values and commitment to the true Way. With his downfall the *sarim* movement was for a time eclipsed, only to emerge half a century later finally victorious. Then, however, it was not the *sarim* as a political movement, but rather the *sarim* mentality itself that won general acceptance as the indisputable orthodox core of genuine Confucianism. This became clear as a mature grasp of the Ch'eng-Chu vision in its interlinked intellectual and ascetical dimensions emerged in the Korean world. The central figure in this development was the author of the *Ten Diagrams,* Yi Hwang (T'oegye).

Yi Hwang (T'oegye, 1501–1570)

T'oegye had no direct connection with Cho Kwangjo or members of his group, but he is nonetheless considered Cho's spiritual heir. His immense learning reconstructed for the first time the complete edifice of Ch'eng-Chu thought on the peninsula, and at the center of that edifice stands the profound moral concern and emphasis on self-cultivation that was the *sarim* hallmark. In T'oegye's legacy this orientation is so thoroughly worked out in relation to all the elements of Chu Hsi's teaching that its rightful place was henceforth beyond question.

The events we have described in the foregoing pages set the milieu of T'oegye's life. The period of his early childhood coincided with the debacle of the Yŏnsan'gun's final purge. He was in his teens when the resurgent *sarim* movement became the center of attention and hopes, and just beginning serious involvement in Neo-Confucian learning when Cho Kwangjo was purged. Most of his active career as an official was under King Chungjong, who reigned until 1544. These circumstances, as we shall see, strongly affected the development of T'oegye's life and thought.[14]

HIS LIFE

Yi Hwang was born of a relatively modest yangban lineage in the village of Ongyeri,[15] located near Andong in modern Kyŏngsan Pukdo, about 200 kilometers southwest of Seoul. His courtesy name was first Kyeho, but later changed to Kyŏngho. He is universally known, however, by the honorific name he took from the site of his scholarly retreat in later years, T'oegye.

When T'oegye was only seven months old his father died, leaving his wife to raise seven sons and a daughter. The household eked out a meager existence by agriculture and sericulture, but the widow somehow put enough aside to see to the education of her sons. Character deficiencies were commonly supposed in children raised without a father, and she constantly exhorted hers that they must be outstanding in deportment and conduct if they were to escape this stigma.

When he was 11 years old, T'oegye went with his elder brother, Hae (1496–1550), to begin their classical education by studying the *Analects* with their father's brother, Yi U (1469–1517). Their uncle, who had passed the civil service examinations in 1498, was a stern teacher, but he had high praise for the talents of his young nephews. Yi U had a reputation for poetry, and T'oegye quickly developed a deep and lifelong fondness for it; he was particularly attracted to the poetry of T'ao Yüan-ming (365–427), the Chinese poet whose themes of rural retirement and closeness to nature deeply resonated with his own inclinations.

Introspective and quiet by nature, T'oegye loved reading and study. Even in these early years he frequently would sit quietly facing the wall, absorbed in his reading while those about him were socializing. At nineteen he tackled the *Book of Changes* and became so engrossed that "he almost forgot to eat and sleep." In this case the conventional phrase was all too accurate: he overdid it to such an extent that he ruined his health and had to drastically curtail his studies for several years. He never fully recovered, and through the remaining years of his long life ill-health was to be a constant burden; later he continually cautioned his own serious young students against repeating his mistake.

T'oegye married at twenty, and remarried at twenty-nine, having lost his first wife shortly after she gave birth to their second son. In 1523 he directly experienced the debilitating effects of the 1519 purge when he entered the Confucian Academy, Sŏnggyun'gwan. His fellow students were unruly and little interested in serious study;

T'oegye, who presented a marked contrast in both respects, was made an object of mockery. Before long he returned home.

In 1527 and 1528 he passed the two lower level civil service examinations. This was enough to maintain the family's tradition of learning; he had no intention of going on to take the final examinations which led to an official career. His brother Hae, however, had passed the final exams in 1528 and embarked upon an official career, and he now prevailed upon his mother to persuade his younger brother to do the same. T'oegye could not refuse: in 1534 he placed second in the exams and entered government service.

For most of the next 15 years T'oegye served in office, rising gradually to a position of Junior Third Rank. In general he was appointed to the ministries concerned with drafting royal documents, compiling dynastic history, or composing documents addressed to the Ming court, that is, the kinds of position that utilized his scholarly and literary talents. As he describes his life during this period, "I was immersed in the dusty world without a day's leisure, and there is nothing else worth mentioning."[16]

During this period T'oegye established a reputation as a conscientious official and a man of integrity, but in general did not attract much attention. He began his career somewhat under a cloud by refusing an invitation to visit the corrupt but powerful Kim Allo (1481–1537). In 1542 he was responsible for the impeachment of a high official whose corruption he discovered on a provincial tour as a royal inspector. In 1545 he stood almost alone in memorializing in favor of accepting proffered peace overtures from the Japanese, rightly assessing the potential for disaster from those quarters.[17] Such instances reflect his consistent courage and integrity, but they were exceptional moments in a routine life of bureaucratic chores that was not particularly noteworthy.

In any case, it was not a period in which an idealist could hope to accomplish much. The decades that followed the downfall of Cho Kwangjo were characterized by a dreary succession of power brokers, each dominating the scene for a few years before being supplanted by another in the constant maneuvering for power. The fervent self-cultivation orientation symbolized by Cho was viewed with suspicion, and men like T'oegye were well advised to keep a low profile. Within a few decades he was to become famous as the foremost scholar of Ch'eng-Chu thought and and outstanding representative of the School of the Way *(tohak, tao-hsüeh)*, but during this period, as a disciple remarked, "even his friends did not yet realize he was a Confucian of the School of the Way,"[18] and another comments that most thought of him primarily as a poet.[19]

In fact, the scholarship that was to bring him fame was a late accomplishment, beginning in earnest with his years of retirement after 1549. His love of learning was constant, but the circumstances of his life and time had deprived him of the opportunity for teachers or intercourse with learned friends. Then in 1543 the *Chu Tzu ta-ch'üan* (Chi Hsi's Complete Works) was finally printed in Korea. T'oegye had not previously known such a work existed, and now burned with a desire to immerse himself in its study. His resolve to resign from public life dated from this time.

In 1539 the oppressive political atmosphere began to change and *sarim* figures again found their way into government. But the clouds soon began to gather as rival factions gathered around the uncles of Chungjong's two potential heirs. Chungjong died in 1544, and was succeeded by Injong, but Injong died after only 8 months and was succeeded by Myŏngjong (r.1546–1566). This reversal brought on the final literati purges of 1545 and 1546, for the majority of the literati had been arrayed against the faction of Myŏngjong's uncle, Yun Wŏn-hyŏng (? – 1565). Myŏngjong was just a boy when he ascended the throne, and Yun and his faction dominated the political scene for the next twenty years.

T'oegye's name was on the list of those to be dismissed from office in the 1545 purge, but was removed when someone in Yun's faction defended him: to dismiss a conscientious official who kept as far from factional politicking as T'oegye would have undercut the plausibility of charges being brought against others. The aftermath of the purge touched him painfully, however, when in 1550 his brother Hae was sentenced to beating and exile, but died from the severity of the beating. T'oegye had already taken steps to extricate himself from public life.

In 1548 and 1549 he had obtained posts as magistrate of Tan-yang and P'unggi counties, from whence he planned to move into full retirement. In 1549, after three resignation requests sent to the province governor went unanswered, T'oegye finally packed up his bags and left his post without permission. The result was a reprimand and a two grade reduction in rank, but that meant little. T'oegye had never really desired an official career, and now his longing for an opportunity to immerse himself in study, coupled with a strong distaste for the political climate, overrode all other considerations. His period of scholarly retirement had begun.

Students quickly gathered about him at the retreat he had prepared at T'ogye (renamed T'oegye), a stream not far from his birthplace. He outgrew this, however, and built another with more ample quarters for students on Tosan, a neighboring mountain, where he moved in 1561.

He was not allowed to simply retire and immerse himself in his studies and teaching, however. Throughout the twenty-one years of his retirement period he was hounded by a series of appointments that rose in rank as his reputation grew. During these years he wrote some fifty-three documents either resigning from or refusing official appointments. From 1552–1555 he was again in office, and again served for five months in 1558. Myŏngjong's uncle finally fell from power in 1565 and T'oegye's friends and disciples soon began to fill the government and exert pressure for his return. He returned in 1567, but the king died just three days after T'oegye arrived at Seoul. Hearing reports that his friends were urging the young successor, Sŏnjo (r. 1567–1607) to appoint him Prime Minister,[20] he fled the capital without notice or leave, even before the final rites for Myŏngjong had been completed, a serious breach of propriety that caused much comment. Pressure continued, however, and he returned to accept a position in the Royal Lectures. His stay of eight months produced two famous documents, the *Six Section Memorial* advising the young ruler on fundamental matters of conduct and policy, and the *Ten Diagrams,* a summation of Neo-Confucian learning proffered to the king on the eve of T'oegye's return to retirement. These, famous as his last political and intellectual testaments respectively, were subsequently often published bound together as the epitome of his learning.

He returned to Tosan in very ill health, but continued his

study and teaching during the year left to him. He died in the last month of 1570, sitting up in bed, peaceful and alert to the very end.

T'OEGYE'S LEARNING

The literati purges of T'oegye's childhood and youth effectively destroyed the spiritual and intellectual milieu which would have furnished the indigenous roots of his learning. He himself states that in his formative years he had no teachers or intellectual friends.[21] The *sarim* movement may have deeply affected his general orientation, but its representatives were purged and their writings destroyed. The intense fervor with which he immersed himself in Chu Hsi's *Complete Works* when it became available to him in middle age was fueled by the frustration of years he felt to be sterile. In the thousands of pages of Chu Hsi's correspondence he finally found the kind of guidance and dialogue that addressed his own questions and doubts. Having no teacher, Chu Hsi became his master, and the absolute respect and reverence he held for Chu Hsi was but a reflection of what he experienced as a direct and personal master-disciple relationship.

T'oegye did not grow up with access to broad collections of Neo-Confucian works, but a few that he did manage to obtain left a deep impression on him. Undoubtedly the most important of these was the *Hsin-ching (Simgyŏng)* or *Classic of the Mind-and-Heart* by Chen Te-hsiu (1178–1235),[22] a leading scholar of the late Sung period. This work, a collection of passages dealing with self-cultivation compiled from classical and major Sung Neo-Confucian sources, circulated in Korea in a greatly expanded version, the *Hsin-ching fu-chu* (Classic of the Mind-and-Heart Supplemented and Annotated), by the Ming scholar, Ch'eng Min-cheng (1445–1499). T'oegye obtained a copy sometime in his early twenties, and it became his constant and daily reading matter to the end of his life. Although it was later lost in China, T'oegye's love for this work helped it attain a permanent and important place in the Korean Neo-Confucian world, where it went through some twenty-five printings from the sixteenth to nineteenth centuries.[23]

The *Classic of the Mind-and-Heart* is a crystallization of Ch'eng-Chu thought dealing with personal self-cultivation, an aspect often called *hsin-hsüeh (simhak)*, "the learning of the mind-and-heart," or *hsin-fa (simbŏp)*, "the system of the mind-and-heart." It deals almost exclusively with the inward cultivation of the spiritual life, and emphasizes above all *ching (kyŏng)*, "mindfulness,"[24] as the central practice of all self-cultivation. The last five chapters of the *Ten Diagrams* are devoted to various aspects of the learning of the mind-and-heart and T'oegye deliberately makes mindfulness the central theme of the whole work, a clear reflection of the lasting impression of Chen's *Classic* on his thought. In his later reading of Chu Hsi's works, he likewise continued to make these themes the special object of his attention, leading him to value Chu's letters as the central portion of his *opus*.

The centrality of these matters is well-substantiated in Chu Hsi's own writings. But the *Classic* devotes little attention to study, "the investigation of principle," the external inquiry that must balance and complement internal asceticism in Chu Hsi's approach to self-cultivation. Ch'eng Min-cheng's preface explains this one-sided emphasis as Chen Te-hsiu's deliberate attempt to correct the scholastic intellectualism that had arisen among Chu Hsi's followers. T'oegye accepted this view wholeheartedly and constantly warned against separating study from its mooring in self-cultivation and making intellectual concerns an end in themselves.

But Ch'eng went further, suggesting in an annotation that late in life Chu Hsi repented his earlier emphasis on the role of study in the self-cultivation process.[25] Toward the end of T'oegye's life certain flaws in Ch'eng's character became known and this passage was recognized as an effort to steer Chu Hsi's school toward a rapprochement with the Lu-Wang approach. This deeply distressed T'oegye, but he was unwilling to reject the *Classic*. Instead, he wrote an epilogue to explain the error and redress the balance. This epilogue was published in all subsequent Korean editions, making this popular work, in effect, a part of the bulwark protecting Ch'eng-Chu orthodoxy from the penetration of the Lu-Wang school into the peninsula.

Another important influence in T'oegye's early years was the *Hsing-li ta-ch'üan* (Great Compendium of Neo-Confucianism),[26] an encyclopedic compendium of the discussions of Sung and Yüan Neo-Confucians topically arranged to cover the most fundamental works, concepts, and issues in the Ch'eng-Chu tradition. Containing extensive quotations from over one hundred authors, it was a predigested reference library that was of major importance in fixing the orthodox parameters and reference points of Neo-Confucian thought in both China and Korea.

T'oegye later became thoroughly familiar with this work; references to it are scattered throughout his correspondence with his students and most of the quotes of authorities other than Chu Hsi and the Ch'eng brothers in the *Ten Diagrams* can be traced to its pages. But in his early years he possessed only the first and last of its seventy fascicles, which he obtained when he was nineteen years old. The first, containing the *Diagram of the Supreme Ultimate,* together with Chu Hsi's commentary and extensive additional comments, was of special importance, for it provided him with a fundamental grounding in Neo-Confucian metaphysics. He later told his students that it was this that first really opened his eyes and provided him his point of entry to the Way.[27] Although some looked askance at introducing young students to such "lofty" matters, he regarded it as so fundamental that it figured prominently in his lectures to his students, and he made it the subject of the first chapter of the *Ten Diagrams.*

Those familiar with the system of Ch'eng-Chu thought will find this quite unexceptional, even basic. But there is little indication that Neo-Confucian intellectuality was securely integrated with the ascetical, self-cultivation aspects of the tradition that had occupied the *sarim;* one of T'oegye's most important contributions was to make this systematic integration of the Ch'eng-Chu vision henceforth a commonplace.

The third work that was of decisive importance to T'oegye's formation has already been mentioned: the *Chu Tzu ta-ch'üan,* (The Complete Works of Chu Hsi), which he discovered only in his forty-third year. The study of this work became his consuming interest, and at every opportunity he shut himself away to pour over it. About one-third of its 120 fascicles are made up of Chu Hsi's voluminous correspondence; this portion he read and reread so often that his disciples several times had to replace his worn-out copies with new ones. He absorbed the ideas, attitudes, and phraseology of the letters until they became virtually second nature to him, constantly echoed in his own discourse. In the words of a disciple, "he employed them [as naturally as] the grasping of the hand, the stepping of the foot, the hearing of the ear, or the seeing of the eye."[28]

The letters are an invaluable source for understanding the history and development of Chu Hsi's ideas, but for T'oegye this was not their main import. Self-cultivation, not theory, was ever the center of his concern, and he prized the letters because they offered a personal encounter with a master spiritual director whose response and advice was unfailingly appropriate to the many circumstances, personalities, and spiritual/intellectual levels of those he addressed.[29] In the letters he sought out not so much the theoretical system as the mind and spirit of Chu Hsi, and it is this that enabled him to recreate Chu Hsi's vision with rare accuracy and balance.

From 1549 until his death in 1570 T'oegye's life in the main was devoted to study, writing, and teaching the ever-growing number of disciples who sought him out. In spite of continual problems with his health, his output during these years was prodigious.

T'oegye's intense involvement with Chu Hsi's letters is reflected in his first major work, a recension of the letters, the *Chu sŏ chŏryo* (The Essentials of Chu Hsi's Correspondence). It is a selection of about one-third of the original corpus of Chu Hsi's letters emphasizing particularly his discussions of matters related to self-cultivation.

T'oegye's second work relates to his early interest in the *Book of Changes.* He had great respect for Chu Hsi's analysis of this work, found in his *Chou-i pen-i* (Fundamental Meaning of the *Book of Changes*), and his *I-hsüeh ch'i-meng* (Instruction for Beginners on the Study of the *Changes*). The complex and obscure emblematic and numerological interpretation found in the latter work, however, left him with many questions. Over the years he pondered these and searched the ancient sources of this tradition of interpretation to discover the origins of Chu Hsi's comments or shed further light on obscure points. In 1557 he arranged the hundreds of pages of notes he had accumulated on this, producing the *Kyemong chŏnŭi* (Problems Relating to the *Ch'i-meng*).

In 1559 he began the massive task of compiling a record of

everyone involved in the transmission of Chu Hsi's learning. The result was the *Songgye Wŏn Myŏng ihak t'ongnok* (Comprehensive Record of Southern Sung, Yüan, and Ming Neo-Confucianism). In ten fascicles he passes in review some 517 persons, recording the available data on their biographies and the character of their learning. It is an invaluable historical source, but T'oegye's motivation, as indicated in his introductory remarks,[30] was not merely to preserve the historical record, but rather to make the essence of the true Way apparent through the record of the twists and turns, depths and shallows of its actual historical transmission down from Chu Hsi. The sense of responsibility for preserving the true Way was heightened by the spectacle of the rising tide of Lu-Wang popularity in China, and T'oegye directly addressed the problem in several influential essays attacking Wang Yang-ming and his forerunner, Ch'en Hsien-chang (Po-sha, 1428-1500).[31] T'oegye's concern with defending and transmitting the imperiled Way was inherited by his students and contributed greatly to making Korea a self-conscious bastion of Ch'eng-Chu orthodoxy.

In 1559 T'oegye also became involved in what was to become the most celebrated and important controversy in Korean Neo-Confucian history: the "Four-Seven Debate," which he carried on in correspondence with Ki Taesŭng (1527-1572).[32] In this debate he broke new ground in the metaphysically based psychological theory of the Ch'eng-Chu school and launched a theory that was to divide the Korean intellectual world and set the intellectual agenda for generations to come. It is fully discussed in chapter 6. The correspondence relating to the debate is unmatched in its quality of argumentation, clarity of focus, and level of mutual understanding.

Finally, mention must also be made of T'oegye's extensive correspondence, which fills thirty-six fascicles of his *Complete Works (T'oegye Chŏnsŏ).* As is the case with Chu Hsi, whom he was undoubtedly emulating, in the letters one gets a full view of T'oegye as a teacher, guide, and friend; they are the best resource for assessing not only the intellectual, but the personal and human quality of his learning. He himself collected those he considered especially important—less than one hundred in all—into a separate compilation, the *Chasŏngnok* (Record for Self-Reflection).[33]

By the end of his life T'oegye was already referred to as the "synthesizer and complete integrator" *(chipdaesŏngja)* of the Ch'eng-Chu school in Korea, and this assessment has stood the test of time. Korea's mature and integral appropriation of the Ch'eng-Chu vision in both its intellectual and spiritual dimensions began with T'oegye. This maturity would ubdoubtedly have come in any case, but perhaps with a balance other than the one he gave it by emphasizing the learning of the mind-and-heart while not neglecting "the investigation of principle." And most decisively, his Four-Seven Debate shaped the future of Yi dynasty intellectual endeavor, focusing its attention on fundamental questions of the relationship of principle *(li)* and material force *(ki, ch'i)* in their vital application to understanding the constitution of human beings. His influence also extended to Japan, where the self-cultivation orientation of his learning of the mind-and-heart became fundamental in the important school of Yamazaki Ansai (1618–1682).

The Ten Diagrams on Sage Learning

The *Ten Diagrams* is T'oegye's last great work, and of all his writings it has perhaps been the best known and most popular. It went through some twenty-nine printings during the Yi dynasty, and now circulates in at least three modern Korean translations. Generally regarded as expressing the essence of T'oegye's learning, it is at once profound and fundamental. Generations of students have appreciated the clarity with which this brief work presents the essential framework and basic linkages of Neo-Confucian metaphysics, psychological theory, and ascetical practice. Mature scholars returned to it continually for the subtlety, balance, and soundness of this integral presentation of the vision by which they lived.

This is indeed a summation of what T'oegye thought it essential to understand. He composed it in 1568 to leave behind with the young King Sŏnjo as he retired. Worn out and ill, he could not continue to instruct the king, and the *Ten Diagrams* was his substitute for the teaching he could no longer offer in person. Its composition was by no means an erudite research project, though it expresses the learning of a lifetime. The old teacher carefully arranged and ordered materials he had long used in his teaching and personal life, weaving them together to encompass the scope of a learning by then self-evident to him.

"Sage Learning" is a term frequently used in a genre of Neo-Confucian literature designed for the instruction of rulers. Its usage reflects the particular duty of the ruler to learn from and model himself after the ideal sage rulers of the past. The circumstances of its origin clearly place the *Ten Diagrams* within this provenance. This fact is somewhat misleading, however, for as T'oegye himself says, when it comes to questions of learning and self-cultivation, there is no essential difference between the ruler and everyman.[34] The king needs particular kinds of knowledge to govern, but Confucians traditionally considered the essential learning for all government to be the cultivation of oneself as a full and proper human being, and it is to this that the *Ten Diagrams* is addressed.

While it belongs to the learning of rulers, "sage learning" also had a particular place in the new kind of learning developed by Neo-Confucians. In a famous passage in his *T'ung-shu* (a chapter itself entitled "Sage Learning")[35] Chou Tun-i put the question, "Can one learn to become a sage?" He answered with a resounding "Yes!" and set out to explain how. This reflects a new and important development. Traditionally Confucians had affirmed that any man could become a sage, but had let it remain a theoretical ideal. Now they elaborated a metaphysical, psychological, and ascetical framework that showed the path to sagehood, making this lofty ideal as realistic and immediate as was enlightenment for the Buddhist. The term "sage learning" in T'oegye's title signifies his intent to present that framework and path.

The *Ten Diagrams* is an extremely compressed work, more a distillation of the essential elements of the Ch'eng-Chu vision than an exposition of them. The commentary that accompanies this translation draws heavily on T'oegye's more expository writings to fill in the background modern readers will need. The format of the *Ten Diagrams* is ten sections or chapters. Each begins with a diagram and related text drawn from Chu Hsi or other leading authorities, and concludes with a few brief remarks by T'oegye. The brevity is in part due to his intention that it be made into a ten-paneled standing screen as well as a short book.

The brief format and the idea of presenting it on a screen are closely related to the purpose of the *Ten Diagrams.* It is intended for repeated reading and reflection. In moments of leisure the eye could play over the screen and the mind be gently but constantly engaged with its contents, so that one might finally totally assimilate this material and make it a part of himself.

T'oegye sees the structure of the *Ten Diagrams* in several ways. Basically it is split down the middle: the first five chapters present the essential framework, "based on the Tao of Heaven," as he says. They include a description of the universe (metaphysics), society (ethics), and their import for human life (learning). The remaining five chapters deal directly with self-cultivation, the "learning of the mind-and-heart." They begin with an analysis and characterization of man's inner life (psychology) and conclude with concrete practice (ascetical theory).[36] Or from a slightly different perspective, the chapters on learning are the core of the whole work; the first two chapters present the great foundation which must be properly understood and the later chapters detail the fruition of learning in the actual process of self-cultivation.[37] This perspective brings out the underlying unity of the two halves of the *Ten Diagrams,* in which intellectual considerations and moral practice are the interdependent and dialectically related facets of the single process of self-transformation called learning. T'oegye makes a special point of this in his remarks presenting the *Ten Diagrams* to King Sŏnjo.

T'oegye explicitly makes mindfulness *(kyŏng, ching)* the central theme of the whole *Ten Diagrams.*[38] It is absolutely fundamental for both study and practice. On the side of intellectual investigation, it stands for the mental recollection and concentration necessary for such pursuits. As for moral practice, the same mental recollection is a token of the self-possession and reverential seriousness that are the basis of a sound and proper response to the world around us. The final two chapters are devoted entirely to the topic of mindfulness, but it is a constant subject throughout the other chapters as well.

Most of the material used for the first five chapters, those dealing with the basic framework, are so fundamental and well known as to be virtually self-selecting. The *Diagram of the Supreme Ultimate,* the *Western Inscription,* and the *Great Learning* certainly are such. In Korea, as in Yüan China, the *Elementary Learning* was esteemed as a classic, so pairing it with the *Great Learning* was also a matter of course. The rules Chu Hsi wrote for his White Deer Hollow Academy were likewise well known, being inscribed on the walls of Korea's own Confucian Academy. But to extend the discussion of learning to three chapters by including them is a bit surprising. One explanation may be T'oegye's great concern with these issues, which were currently being seriously challenged in China by the Lu-Wang school. Further motivation may have been T'oegye's concern for private academies, a Neo-Confucian institution that with his help was just getting underway in Korea.

Personal preference played a larger role in compiling the last five chapters which deal with the learning of the mind-and-heart. This was a fundamental aspect of the Ch'eng-Chu school, but by nature it was more diffuse and personal and did not crystallize into universally recognized reference points such as the *Diagram of the Supreme Ultimate.* Chen Te-hsiu's *Classic of the Mind-and-Heart* was, of course, a major reference point for T'oegye. It's influence is clear in the central position accorded mindfulness throughout the *Ten Diagrams,* and the *Diagram of the Study of the Mind and Heart* (chapter 8) prefaces the *Classic* as an expression of the essence of the work. Chu Hsi's *Admonition for Mindfulness Studio* (chapter 9) likewise appears in its pages. Chu Hsi's famous *Treatise on Jen* does not appear in the *Classic* itself, but it epitomizes a formulation of *jen* (humanity) that was prominent in the thought of Chen Te-hsiu and occupied an important position in the *Classic.*

The sixth chapter, however, merits special attention. Chen's *Classic* avoided intellectualism, but T'oegye here reintroduces it to the learning of the mind-and-heart by a chapter that serves to establish a metaphysical framework for man's inner life. It is actually three diagrams, each with its own text. The first is a fairly standard presentation of basic Ch'eng-Chu psychological theory. The second and third, however, are T'oegye's unique contribution, a summation, in effect, of his final position in the Four-Seven Debate. In an unprecedented way they undertake a metaphysical analysis of the function of different feelings, the active life of the mind. Far from being cut off from intellectuality, the learning of the mind-and-heart was henceforth to become the central and distinctive area of Neo-Confucian intellectual discussion in Korea.

ADDRESS PRESENTING THE TEN DIAGRAMS ON SAGE LEARNING *TO KING SŎNJŎ*

The Minister Without Portfolio,[1] Your subject Yi Hwang, reverently bows twice and addresses Your Majesty.

The Tao is without form and Heaven does not employ speech;[2] when the River Diagram and the Lo Writing appeared the Sage [Fu Hsi], basing himself upon them, made the trigrams [of the *Book of Changes*] and then for the first time the Tao was made manifest to the world.[3] But the Tao is broad and vast; where can one lay hold of it? The ancient teachings are beyond count; where shall one begin?

But there are major premises involved in sage learning and absolute essentials in the method of cultivating one's mind-and-heart. The wise men of later times could not but take up the task of setting these forth in diagrams and pointing them out in treatises in order to show others the gate for entering the true Tao and the foundation for accumulating virtue.

This is even more important in the case of one who rules others. His single mind is the place where the beginnings of a myriad affairs originate, the place where a hundred responsibilities come together. Manifold desires attack it in unison and all sorts of deceits try to bore their way in. If one is but once slack and heedless it will run wild, and if this continues it becomes like the collapse of a mountain or the boiling of the sea: who can control it then!

The Sage Emperors and wise Rulers of old[4] were much concerned by this, and hence were wary and fearful, cautious and reverent. [But although they kept this attitude] day after day, they yet regarded it as insufficient; therefore they instituted the offices of tutors to instruct them and officials with the duty to remonstrate with them. Before them there was questioning, behind them assistance; to their left there were those who could remedy [their shortcomings], to their right those who could help. "When they rode in a carriage, there were the rules concerning the bodyguard, and at court there were the regulations of the officials and tutors; when at their desks there was the remonstrance of the Master of Recitation, and in their chambers there were the admonitions of their Chamber Councilors; when attending to affairs they had the guidance of the Music Master and Court Astrologer, and when at leisure there were the recitations of the Minister of Works."[5] Even on their wash basins, rice bowls, writing desks, staffs, swords, and window lattices—wherever the eye might rest, wherever they might be, everyplace there was an inscription or admonition.[6]

Such were the lengths to which they went in their measures to maintain proper dispositions and defend their persons [from errant tendencies]. Thus day by day their virtue was renewed and their accomplishments increased; they made not the slightest mistake and enjoyed great renown.

As for the rulers of later times, when they receive the Mandate of Heaven and occupy the throne, the extreme gravity and greatness of their responsibilities is no less than that [of the rulers of ancient times], but of the measures they take to properly regulate and control themselves, not one is as stern as were these. So they complacently consider themselves sages and arrogantly assume a haughty air as they preside over the nobles and occupy the position at the head of the multitudes; and when they thus come in the end to ruin and rebellion and are completely wiped out, what is there to cause surprise!

At such times therefore, one who as a true subject would draw his ruler back to the true Tao certainly cannot but apply himself to the task. Chang Chiu-ling's proffering his *Record of the Golden Mirror,*[7] Sung Ching's offering his *Diagram on Being without Idleness,*[8] Li Te-yü's presenting his *Six Maxims of the Crimson Screen,*[9] Chen Te-hsiu's offering his *Diagram of the Seventh Month Ode,*[10] all such deeds have stemmed from the diligent and profound loyalty of those who love their ruler and are concerned for the nation; they come from the sincere and perfect intention to present the good and offer guidance. How then could the rulers but deeply ponder and reverently submit themselves [to the teachings presented in such works]

My extreme ignorance and lowliness were a dishonor to the royal favor shown me through successive reigns. Sick and disabled, I was in the countryside planning to rot away there along with the plants and trees. Then unexpectedly my empty reputation mistakenly spread and Your Majesty summoned me to assume the weighty responsibility of the Royal Lectures.[11] Shaking with fear and terrified, I wished to decline and avoid it, but there was no way. Since I was unable to avoid unworthily assuming this position, then as for [the duty of] urging and guiding Your Majesty in sage learning and assisting in the nurture of Your Majesty's virtue in the hope of again bringing about the perfection of the reigns of Yao and Shun, though I might wish to decline the undertaking as beyond my powers, how could I do so? But in addition to the fact that my learning is coarse and sparse and my speech clumsy and awkward, due to continued ill health I have been able to attend upon Your Majesty but rarely, and since the onset of winter even this has ceased entirely. My crime deserves ten thousand deaths, and I have no way to settle the anxiety and confusion I feel.

Humbly reflecting, I am aware that the writings discussing

learning that I presented initially were not such as might move Your Majesty's will, and that later the explanations I gave on repeated occasions in Your Majesty's presence were not able to benefit Your Majesty's wisdom. Your humble subject in all honesty and sincerity does not know what to say.

There are, however, the wise men and superior persons of former times who have clarified sage learning and apprehended the method of cultivating the mind-and-heart. There are the diagrams and treatises by which they showed others the gate through which to enter the Tao and the foundation for accumulating virtue; these circulate in our times, shining forth like the sun and stars. Now then, I venture to bring these forward and present them to Your Majesty that they might substitute in the role played by the recitations of the Minister of Works and the inscriptions on the utensils of the Emperors and Rulers of old, hoping that by borrowing from the past there might be profit for the future.

Therefore I have selected from these materials the most outstanding; this furnished seven [diagrams]. [In treating the saying], "The mind combines and governs the nature and the feelings," I have used the diagram of Ch'eng [Fu-hsin] and added to it two small diagrams of my own.[12] As for the other three diagrams,[13] although I myself made them, their words, their meaning, their categories and their arrangement are derived entirely from the wise men of earlier times and are not my creation. Combined, these make up ten diagrams on sage learning; to each diagram I have also presumed to add my own inadequate explanation. I reverently submit this draft I have made.

I wrote this personally while I was shivering with cold and hampered by illness; my sight is not good and my hand is unsteady. Thus the writing is not neat and precise, the lines not even, and the characters are not uniform. If nonetheless Your Majesty does not reject it, I hope he will send this copy to the Bureau of the Royal Lectures to be minutely examined and have the mistakes corrected, then have a calligrapher make a good final copy and have it sent to the proper office to be made into a screen to be placed where Your Majesty spends his quiet leisure. And perhaps another copy might be made in a smaller format as a handbook which Your Majesty might always keep on his desk.[14] Thus whether looking up or down, to the side or back, there will always be matter for Your Majesty to reflect upon and be cautioned by; for one whose earnest intent is your loyal service there could be no greater joy than this.

There are however, points which have not been completely explained. I beg leave to expound them further.

Mencius said, "The office of the mind is thinking; if one thinks, one will apprehend [what is proper]; if one does not think, he will not apprehend it."[15] And Chi Tzu (Kija) in setting forth the Grand Plan for King Wu said in a similar vein, "Thought means wisdom; wisdom makes one a sage."[16] Indeed, the mind is embodied in the heart and is perfectly empty, perfectly spiritual;[17] principle *(li)*[18] is manifest in diagrams and writings; it is perfectly evident, perfectly true and real. If with a mind that is perfectly empty and perfectly spiritual one seeks principle that is perfectly evident and perfectly true and real, there rightly should be no failure in apprehending it. Thus as for thinking and so apprehending [what is proper], or being wise and so becoming a sage, how can there be any lack that would prevent one's actually experiencing this in our own times? Nevertheless, although the mind is empty and spiritual, if it is lacking the proper self-mastery, matters will present themselves and not be thought out. And even though principle is evident, true, and real, if one does not perceptively attend to it, though it is constantly right before one's eyes he will not see it. This applies likewise to these diagrams; Your Majesty cannot be negligent in thinking them out thoroughly.

There is also the saying of Confucious, "He who learns but does not think is lost; he who thinks but does not learn is endangered."[19] To learn means to make oneself thoroughly versed in a matter and actually put it into practice. For in the kind of learning pursued in the school of the Sages, if one does not seek it out in his own mind-and-heart he will be blind and not accomplish his objective; therefore it is absolutely necessary to think it out in order to fully comprehend even the most subtle aspects of the matter. If one does not make himself thoroughly versed in a matter, he will be endangered and not at ease; therefore it is absolutely necessary to learn in order to carry it out in actual practice. Thus thinking and learning mutually advance and mutually complement one another. My humble hope is that Your Majesty will deeply understand this principle. First of all, one must establish a firm intention [to pursue learning] with the thought, "What sort of man was [the sage] Shun? What sort of man am I? If I try, I too can be as he was [for he too was an ordinary human being]," [20] and with a surge of strength vigorously apply oneself to both [thinking and learning].

And it is by the constant practice of mindfulness (*kyŏng, ching*) that one combines thought and learning; it is the single, consistent thread which runs through the states of both activity and quiet, that whereby one may harmonize and unify his inner [dispositions] and outward [activity], making that which is manifest one with that which is subtly latent.[21] As for how one is to do this, he must preserve [the proper dispositions of] the mind by exercising strict composure and quiet recollection, and exhaustively investigate principle through study, inquiry, and the exercise of thought and discernment. "Before one is seen or heard [by others] is the time for one's heedfulness and caution to be all the more strict, all the more mindful; when one is in a hidden, secluded, solitary place is the time for one's self-examination to be all the more minute, all the more exact."[22] If one takes up one diagram for consideration, he should entirely focus his attention on that diagram, as if he did not know there were any others; if one takes up one matter for practice, he should entirely focus his attention on that one matter as if ignorant that any other existed. Whether morning or night, there should be constancy; from one day to the next there should be a single continuity. At times one should go over [what one has learned] and become steeped in its savor in the restorative atmosphere of the early predawn hours when the mind is clear;[23] at others he should deepen his personal experience of it, nurturing and cultivating it in his intercourse with others in daily life.

At first [in trying to practice continual mindfulness] one may not be able to avoid an uncomfortable feeling of constraint and contradiction, and at times one may be afflicted with feelings of extreme discomfort and dreariness. The ancients spoke of such difficulties as "the subtle beginnings of a great advance" and the "beginning of a good condition."[24] One should absolutely not give up on this account, but rather with all the more confidence devote even more effort to the practice.

Finally, after one has accumulated much truth and exerted oneself for a long time, the mind and heart will naturally and spontaneously become steeped in principle, and without being aware of it everything will coalesce and be thoroughly penetrated. Study and practice will mutually ripen one another and gradually become smooth and easy. While at the beginning one had to take each matter and focus his attention on it alone, now he will be able to combine [all matters] into a simple unity. This is truly the condition Mencius had in mind when he said that one who "advances with deep earnestness . . . gets hold of it within himself,"[25] the experience of what he meant when he said, "When [virtue] grows, then how can it be repressed!"[26]

If one follows this practice and is earnest in it, if he is diligent in perfecting that with which he is endowed, he will be like Yen Hui, in whose mind there was nothing contrary to humanity [for three months][27] and who therefore was fit to govern,[28] or like Tseng Tzu, who understood how loyalty and an empathetic understanding of others were the single thread which ran throughout the Tao [of Confucius] and who thereby bore the responsibility of transmitting the Tao.[29]

The practice of this kind of reverent fear and mindfulness is nothing extraordinary; it is simply part of everyday life, but it can bring about the "perfect equilibrium [of the mind before it is aroused] and perfect harmony [after it is aroused]," "establish [heaven and earth] in their proper positions and accomplish the nurture [of all things]."[30] Virtuous conduct is simply a matter of proper human relationships, but through it the wondrous unity of Heaven and man is attained.

This is the purport of these diagrams and the explanations [which accompany them]. I have arranged them and set them forth on ten sheets of paper. If Your Majesty will ponder them and become thoroughly versed in them, simply applying himself to their study in moments of leisure during the course of his daily routine, he will find that the essential foundation for accomplishing the Tao and becoming a sage, and the source for exercising proper governance are contained therein. If Your Majesty will set his mind and intent on them and go over them repeatedly from beginning to end, neither taking them lightly and neglecting them, nor becoming bored and annoyed with them and setting them aside, then great will be the joy of the nation, great the joy of the people!

In presenting this I can but emulate the sincerity of the ignorant peasants [who offered the king] parsley and the warmth of the sun [believing these to be the finest and most precious things in the world].[31] I presume to offer this to Your Majesty, although I am aware that [it is so unworthy that to present it] is an offense to the Royal Dignity; fearful and anxious, with bated breath I await Your Majesty's disposition.

Chapter 1: DIAGRAM OF THE SUPREME ULTIMATE

This chapter presents Chou Tun-i's Diagram of the Supreme Ultimate *and his* Explanation of the Diagram of the Supreme Ultimate.[1] *These works, as interpreted by* Chu Hsi, *became the cornerstone of Neo-Confucian metaphysical thought; here we find the essential framework for understanding both man's place in the universe and the process by which he achieves his ultimate perfection and fulfillment—matters which will be taken up at length in the remainder of this work. Two of the most important Chinese compilations of Neo-Confucian thought, the* Chin ssu lu *and the* Hsing-li ta ch'üan *begin in a similar manner;*[2] *this is the natural starting point for a systematic understanding of Chu Hsi's project. T'oegye has abridged Chu Hsi's analysis of the graphics of the* Diagram of the Supreme Ultimate[3] *and incorporated it as a gloss into the diagram itself.*

Chou Tun-i's Explanation of the Diagram of the Supreme Ultimate

The Indeterminate and also the Supreme Ultimate: The Supreme Ultimate through activity produces yang. Activity having reached its limit, there is quiet. Through quiet [the Supreme Ultimate] produces yin. When quiet reaches its limit there is a return to activity; thus activity and quiet each in turn becomes the source of the other. In this way the distinction between yin and yang arises and the two modes are established. Yang changes and yin corresponds, and thus are produced Water, Fire, Wood, Metal, and Earth; these Five Agents are harmoniously arrayed and the four seasons proceed in their course.

The Five Agents are the one yin and yang; yin and yang are the one Supreme Ultimate; the Supreme Ultimate is fundamentally the Indeterminate. But in the production of the Five Agents, each has its own nature.

The reality of the Indeterminate and the essence of the two modes [i.e., yin and yang] and the Five Agents wondrously unite and consolidate. *Ch'ien* (Heaven) constitutes the male element and *K'un* (Earth) constitutes the female element.[4] These two forces by their interaction transform and produce the myriad creatures. The myriad creatures produce and reproduce and so change and transformation go on without end.

Man alone, however, receives [the Five Agents] in their highest excellence and so is endowed with the fullest spiritual potential. His physical form is produced and his spirit manifests intelligence. His five-fold nature is stirred [in response to external phenomena] and acts; thus the distinction of good and evil arises and human affairs take place.[5]

The Sage properly orders these [affairs] according to the mean, correctness, humanity, and righteousness, taking quiet as the essential; in this way he establishes the ultimate standard for man. Therefore the Sage "with respect to Heaven and Earth is at one with their character, with respect to the sun and moon is at one with their brilliance, with respect to the four seasons is at one with their order and with respect to the spirits is at one with the good fortune and the misfortune [which they mediate]."[6] The superior man in cultivating these qualities enjoys good fortune, while the inferior man in violating them suffers misfortune.

Therefore it is said, "In establishing the Tao of Heaven yin and yang are spoken of; in establishing the Tao of Earth the

1 Diagram of the Supreme Ultimate

○ This represents the Supreme Ultimate and the Indeterminate. That is [it gives rise to] yin and yang, but this indicates that in its fundamental substance there is no admixture of yin and yang.

◉ This represents how ○ moves and produces yang, quiesces and produces yin. The ◦ in the center represents their fundamental substance. ☽ is the root of ☾; ☾ is the root of ☽.

This represents how yang by its change and yin by its union therewith produces water, fire, wood, metal and earth.

Yang

Yin

Action

Quiet

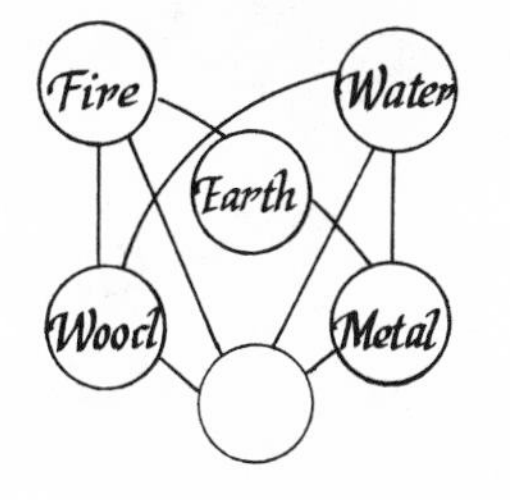

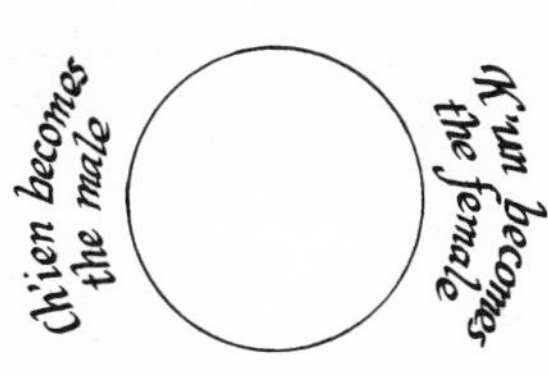

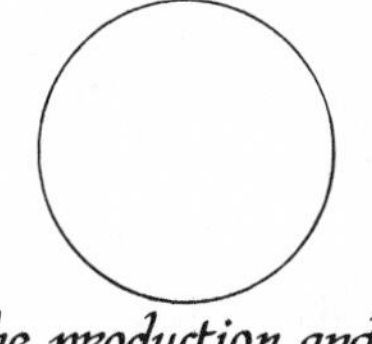
The production and transformation of all creatures

represents how the Indeterminate and yin and yang and the Five Elements wondrously unite and are without separation.

○ This represents how by the transformations of material force Ch'ien becomes the male and K'un becomes the female.

Male and female each have their own natures, but are the one Supreme Ultimate.

○ This represents how all things evolve and are produced by transformations of form.

Each thing has its own nature but all are the one Supreme Ultimate.

soft and the hard are spoken of; in establishing the Tao of man humanity and righteousness are spoken of."[7] And again, "[The *Book of Changes*] traces things to their origin in the beginning and back again to their final end; therefore it understands life and death."[8] Great indeed is the *Book of Changes*![9] And herein lies its highest excellence!

Chu Hsi's Comments

Chu Hsi says: "In [Chou Tun-i's] explanation of the *Diagram,* first he describes the origin of yin and yang, change and transformation; then he clarifies the matter, namely in terms of [the corresponding] endowment and constitution of human beings. When he says, 'Man alone receives [the Five Agents] in their highest excellence and so is endowed with the fullest spiritual potential,' [a reference to] man's pure and perfectly good nature, what he is speaking of is the Supreme Ultimate. 'His physical form is produced and his spirit manifests [intelligence]' is the doing of the activity of yang and the quiet of yin. 'His five-fold nature is stirred and acts' is the nature of Water, Fire, Wood, Metal, and Earth produced when yang changes and yin corresponds. 'The distinction of good and evil arises' is the likeness of the male and the female elements. 'Human affairs take place' is the likeness of the production and transformation of the myriad creatures. And finally when we come to, 'The Sage properly orders these [affairs] according to the mean, correctness, humanity, and righteousness, taking quiet as the essential; in this way he establishes the ultimate standard for man.' This again refers to man's having received the integral substance of the Supreme Ultimate, with the result that he is conjoined with Heaven and Earth in a perfect unity. Therefore the text goes on to say that with regard to Heaven and Earth, the sun and moon, the four seasons, and the spirits, there is none with which he is not at one."[10]

And again [Chu Hsi] says: "The sage has no need to cultivate these qualities but possesses them naturally. Not yet having attained such perfection but cultivating it is that wherein the superior man finds his good fortune; being ignorant of this [perfection] and violating it is that wherein the inferior man suffers misfortune. Whether one cultivates it or violates it is simply a matter of the difference between practicing mindfulness and licentiousness. If one is mindful one's desires will be few and principle will be clear. If one reduces one's desires and then reduces them yet further until he approaches the condition in which they are totally absent, then in quiet [one's mind and heart] will be empty [of self-centered impulses] and in activity [one's conduct] will be correct; one will thus be fit to learn to become a sage."[11]

T'oegye's Comments

This diagram and its accompanying explanation are both the work of Chou Lien-hsi [Tun-i]. Yeh Ping-yen[12] spoke of this diagram as follows: "It takes the words of the Appended Remarks [of the *Book of Changes]*, 'The *Book of Changes* has the Supreme Ultimate; this produced the Two Modes; the Two Modes produced the Four Forms,'[13] and expands and clarifies its meaning. The only difference is that the *Book of Changes* speaks in terms of the hexagrams and their lines, while the *Diagram* speaks in terms of the creation and transformation [of the physical universe]."[14] Master Chu called it, "the great fountainhead of moral principle,"[15] and again referred to it as "the source of proper understanding of the Tao through all ages."[16]

This diagram has been placed at the very beginning of

this work for the same reason that its explanation was placed at the beginning of [Chu Hsi's] *Reflections on Things at Hand.* That is, one who would learn to be a sage should seek the beginning here in this [diagram] and apply his efforts to the practice of [what is presented in] such works as the *Elementary Learning* and the *Great Learning.*[17]

When the day of reaping the fruits arrives and one completely returns to the Single Origin, he will have arrived at the condition described as having "exhaustively comprehended principle, fully realized his nature, and so completely fulfilled the Mandate";[18] he will have become "the person of perfectly accomplished virtue who exhaustively comprehends the realm of the spirit and understands the transformations [of the universe]."[19]

Commentary

On Beginning with the Diagram of the Supreme Ultimate

When T'oegye was nineteen years old he first obtained a copy of the first *chüan* of the *Hsing-li ta ch'üan,* which presents this material along with Chu Hsi's commentary on it and extensive annotations from other sources; this, he says, first opened his eyes and provided him a real entrée to the Neo-Confucian path.[20] Although he was criticized by some for engaging his students in such lofty matters rather than concentrating on the basics of moral cultivation such as are found in the *Elementary Learning* (see below, ch. 3), he considered this material as basic and frequently lectured his students on it.[21] We shall see that fundamental moral cultivation rather than philosophical theory is the essence of his approach to learning; but his own mind needed the support of grasping the overall framework, and he assumed the same for others:

[T'oegye] said: "Studying things on the lower level to arrive at the higher is certainly the constant order [of learning]. Nevertheless if those who pursue learning practice for a long time without attaining much, they easily reach the point of giving up in the middle. It is better to show them the basic foundation [of this whole endeavor]." Thus in guiding his students he showed them the fundamental well-springs. (*OHN* 1.21a,B, p. 799)

On the Relationship of Principle and Material Force

Li and *ki* (Chinese: *li* and *ch'i,*) principle and material force, are the two essential constituents of existence. They are explained in the Appendix on Terminology. The following passage summarizes the basic aspects of their relationship that are critical in the interpretation of this diagram:

Someone asked Master Chu, "What is the meaning of saying there must be principle and only then can there be material force?" [Master Chu] replied: "Fundamentally this cannot be spoken of in terms of prior and posterior; nonetheless if one must pursue the question of whence comes material force, then it is necessary to say that first there is this principle. But principle is not a separate thing: it exists in the midst of material force, and without this material force principle would have nothing to which to adhere."[22] Now if one considers the matter in terms of these three statements, then principle and material force fundamentally are not mixed together and likewise are not separate from each other. If one does not speak of them separately, they flow together as a single thing and one fails to understand that they are not mixed; if one does not speak of them together, they become divided as two things and one fails to realize that they are not separate. (*OHN* 4.5a, B, p. 838)

The emphasis upon the separateness but inseparability of principle and material force reflects a critical balance necessary to a vision which might be described as a dualistic monism. In the monistic direction, there is a tendency to a monism of material force in which principle is reduced to the order inherent in material force, an interpretation instanced by the philosophies of Chang Tsai and Lo Ch'in-shun (1465–1547)[23] in China and Sŏ Kyŏngdŏk[24] in Korea. T'oegye was acutely aware of this tendency and criticized it strongly;[25] the dualism which he defends separates principle and gives it priority, as reflected in this passage. As the inborn norm of everything in the universe principle has a clear value priority; as the inborn nature of things it has a logical priority over any concrete instance of that nature. A third kind of priority, priority in the existential order of causality, is a vexatious issue in Chu Hsi's writings that has led historically to quite varied interpretations and developments of his thought.[26]

Principle as the Indeterminate and the Supreme Ultimate

Chou's diagram was derived from Taoist sources. The phrase, *wu-chi,* in the first line of his *Explanation* would be translated as "the Ultimate of Non-Being" in a Taoist context, a reflection of that tradition's derivation of being from nonbeing. Chu Hsi, in adapting this work to his own purposes, could not accept such an interpretation and strongly argued against it in his famous debate with Lu Hsiang-shan.[27] He disarms the Taoist implications of *wu-chi* by interpreting the phrase as a qualification of the Supreme Ultimate clarifying its unlimited and nonconcrete nature. Thus I have rendered *wu-chi* as "the Indeterminate." T'oegye presents the rationale of this interpretation as follows:

Master Chu in discussing the Indeterminate and the Supreme Ultimate says: "If one does not say 'the Indeterminate,' then the Supreme Ultimate would become the same as a single thing and would not suffice as the root of the ten thousand transformations; if one does not say 'supreme ultimate' then the Indeterminate would be confused with a quiescent emptiness and would not be able to serve as the root of the ten thousand transformations."[28] Ah! Ah! This saying can be said to perfectly encompass the matter in every respect. (A, 16.40b, p. 421, Letter to Ki Myŏngŏn)

The Supreme Ultimate is identified as principle, or the total sum of all specific principles. As the above passage indicates, it is in itself nonspecific, not concrete, not a *thing,* but nonetheless *real.* In the following discussion of principle T'oegye elaborates further on these qualities:

The differences between the ancients and people nowadays with regard to the learning and understanding of the Tao are simply due to the fact that the word "principle" is hard to understand. What I mean by saying the word "principle" is hard to understand is not that a general understanding is difficult, but that truly knowing it with a wondrous understanding that reaches 100 percent is difficult. If one is able to exhaustively investigate all principle with 100 percent penetration, he will clearly perceive that it is perfectly empty but perfectly real, perfectly nonbeing but perfectly being; it acts but does not act, it is quiescent but not quiescent; it is so pure and clear that not the slightest bit could be added to it nor the slightest bit taken from it; it is able to be the foundation of yin and yang, the Five Agents, and of all things and all affairs, and yet it is not encompassed within yin and yang, the Five Agents, or all things and affairs. How could one mix it with material force and consider them as a single substance or see them as just one thing? (A, 16.46b, p. 424, Letter to Ki Myŏngŏn).

The negations reflect what is implicit in the "indeterminate" side of principle and establish its transcendence; the affirmations indicate the reality of the "supreme ultimate" side, based upon its function as immanent within the concrete beings of the universe. One cannot seek it out as a thing in itself apart from its manifestation in concrete existence, and yet it transcends any of its particular manifestations. The essential message to be drawn from this vision is not mystical absorption in the Supreme Ultimate, which in itself is nothing, but concentration on responsiveness to principle as it is immanent and real in the affairs of daily life. Thus T'oegye says:

In the *Explanation of the Diagram of the Supreme Ultimate,* two phrases are the most important points for application by one who pursues learning: "The superior man in cultivating these qualities enjoys good fortune. The inferior man in violating them suffers misfortune." It is only the difference between being mindful and being licentious; can one but be fearful! (*OHN,* 1.20b, B, p. 798)

The Supreme Ultimate and Material Force

Yin and yang, representing quiet and activity, are the most fundamental characteristics of concreteness, i.e., material force. When Chou Tun-i said in his explanation, "The Supreme Ultimate through movement produces yang. . . . Through quiet [the Supreme Ultimate] produces yin," the statement was not problematic, for his thought was not formed in the context of the philosophy of principle elaborated by his younger contemporaries, the Ch'eng brothers (especially Ch'eng I), and he was probably thinking of the Supreme Ultimate in terms of material force. But when the statement is viewed in the light of the assumption that the Supreme Ultimate is principle, it becomes exceedingly problematic: it seems to indicate that material force is produced by principle and to attribute a kind of activity to principle that belies its condition of being above all concreteness and hence action. On a deeper level, it poses the question of how one can conceive the causal function of principle at all, since material force is the single concretizing and energizing element in the universe.

Chu Hsi responds to this problem in a variety of ways which have in common the tendency to avoid giving existential independence to principle while at the same time giving it some kind of nontemporal priority. T'oegye picks up one of his main leads in this matter as follows:

Master Chu once said: "Principle has motion and quiet and therefore material force has motion and quiet; if principle did not have motion and quiet, whence would material force have motion and quiet?"[29] For principle moves and material force accordingly arises (*saeng*); material force moves and principle accordingly is manifested. Lien-hsi [Chou tun-i] says, "The Supreme Ultimate through movement produces (*saeng*) yang." This means principle moves and yang arises (*saeng*). (A, 25.35a, p. 608, Letter to Chŏng Chajung)

Logically and causally there must be a principle of motion before there can be motion. T'oegye's analysis addresses the casual question by moving the verb "*saeng*" (Chinese, 'sheng') from the SVO position where it reads subject "produces" object, to an SV position where it may mean subject "arises," i.e., arises of itself in accord with, but not actually produced by, what is contained in principle. In the last years of his life T'oegye accepted a current of thought among the younger generation of Korean scholars that made him feel this rearrangement to be somehow superfluous:

[Question:] The Supreme Ultimate through movement produces yang and through quiet produces yin. Master Chu says, "Principle has no feelings or intent, no productive activity."[30] If it has no feelings or intent, no productive activity, then I fear it could not produce yin and yang. And if one says it can produce them, would it not mean that at the beginning originally there was no material force—that there would be material force only after the Supreme Ultimate produced yin and yang? [Huang] Mien-tsai[31] says, "producing yang, producing yin" is the same [as saying] "yang arises, yin arises";[32] but is this not also going too far in disliking [any attribution of] activity [to principle]?

T'oegye replies as follows:

Master Chu once said: "Principle has motion and quiet and therefore material force has motion and quiet; if principle did not have motion and quiet whence would material force have motion and quiet?"[33] If you understood this you would not have this question. For the "having no feelings or intent" passage refers to [principle's] original substance; being able to activate and being able to produce is its extremely wondrous function. [Huang] Mien-tsai's explanation need not be like that, for principle itself has function and therefore naturally (spontaneously) there is the production of yang and the production of yin. (A, 39.28a-b, p. 889, Letter to Yi Kongho)

There are ambiguities in this passage that call for more discussion than would be appropriate here. Suffice to say that two of the leading contemporary Korean scholars who have devoted lengthy analyses to this aspect of T'oegye's thought concur in the opinion that he ultimately still assumed a material force that is self-originating and hence without beginning.[34] But it is notable that he now dispenses with Huang's interpretation, which is virtually identical with his own earlier position. One can only conclude that he is now seeing in principle's "extremely wondrous function" a more active sort of role for principle than he had hitherto envisioned, and hence sees a more dependent role for material force which leads him to want to avoid expressions that too clearly point to its self-origination. While it is still a matter of material force naturally originating itself in dependence upon principle, he is now seeing the casual function of principle in a way that is leading him to stress the dependence side and play down the self aspect of that origination.

T'oegye's application of "the extremely wondrous function" of principle to this question is related to a discussion which was really focused on seeing a more active role for principle in "the investigation of things" as presented in the *Great Learning.* This will be taken up in our discussion of the fourth diagram.

Although the emphasis on the active function of principle comes only at the very end of T'oegye's life—instigated by Ki Tae-sŭng,[35] his friend and disciple—it is congruent with an emphasis on principle that is present in all of his thought. At the same time, in Ki's generation, which succeeded T'oegye's, there was present Yi I (Yulgok),[36] who came to stand with T'oegye as one of the two greatest Korean Neo-Confucian thinkers. While T'oegye and his disciples tend to grant ever more priority to principle, Yulgok emphasizes more the strict interdependence and mutuality of principle and material force and, by contrast to T'oegye's school, the school of Yulgok is often characterized as "the school of material force." These differing emphases become the source of the two major currents which run throughout the remainder of Yi dynasty Neo-Confucian thought.

The One and the Many

The multiple circles of the *Diagram of the Supreme Ultimate* are really an analysis of a single phenomenon, the universe. Read from the top down it is an unfolding of the Supreme Ultimate to its diversified manifestation in the many creatures; considered from the bottom up, it is a revelation of the ultimate unity within the manifest plurality of those creatures. In Chu Hsi's analysis of the graphics of the *Diagram* which T'oegye has added to it, the final sentence deals with the bottommost circle, which represents the multiple creatures of the universe. It says: "Each has its own nature and all things are the one Supreme Ultimate." The following passage addresses the basic question implicit in this statement:

Question: In the commentary on the *Diagram* an annotation containing the explanation of Huang Mien-tsai says that the expressions, "the total sum of all principles" and "the fundamental origin of all transformations" refer to the Supreme Ultimate.[37] As for the statement that all creatures are each endowed with the one Supreme Ultimate, can one then also say [each is endowed with] the total sum of all principles and the fundamental origin of all transformations? Persons indeed are endowed with all principles; but as for things, each is endowed with the single principle suited to its use and that is all. How could they be fully endowed with all principles?

[T'oegye] said: In the case of a single thing, it seems one could not call it the total sum of all principles. Nevertheless, that with which it is endowed is the principle of the Supreme Ultimate, so why can one not say that each is endowed with the one Supreme Ultimate? How could [one regard] the Supreme Ultimate as a collection of the total sum of all principles, [as if] it cuts off single principles and applies each to one thing? It is like a single ray of moonlight which shines all around: whether it be the vastness of a river or the sea, or a single cup of water, it shines in all. In the case of the moonlight in a single cup, how could one, because of the small amount of water, go on to say it is not the moon shining? (*OHN*, 1.11b-12a, B, p. 794)

This is further clarified when one is reminded not to transfer the specificity of principle as encountered in the nature of concrete beings to considerations related to principle as such, which transcends form and specificity:

Question: The principles of ruler and subject are certainly endowed in my person; but are the principles of plants and trees likewise the same as [the principle of my] person? [T'oegye] said: One should not use the word "same": it is just one and that is all. In the case of things which have form, there is necessarily a difference between this and that. But principle is something without form, so how could it ever be divided as this and that? Tzu Ssu in the *Doctrine of the Mean* [ch. 1] only speaks of "the great foundation of the world." Among all those seated here, I have the great foundation, you have the great foundation, and besides us however many millions of persons there may be, they all have the great foundation. They do not borrow it from me and I do not borrow it from them. In the case of things with form, one having more of something means another is lacking; if I have it then you do not have it. But this is a thing without form; how could there be distinctions between this and that, others and myself? (*OHN*, 4.5a-b, B, p. 838)

The one principle, then, transcends distinctions; its diverse manifestation as the specific natures of different creatures is due rather to differentiations, typically expressed in terms of purity and fineness versus turbidity and coarseness, that arise in material force, the vehicle of its manifestation.[38]

Chapter 2: DIAGRAM OF THE WESTERN INSCRIPTION

The Western Inscription *is the work of Chang Tsai (1020–1077), and it stands with the* Diagram of the Supreme Ultimate *as one of the most fundamental documents of the Neo-Confucian tradition.*[1] *It puts flesh and blood on the bare bones of metaphysics, reflecting upon Heaven and Earth as the common parents of all creatures; stemming from a single common origin, all of creation is therefore a single body, and all people form a single great family. With the* Western Inscription *the level of discourse shifts from metaphysics to ethics: granted this unity which pervades the cosmos, what does it mean for the way I relate to others? How should I live, and how should I die?*

Text of the Western Inscription

Ch'ien [Heaven] is called the father and *K'un* [Earth] is called the mother. I, this tiny being, am commingled in their midst; therefore what fills up all between Heaven and Earth, that is my body, and that which directs Heaven and Earth is my nature.[2]

All people are from the same womb as I, all creatures are my companions. The Great Ruler is the eldest son of my parents, and his great ministers are the household retainers of the eldest son. By honoring those who are advanced in years, I carry out the respect for age which is due my aged,[3] and by kindness to the solitary and weak, I carry out the tender care for the young which should be paid to my young.[4] The Sage is at one with the character [of Heaven and Earth],[5] and the wise man is of their finest [stuff]. All persons in the world who are exhausted, decrepit, worn out, or ill, or who are brotherless, childless, widowers, or widowed, are my own brothers who have become helpless and have none to whom they can appeal.[6]

To maintain [our awe of Heaven] at the proper time is to show the respect of a son;[7] to feel joy [in what Heaven allots] without anxiety is to exemplify filial piety in its purity.[8] Deviation from [the will of Heaven] is called a "perverse disposition";[9] doing injury to humanity *(jen)* is called "villainous."[10] One who promotes evil is lacking in [moral] capacity;[11] he who fulfills his bodily design [by doing good] resembles [his parents, Heaven and Earth].[12] Understanding the transformations [of the universe] is being skillful in carrying forward [one's parents'] activities; plumbing the spiritual exhaustively is being good at perpetuating their intentions.[13] He who even in the recesses of his house does nothing shameful will bring no shame;[14] he who is mindful and fosters his nature will not be negligent.[15]

Through disliking fine wine, the son of the Earl of Ch'ung [i.e., the sage, Yü] looked after the nurture [of his parents];[16] through his development of the fine talents of others, the frontier guardian at Ying extended [his filial piety] to others of his kind.[17] It was the merit of Shun that by being unceasing in his exhausting labors, he caused his father to find delight [in what was good][18] it was the reverence of Shen-sheng that caused him to await death without attempting to flee.[19] Shen [i.e., Tseng Tzu] was one who, having received his body intact from his parents, returned it intact at death.[20] Po-ch'i fearlessly obeyed and conformed to the commands [of his parents].[21]

Wealth, honor, good fortune, and abundance have as their aim the enrichment of our lives. Poverty, meanness, grief,

2 Diagram of the Western Inscription

Part A The theme of this section is the clarification of how principle is one but it's manifestations are diverse.

Ch'ien — K'un

called

Father — Mother

That which fills up all between Heaven and Earth, that is my body

I, this tiny being am commingled in their midst; therefore

That which directs Heaven and Earth, that is my nature

In terms of humanity arising from common birth

All people are from the same womb as I;

All creatures are my companions.

Division between man and creatures

*All others and I, the people and other creatures, are brothers; their principle is all one.

In terms of putting humanity into practice

The Great Ruler is the eldest son of my parents, and his great ministers are the household retainers of the eldest son.

Division between ruler and minister

Honoring those who are advanced in years, I carry out the respect for age which is due to my aged; by kindness to the solitary and weak, I carry out the tender care for the young which should be paid to my young.

Distinction of Elder and younger

The sage is at one with the character [of Heaven and Earth], the wise man is of their finest stuff.

Distinction of Sage and Worthy

All persons in the world who are exhausted, decrepit, worn out, or ill, or who are brotherless, childless, widowers or widows are my own brothers who have become helpless and have none to whom they can appeal.

Distinction of Noble and base

*Principle returns to Unity

Part B This section discusses the sincerity of for clarifying the Tao of serving Heaven.

To maintain [our awe of Heaven] at the proper time is to show the respect of a son;

Deviation from [the will of Heaven] is called a "perverse disposition;" doing injury to humanity is called "villainous."

Understanding the transformations [of the universe] is to be skillful in carrying forward [one's parents'] activities;

He who even in the recesses of his house does nothing shameful will bring no shame;

Through disliking fine wine the son of the Earl of Chung [i.e. the sage Yü] looked after the nurture [of his parents];

It was the merit of Shun, that by being unceasing in his exhausting labors, he caused his father to find delight [in what was good];

Shen [i.e. Tseng Tzu] was one who, having received his body intact from his parents returned it intact at death;

Wealth, honor, good fortune, and abundance have as their aim the enrichment of our lives;

In life I shall serve [my parents, Heaven and Earth] compliantly;

one's service to one's parents as a basis

— to feel joy [in what Heaven allots] without anxiety is to exemplify filial piety in its purity.

— One who promotes evil is lacking in [moral] capacity; he who fulfills his bodily design [by doing good] resembles [his parents, Heaven and Earth].

Distinction of fulfilling and not fulfilling the Tao

— plumbing the spiritual exhaustively is to be good at perpetuating their intentions.

The sage is at one with the character [of Heaven and Earth] and therefore fulfills the Tao

— he who is mindful and fosters his nature will not be negligient.

The Worthy, being of their most excellent stuff, seeks to fulfill the Tao

— through his development of the fine talents of others the frontier guardian at Ying extended [his filial piety] to others of his kind.

— it was the reverence of Shen-sheng that caused him to await death without attempting to flee.

— Po-ch'i fearlessly obeyed and conformed to the orders [of his parents].

Sage and Worthy each fulfills the Tao

— poverty, meanness, grief, and sorrow serve to discipline us so as to make us complete.

— in death I shall be at peace.

With this exhaustively [fulfilling] the Tao reaches it's ultimate perfection and sorrow serve to discipline us so as to make us complete.[22] In life I shall serve [my parents, Heaven and Earth] complaintly and in death I shall be at peace.

Comments of Chu Hsi *and Others on the* Western Inscription

Master Chu says: "Ch'eng I regarded the *Western Inscription* as clarifying the fact that principle *(li)* is one but its manifestations are diverse.[23] That is, as for regarding *Ch'ien* as father and *K'un* as mother, among living beings there are none of which this is not so; this is what is meant by saying that principle is one. But among men and other living creatures which have blood in their veins, each has [particular] affection for its own parents, each treats its offspring as its own; thus how can the distinct manifestations but be diverse! [If one sees that] there is a single, comprehensive unity but with ten thousand diversities, then although the world be as a single family and China as a single person, one will not fall into the mistake of [Mo Tzu's doctrine] of universal, egalitarian love.[24] [If one realizes that] there are ten thousand diversities, but a single unity runs throughout, then although there are distinctions of feelings according to the proximity or distance of relationships and the noble and the base belong to distinct levels, one will not be bound up in the selfishness of acting only for self-interest. This is the main idea of the *Western Inscription.*

[Chang Tsai] analogically extends the closeness of the affectionate relationship one has with one's parents [to the universe] in order to show the great compass of the impartiality of the selfless person; he takes the sincerity of one's service to one's parents as a basis for clarifying the Tao of serving Heaven. Reflecting on this, [one sees that] there is no aspect of it that cannot be characterized as distinctions standing established, while the pervasive unity of principle extends throughout."[25]

[Chu Hsi] also says, "The first half of the *Western Inscription* is like a chess board; the second half is like actually playing the game."[26]

Yang Kuei-shan[27] says: "The *Western Inscription* [explains how] principle is one but its manifestations are diverse. It is by understanding that principle is one that one practices humanity; it is by understanding that its manifestations are diverse that one practices righteousness. As Mencius says, 'Be affectionate to your parents and humane to the people; be humane to the people and value other creatures':[28] the diverse manifestations are not the same, and therefore the [kind of love] one shows cannot but have different levels."[29]

Yao Shuang-feng[30] says: "The first half of the *Western Inscription* explains how man is the son of Heaven and Earth; the second half speaks of how man's service to Heaven and Earth should be like that of a son to his parents."[31]

T'oegye's Comments

The above inscription is the work of Master Chang Heng-ch'ü [Tsai]. At first it was entitled "Correcting Obstinacy"; Master Ch'eng [I] changed it to "Western Inscription." Ch'eng Lin-yin[32] made this diagram of it. For the learning of the sages consists in the seeking of humanity. It is necessary to deeply inculcate in oneself the intention [of becoming humane], and then understand that one makes up a single body with Heaven and Earth and the myriad creatures. To truly and actually live this way is what is involved in becoming humane. One must personally get a taste [of this experience]; then he will be rid of the problem [of thinking that] it is something so vast as to be unobtainable and also will be free from the mistaken notion that other things are identical with himself, and the inner dispositions of his mind and heart will thus become perfect and complete. Thus Master Ch'eng says, "The meaning of the *Western Inscription* is exceedingly perfect and complete; it is the substance of humanity."[33] And again, "When one has fully attained to this, he will be a sage."[34]

Commentary

Confucian Ethics on a New Foundation

The Confucian tradition had always made human relationships its central concern, focusing its attention particularly upon government and family as the principal forms of human interrelatedness. The family in particular provided the paradigm for proper relationships and served as a model for government. The virtue of filial piety, the norm for the relationship of children to parents, stood at the heart of this ethics; one schooled in an affectionate and attentive relationship to parents could be expected to transfer these attitudes appropriately to other forms of relationships in society and thus become a person of *jen,* humanity (often translated as "love" or "benevolence"), the crowning virtue of the Confucian tradition that expressed the essence of all properly human relationships.

In the two short sentences with which the *Inscription* begins, Chang Tsai casts the emergent Neo-Confucian metaphysics in a form which relates directly to this ethical tradition, catching it up and reestablishing it for the first time on a cosmic level. This not only creates a new philosophical grounding for Confucian ethics, but transforms them by opening up a vision of a unity among humans and also among all creatures of a sort that the earlier tradition had granted only to the members of a single family, a single body made up of those who share the same flesh and blood. The one-body concept—it is much more than a metaphor—subsequently came to occupy an important place in Neo-Confucian thought.

The conceptualization of all creatures as forming one body stemming from a single shared origin is a powerful foundation for attitudes of selfless affection for others and identification with their well-being, i.e., humanity *(jen)*. But it entails the danger of slipping into the kind of undifferentiated, universal love advocated by Mo Tzu; this was anathema to Confucians, who were much concerned with the appropriate differentiation of love according to the different kinds and degrees of human relationships. Such fears were voiced by Yang Shih (1053–1135), a principal disciple of the Ch'eng brothers. Ch'eng I decisively settled this problem by applying a crucially important dictum to the *Western Inscription:* it is, he responded to Yang, a perfect expression of how "Principle is one but its manifestations are diverse."[35] This dictum plays a central role in both the interpretive framework of the diagram of the *Inscription* and in the comments which T'oegye has drawn from various sources. While unity is indeed the central theme of the *Western Inscription,* looked at in this framework, one sees that differences are indeed also expressed. The Confucian doctrine of graded love, even in the new ambience, is preserved.

Although Chang Tsai's own philosophy was a monism of material force, his essential insight was successfully translated into the language of the philosophy of principle elaborated by the Ch'engs and completed by Chu Hsi. "Principle is one but its manifestations are diverse," is both metaphysical and ethical and could be applied to the Supreme Ultimate as well as to this work. In Neo-Confucian thought a metaphysically grounded ethics and an ethically significant metaphysics make up a single discourse with a shared terminology. There is in fact a close relationship between the metaphysical concern to maintain a realistic pluralism with a monistic basis, and the ethical concern to maintain appropriately differentiated forms within an all-encompassing love. The dual applicability of Ch'eng I's dictum is an apt reflection of this mutual articulation.

The Substance of Humanity

The root of all evil in Confucian ethics is self-centeredness or selfish desires that cause disorder and disruption in the interrelated human community. The opposite of selfishness is *jen,* variously translated as "humanity," "love," or "benevolence"; in effect it is a matter of treating others with the care and concern with which we treat ourselves. The *Western Inscription* is considered a breakthrough expression of the "substance of *jen*" because it exposes the ultimate metaphysical grounds of the human condition which make selfishness a basic misapprehension of the nature of one's existence by showing that humanity *(jen)* is a reflection of a universe which is truly united as a single body. This is clear in the following passage, in which T'oegye discusses the meaning of the original name of the *Western Inscription*, "*Ting wan* (Correcting/Obstinacy)":

> *Ting* means "to discuss"; it also has the meaning of settling and setting aright errors and mistakes. *Wan* [meaning "wicked" or "obstinate"] is the term for being not humane. [The mind of] one who is not humane is obscured and blocked up by selfish desire; he does not know the connection between himself and others or understand how to extend [to others] his mind's [innate] disposition to commiseration.[36] His mind is obstinate, like a rock, and so [Chang Tsai] termed it "obstinacy" [in his title]. For Heng-ch'ü [Chang Tsai] in this inscription repeatedly reasons out and clarifies how the principle shared by oneself, Heaven and Earth, and all creatures is fundamentally one. He formulates the substance of humanity in order to break down the selfishness of the self, expand on the impartiality of selflessness, and make the stonelike, obstinate mind-and-heart dissolve and fuse with no separation between the self and others, allowing no place for the least bit of self-centered intentions between them. One can thus see that Heaven and Earth are as a single family, the whole nation as a single person, and that the suffering and distress [of others] is truly that of one's own person; [understanding this] one attains the Tao of humanity. Therefore he named [this inscription] "Correcting Obstinacy," meaning it corrects the obstinacy [of self-centeredness] and makes one truly human. (A, 7.49a-b, p. 218)

Weaving a New Cloth of Old Threads

As the multiplicity of the footnotes makes clear, the *Western Inscription* is a tissue of quotations from classical sources. Chang Tsai's use of these materials is a more potent tool for the transposition of the old tradition to a new key than any exposition in his own words could have been. T'oegye describes how one is to approach this work:

Master Chu characterized this work as being entirely composed from the sayings of the ancients.[37] In reading it, one must for every phrase investigate whence it comes, and after considering its basic meaning in its original context, move [to consider its meaning] in the context of this work; then one will recognize the inexhaustible subtlety of Heng-ch'ü's use of words and phrases. Only when both of these are evident will one be able to catch the drift [of his meaning]. (A, 7.51b, p. 219)

The basic shift, of course, is the transposition of the filial piety tradition to a cosmic context. The second part of the *Inscription* in particular weaves together cosmological references from such works as the *Book of Changes* with well-known passages dealing with filial piety. The modern reader can easily get the basic meaning, but it is difficult to recapture the original savor of Chang's suggestive juxtaposition of phrases that had deep meaning and broad connotations for his Confucian readers. A good example of this is T'oegye's comment on "Understanding the transformations [of the universe] is being skillful in carrying forward [one's parents'] activities; plumbing the spiritual exhaustively is being good at perpetuating their intentions":

The *Book of Changes,* in the Appended Remarks [pt. 2, ch. 3] says, "Plumbing the spiritual exhaustively and understanding the transformations [of the universe] is the fullness of virtue." The *Doctrine of the Mean* [ch. 19] says, "Filial piety is being good at perpetuating others' intentions and being skillful in carrying forward others' activities." The *Doctrine of the Mean,* in speaking of "others," meant to refer to one's parents, but [Chang Tsai] has here changed these words so that, although the saying still refers to parents, the referent is Heaven [rather than human parents]. His meaning here is profound and marvelous! (A, 7.55b, p. 221)

The *Western Inscription,* elegant, inspirational, and endlessly suggestive, occupies a permanent place as one of the most fundamental expressions of Neo-Confucian ethics. But the impact of the new metaphysics instigated a further, many-faceted exploration of the cosmic significance of *jen.* This led to developments only foreshadowed here; we will see the culmination of this development when we take up Chu Hsi's *Treatise on Jen* in the seventh chapter.

Principle as Objective Norm and Subjective Identity

Principle, or, in more traditional terms, the Tao, serves as the objective norm of the way things should be, and as we have seen in the *Western Inscription,* the unity of principle establishes an objective, cosmic ground for an ethics of selflessness in human relationships. But T'oegye notes that the *Inscription* should not be read in a merely objective, nonpersonal sense:

[Chang Tsai] employs the terms people use to refer to their own persons; all who read this work should consider these ten [first person pronouns] not as references to the self of Heng-ch'ü, nor put them off as referring to the self of others: they must all be seen as indications of one's personal responsibility for what is one's own affair. Only then will one be able to grasp how the *Western Inscription* is fundamentally a formulation of the substance of humanity. . . . Heng-ch'ü also regards humanity as something that, although [it means] being as one body with Heaven and Earth and all creatures, must nevertheless first come from the self as its fundamental source and master; one must attain a personal realization of the interrelatedness of the self and others in the unity of principle. When the disposition of commiseration which fills the heart penetratingly flows forth, unblocked by anything and with nothing which it does not encompass, then this finally is the true substance of humanity. If one does not understand this principle and just broadly considers humanity as a matter of Heaven and Earth and all creatures being as a single body, then what is called the substance of humanity will be something vast and distant; what connection will there be with one's own body and mind! (A, 7.50a-b, p. 218)

There is a world of difference between looking at principle as something objective, "out there," and realizing that it is actually the substance of one's own being, the heart of one's own identity. The first section of the *Western Inscription* brings this out naturally because filial piety is fundamentally based in the question of a proper understanding of one's own identity.[38] But systematically it is broadly founded on the metaphysics of principle, which locates principle both in the realm of objective norms and in one's own nature as the substance or basis of personal consciousness and identity. We shall see that T'oegye's emphasis here on the absolute necessity of a personal grasp and personal experience runs throughout his discussion of study and the investigation of principle. In this framework, understanding the universe and what is proper in the conduct of affairs is also, ultimately and most urgently, a matter of understanding oneself.[39]

Chapter 3: DIAGRAM OF THE ELEMENTARY LEARNING

The Elementary Learning is a compilation of 386 passages, a little more than half of which are drawn from the Classics and the remainder from the writings of outstanding Confucians of the postclassical period, including a liberal selection from the early Sung dynasty Confucians. Its purpose was to present the most fundamental teachings and values of the Confucian tradition for the instruction of the young; it includes extensive materials dealing with the Five Relationships,[1] which constitute the core of traditional Confucian ethical teaching.

This work became the gateway to serious study for generation upon generation of Confucian scholars. In Korea it was considered virtually one of the Classics, and from the first decades of the Yi dynasty its memorization became a prerequisite for admittance to the lowest level of the civil service examinations.[2] The high point of its importance was reached in the generation immediately preceding T'oegye's, when it became a symbol of the distinctive moral seriousness of the burgeoning Neo-Confucian movement. Kim Koengp'il (1454–1504), one of the foremost scholars and teachers of that period, made it his boast that he devoted himself exclusively to the Elementary Learning until he was thirty years old and was a member of a club of prominent scholars and officials dedicated to maintaining and practicing the principles taught in it.[3]

Although the Elementary Learning is generally attributed to Chu Hsi, the actual compilation was done at his direction by one of his disciples, Liu Ch'ing-chih (1139–1189); Chu Hsi himself then rearranged it, added a few passages, and wrote a preface and an introduction for it. His introduction constitutes the main portion of the text which accompanies this diagram.[4]

This chapter is much concerned with the relationship of the Elementary Learning *and the* Great Learning, *which is the topic of the next chapter. Or, better, one might say it is concerned with* Chu Hsi's *view of the character of the learning process and the interrelated nature of its two stages, the elementary learning in which the young are engaged and the "great" or "adult" learning pursued by young adults (see below,* Commentary, *first sec.). The two texts, the* Elementary Learning *and the* Great Learning, *stand for these two stages, and the Chinese terms* ta-hsüeh *and* hsiao-hsüeh *are inherently ambiguous in this discussion, since they can be taken either as references to the stages or as titles of the two works which symbolize the stages. English language typographical convention forces a choice here; I have decided to italicize the terms only when the books are unmistakably the referent, for it is important to be aware that the discussion involves more than the relationship of two texts. In other cases I shall capitalize the terms, an indication that the books, particularly the* Great Learning, *hover in the immediate background, giving a very specific shape to the content of what might otherwise seem very general references to stages of the learning process.*

Chu Hsi's "Introduction to the Subject Matter of the Elementary Learning"

Origination, flourishing, benefiting, and firmness are the constant characteristics of the Tao of Heaven; humanity, righteousness, propriety, and wisdom are the [inherent] guidelines of human nature; in all of these, from the very beginning there is nothing which is not good. Thus like a verdant growth the Four Beginnings are stirred and move in response [to external phenomena] and appear.[5] Loving one's parents, reverencing one's older brother, being loyal to one's ruler, and showing respect to elders is called "holding to one's inborn nature";[6] [such conduct] is in accord [with one's natural dispositions], not forced.

3 Diagram of the Elementary Learning

Establishing Instruction

Establishing instruction in womb nurture, fostering and rearing

Establishing instruction: the Small and the Great the beginning and the end

Establishing instruction: the 'three matters' and the 'four skills'

Establishing instruction: master and disciple giving and receiving

Clarifying Relationships

Clarifying affection between father and son

Clarifying righteousness between ruler and minister

Clarifying distinction between husband and wife

Clarifying order between elder and younger

Clarifying intercourse between friends

Making one's Person Mindful

Clarifying the essential skills of dealing with inner dispositions

Clarifying the norms of proper decorum and dignity

Clarifying regulations regarding clothing

Clarifying proper moderation in food and drink

Examining Ancient Examples

Establishing Instruction — Clarifying Relationships — Making One's Person Mindful

Fine Sayings

Expanding on establishing instruction

Expanding on clarifying relationships

Expanding on making one's person mindful

Fine Deeds

Actual practice of establishinging instruction

Actual practice of clarifying relationships

Actual practice of making one's person mindful

But only the sage possesses the full, vigorous perfection of the inborn nature [in its pure, original condition]; without adding the slightest bit [of further perfection] to it, all goodness is already there in its fullness. The ordinary man is foolish and ignorant; the desire for things beclouds his vision and causes his inborn good qualities to decline, and he is content to thus do violence to himself and throw himself away.[7] The sage, pitying this [miserable condition] set up schools and established teachers in order to fertilize the roots and make the branches arrive at their full growth.

The method in Elementary Learning was to have them sprinkle water and sweep [the hall], answer and respond [to questions],[8] act filially in their homes and obediently when abroad, and to see to it that in their actions there would be no violation [of the rules of propriety]. With what energy was left from this, they recited poetry, read books, sang songs, and danced, so that in all their thoughts there would be no transgression [of the proper norm].

As for exhaustively investigating principle and cultivating one's person [in this way], that was the matter for more advanced learning [i.e., it was taken up in schools for young adults]. [With the pursuit of such learning] the bright Mandate[9] would shine forth; there would come to be no distinction between one's interior dispositions and external conduct; virtue would become lofty and one's accomplishments broaden, and one would finally recover the original [perfection of human nature].[10]

It was not due to some peculiar deficiency in the ancients [that such schooling was necessary]; how can we think that we now are more perfect [and have no need of it]? A great length of time has passed; the Sages perished, the Classics were damaged,[11] and instruction became lax. The rearing of the young lacks a proper foundation, so as adults they just become the more given over to corrupt luxury. The villages no longer have good customs; the times are without men of fine talent; greed dizzies men and entangles them, and deviant teachings set up a great clamor.

Fortunately the inborn good nature of man will not perish as long as Heaven lasts; therefore I have collected together what has been heard of old, that it may serve to enlighten generations to come. Ah! Ah! Little ones! Receive this book with reverence; [it contains] not the feeble words of this old man, but only the teachings of the Sages.

Comments from Chu Hsi's Questions and Answers on the Great Learning (Ta-hsüeh huo-wen)

Someone asked: "Now when you mean to speak about the Tao of Great Learning you also want people to reflect on Elementary Learning. Why is this?"

Master Chu said: "In learning, that which is great and that which is elementary certainly has its differences. Nevertheless, as far as the Tao is concerned, it is one and that is all. Thus if when one is young he does not verse himself in it through Elementary Learning, he will not have the means to recover his errant mind and heart and foster the good qualities of his nature[12] in order to lay the foundation for the Great Learning. And when one is an adult, if he does not advance to Great Learning, he will not have the means to discern moral principle and put it into practice in actual affairs, and thus receive the fulfilling of Elementary Learning. . . .

Now, as a young student one must first completely devote himself to sprinkling and sweeping, responding to questions and properly coming forward and retiring, and also become practiced in ritual, music, archery, charioteering, letters, and mathematics.[13] Only after he has reached adulthood does he advance to clarifying virtue and renewing the people and thereby come to abide in perfect goodness [as is taught in the *Great Learning*].[14] This is the order as it should be, and there is no reason it cannot [be followed in practice nowadays]!

[Someone] said. . . . "If one has already reached adulthood but has not attained [what is to be learnt in youth] . . . then what?"

[Master Chu] said: "Time that has already passed by certainly cannot be recovered. But as for the proper order and items of his study, how can that be taken to mean the deficiencies can no longer be remedied? I have heard it said that the single word, "mindfulness," is the means for accomplishing both the beginning and the final culmination of sage learning.[15] As for one engaged in Elementary Learning, if he does not proceed from this [basis], he will certainly not have the means to attend diligently to developing the proper moderation that is inculcated by sprinkling and sweeping, responding to questions, and properly coming forward and retiring, or to devote himself to the proper instruction that is contained in the Six Arts [i.e., ritual, music, etc.]. And if one engaged in Great Learning does not proceed from a basis in mindfulness, he likewise will not have the means for developing his wisdom and moral understanding, advancing in virtue, and cultivating perfection in his activities so as to finally carry out the task of clarifying virtue and renewing the people. . . .

As for one who unfortunately has lost time and come late to the pursuit of learning, if he is sincerely able to apply himself to [the practice of mindfulness], he may thereby progress in that which is more advanced and not be hindered in simultaneously supplementing his deficiencies in that which is less advanced. In such a case the means by which he progresses is such that he need not be troubled about lacking the proper foundation and not having the capacity to attain success."[16]

T'oegye's Comments

Formerly there was no diagram of the *Elementary Learning*; I have used its table of contents to make this diagram, which is meant to be paired with the diagram of the *Great Learning*. I have also quoted Chu Hsi's general discussion [of the relationship of] Great Learning and Elementary Learning which appears in his *Questions and Answers on the Great Learning* (*Ta-hsüeh huo-wen*) in order to show the general nature of the approach to applying one's efforts as it relates to these two. For Elementary Learning and Great Learning are mutually interdependent and complementary; in this respect they are one and yet two, two, and yet one. Therefore in the *Questions and Answers* they can be encompassed in a single discussion and these two diagrams can be taken together as mutually completing one another.

Commentary

The Relationship of the Elementary Learning *and* Great Learning

Most of the items included in T'oegye's *Ten Diagrams* are deeply rooted in his personal scholarly life. The *Elementary Learning* would appear to be the exception, however, for there is no indication that he was particularly devoted to this work as such, nor did he emphasize its importance as a subject for study for his disciples. The character of the comments he chooses for his text here seem to indicate that foremost in his mind is concern for the fundamental structural relationship of the work with the *Great Learning.* This is important because of its bearing on the interpretation of the *Great Learning* and of the learning/self-cultivation process in general. During T'oegye's lifetime Chu Hsi's views on these matters were being profoundly challenged in China by the rise to prominence of the school of Wang Yang-ming.

Chu Hsi interpreted the *Great Learning* as delineating a twofold process of study (the "investigation of things") and self-cultivation or practice. While learning and practice are dialectically related and interdependent, analytically learning precedes practice, though learning without practice is empty. Congruent with this interpretation is his view that the ancients had schools for the young which taught them the fundamentals of what is fitting for human beings and also inculcated habits in accord with these basic principles; more advanced learning, as instanced in the *Great Learning,* is simply the continuation of this twofold process on a more profound and mature level. While the *Great Learning* is a classical text representing this more advanced level, there was no text representing the more fundamental level, a lack remedied by the compilation of the *Elementary Learning.*

Wang Yang-ming argued that knowledge and practice are the same, a conviction which led him to a very different interpretation of the *Great Learning.*[17] Further, he claimed that Chu Hsi later in life came to hold a similar position and abandoned his earlier emphasis upon the investigation of principle. T'oegye strongly disagreed, and adduced Chu Hsi's view of Elementary Learning, including the *Ta hsüeh huo wen* passage presented in this chapter, as evidence of Chu Hsi's true position:

Furthermore, I would suggest that late in life Master Chu saw that many of his pupils were [excessively] bound up in textual studies, and so he strongly pointed to the original substance and moved his point of emphasis to the discussion of honoring the moral nature.[18] But how could this mean that he meant to entirely abandon following the path of inquiry and study and so destroy principle [as it exists objectively] in things and affairs,[19] as Yang-ming says! Yang-ming's wanting to adduce this in order to relate himself to Chu Hsi's views is erroneous. This is all the more [evident if you consider that] for one beginning Great Learning, Elementary Learning should precede, and that one who wishes to investigate [the principle of] things must devote himself to self-cultivation. This certainly was Master Chu's original intention; it appears in the *Ta-hsüeh huo-wen* and also in his letter in reply to Wu Huei-shu.[20] (A, 41.31a, p. 926)

The materials T'oegye has included in this chapter do not explore the contents of the *Elementary Learning,* but rather constitute an interpretive framework for the *Great Learning* that precludes the Wang Yang-ming position. The philosophical significance of the relationship of these two works (or the two stages of the learning process which they represent) is his primary interest, for it provides an accurate understanding of the nature of Chu Hsi's project at a time when it has been seriously challenged.

On not Teaching the Elementary Learning *to his Pupils*

In the Korean world of T'oegye's time Chu Hsi's thought was not thoroughly assimilated and related to practice; many got a reputation as scholars on the basis of lofty speculations, the emptiness of which was reflected in the mishandling of their personal lives. One response of those closely attuned to the intense moral concern of the Neo-Confucian movement was a kind of back-to-basics focus on fundamental moral teachings and practice as found in the *Elementary Learning;* this was exemplified by Kim Koeng-p'il and his club. T'oegye continued such moral concern, but without the fundamentalist approach; this caused criticism among some who recognized him as a fellow spirit but could not understand what he was doing:

I have recently received a letter from Cho Nam-myŏng[21] which says, "Looking at scholars nowadays, while their hands do not know the order of sprinkling and sweeping, their mouths chat about heavenly principle. They plan to steal the reputation [for learning] and use it to deceive others; but on the contrary they are the ones that get injured, and the damage reaches others as well. How can this but be cause for one who is a teacher and senior to reprimand them and put a stop to this! I ask that you entirely suppress and admonish them." Although this thesis has faults, we cannot but seriously caution ourselves and be diligent, and so I am informing you of it, that is all. (A, 35.27a, p. 809, Letter to Yi Koengjung[22])

While the form of the letter asks T'oegye to correct others, it is implicitly a criticism of T'oegye's own teaching practice, as indicated by comments of his pupils.[23] The "fault" in Cho's view is the implication that Neo-Confucian metaphysics is somehow a lofty matter rather than a means to everyday moral cultivation. T'oegye's own view is quite the contrary:

In general those who study, with regard to that which is before physical form (i.e., principle) and that which is after physical form, always want to divide them and treat them as two [different things]. They only recognize that the things and affairs of daily life are after physical form, and do not recognize that in the midst of the things and affairs of daily life, there is also encompassed in their interior what is referred to as being before physical form. Therefore when it comes to that which is before physical form, they look for it in some mysterious, profound, ecstatic condition. This can be described as not yet being able to abide in mindfulness and exhaustively investigate principle, or perfectly understand the subtle and minute. (A, 32.13a, p. 749, Letter to U Kyŏngsŏn)

T'oegye's pupils were not children, and he did not feel constrained to start them on the rudiments of the *Elementary Learning,* but rather tried to construct a systematic foundation in terms of the *Diagram of the Supreme Ultimate* and the *Western Inscription.* His remedy for Cho's problem is rather an emphasis on the ordinariness and mundane applicability of the "lofty" philosophy of principle. The framework of this philosophy opens new vistas, but the profound understanding and outstanding perfection that becomes available through serious application to this Tao is, in the end, nothing apart from the profundity and perfection of ordinary life:

> In sum, the Confucian way of learning is that in order to ascend to lofty heights one must begin with the lowly, to travel afar one must begin with what is near. Indeed, to begin from the lowly and near certainly is a slow process; but apart from this, whence comes the lofty and distant! In applying one's efforts to gradual advancement one attains what is lofty and distant without parting from what is lowly and near; it is in this that it is different from Buddhist and Taoist learning. (A, 19.26b, p. 479, Letter to Hwang Chunggŏ)

As we shall see, this is an emphasis which runs throughout his work. His pupil Chŏng Yuil[25] sums it up: "The master's discussions and explanations of moral principle were always clear and exact; he never spoke in abstruse, profound, and mysterious terms" (*OHN*, 5.14a, B, p. 856).

Mindfulness, the Classic of the Mind-and-Heart, *and the* Elementary Learning

T'oegye's lifelong devotion to Chen Te-hsiu's *Classic of the Mind-and-Heart* is well known (see Introduction "T'oegye's Learning"). This work, which is a compendium of sayings dealing with virtually every aspect of mindfulness, played a role in T'oegye's life similar to the role of the *Elementary Learning* in Kim Koeng-p'il's, and in his teaching it virtually supplants the *Elementary Learning* as an introduction to the fundamentals of practice:

> [Kim Su][26] asked: "Of the *Elementary Learning,* the *Reflections on Things at Hand,* and the *Classic of the Mind-and-Heart,* which is most essential?" The Master replied: "In the *Elementary Learning* both substance and function are complete; in the *Reflections on Things at Hand* moral principle is subtle and minute; one cannot but read both. But as for the matter to which one who is first beginning to study should apply himself, nothing is more essential than the *Classic of the Mind-and Heart.*" (*OHN,* 1.5b, B, p. 791)

Mindfulness (and hence the *Classic*) is the essential practical foundation of both Elementary Learning and the Great Learning. To bring this out, T'oegye in the *Ten Diagrams* does not stop the citation from the *Huo-wen* with the remarks that relate these two works, but continues it to include Chu Hsi's remarks on the remedial capacity of mindfulness for one who has missed the early introduction to the *Elementary Learning.* He remarked to King Sŏnjo: "Therefore Master Chu, in the first page of the *Ta-hsüeh huo-wen,* regards Elementary Learning as the foundation of Great Learning, and as for the practice which runs throughout both and unites them, then he further regards mindfulness as the great foundation." (*OHN,* 1.8b, B, p. 792).

Mindfulness, the disciplined restraint and self-control which is manifested as both physical and mental self-possession, is the fundamental method which T'oegye makes the central theme of the *Ten Diagrams.* It is inculcated through the basic ethical cultivation of the *Elementary Learning* and at the same time becomes the condition for advancement in both cultivation and understanding at even that level. It becomes the sine qua non for the more sophisticated, metaphysically grounded investigation of principle and the broad scope of cultivation with which the *Great Learning* brings the process to completion. Since both levels are essentially concerned with moral understanding and practice, application to the intellectually and socially more mature level of the *Great Learning* will supplement gaps in the elementary foundation if—and only if—one can approach it with the disciplined self-possession which would ordinarily be the product of this elementary training.

The Four Characteristics of Heaven, The Mandate, and Human Nature

The first line of Chu Hsi's introduction to the *Elementary Learning* describes the correlation between the four characteristics of Heaven and the virtues which constitute human nature. This expresses the philosophy of principle in terminology and categories which had long since become deeply rooted in Confucian discourse.

Mencius, in establishing the goodness of human nature, described "four beginnings" (commiseration, shame and dislike for evil, yielding and deference, and a sense of right and wrong) as inherent qualities which if nurtured developed into the virtues of humanity, righteousness, propriety and wisdom;[27] these virtues thus become the essential features of human nature. The *Book of Changes* begins its comments on the *Ch'ien* (Heaven) hexagram with the words, "Origination, flourishing, benefiting, firmness *(yüan, heng, li, chen),*" which are taken as the essential characteristics of Heaven; they are reflected in the cycle of the four seasons, beginning with spring.[28] Early cosmological speculations developed largely outside of the Confucian school in the originally distinct schools of thought that centered on yin and yang and the Five Agents. But during the Han dynasty (206 B.C.–220 A.D.) all of these elements were incorporated into a Confucian synthesis in which categories of correspondences between the Heavenly characteristics, seasons, yin and yang, the Five Agents, and much else, connected the macrocosm of the universe with man as microcosm. Symmetry between the fours and the fives was achieved by making Earth the center of a four-cornered arrangement of the Five Agents (see the *Diagram of the Supreme Ultimate*), correlating it with the constancy or "sincerity" of Heaven and the virtue of faithfulness, which was added to Mencius' original list of the four essential human qualities.

This powerful traditional synthesis was not overturned by the Neo-Confucians; they rather incorporated it and reformulated it as an expression of the transcendent unity of principle. Thus the explanation of the organic unity of the universe moves from cosmology to metaphysics, and the goodness of human nature is transcendently grounded in the goodness of Heaven (i.e., principle). T'oegye expresses the essentials of the Neo-Confucian version as follows:

Heaven is principle, and it has four characteristics: origination, flourishing, benefiting, and firmness. For origination is the principle of beginning, flourishing is the principle of pervasive continuation, benefiting, the principle of accomplishing, and firmness the principle of fulfillment. And that whereby these revolve unceasingly [as in the four seasons] is that all are endowed with the wondrous quality of real truth in which there is no deceit, and this is called sincerity. Therefore when the two and five [i.e., the material force of yin and yang and the Five Agents] begin to act, these four are always present in their midst and are the source whence things are ordained.[29] Thus all things received the material force of yin and yang and the Five Agents as constituting their physical form, and there is none which is not endowed with the principles of origination, flourishing, benefiting, and firmness as constituting their natures. There are five categories in their nature: humanity, righteousness, propriety, wisdom, and faithfulness. Therefore the four characteristics [of Heaven] and the five constant [virtues of the nature], that which is above and that which is below, are the one principle; there has never been a discrepancy between Heaven and man [in this regard]. (*Ch'ŏnmyŏng tosŏl,*[30] ch. 1, B, 8.12b, pp. 140–141)

The traditional correspondences are readily explained in terms of the unity of principle and serve likewise to substantiate it. But the four(five)-fold categorization of correspondences must also be related to the ultimate unity of principle in order to complete the translation of traditional cosmology into the philosophy of principle. T'oegye does this in his annotation to the above passage:

Principle is originally one; how do its characteristics become four? The response is that principle is the Supreme Ultimate. In the midst of the Supreme Ultimate there is originally no thing or affair, so at first how could there be four characteristics which can be [distinctly] named? But if one considers the matter after activity has commenced, then there necessarily must be a beginning; if there is a beginning there must be its pervasive continuation; if there is pervasive continuation there must be its accomplishment; if there is accomplishment there must be its fulfillment. Therefore it begins and continues, continues and accomplishes, accomplishes and fulfills, and the names of the four characteristics are established. Thus if one speaks of them as combined, then there is the one principle and that is all; if one speaks of them separately, then there are these four principles. Therefore Heaven by means of the one principle ordains all creatures, and each creature has the one principle. (*Ch'ŏnmyŏng tosŏl,* ch. 1, B, p. 141)

Material force and the Difference Between the Sage and the Ordinary Man

Principle is one, but differences in material force give rise to different levels (kinds) of creatures in proportion as the quality of their endowment obstructs or allows the full manifestation of principle. The same explanation accounts for human differences, such as the perfection of the sage or the more problematic condition of the ordinary man that Chu Hsi mentions in his introduction. T'oegye says:

The Way of Heaven is perfectly impartial, and in our being endowed with different degrees of purity and impurity, it is not that there is favoritism. The material force of yin and yang and the Five Agents moves revolvingly, mixing together, descending and ascending back and forth; it becomes confused and mixed with myriad differences. When it wonderfully fuses at the moment of forming things, the types of material force each meets with cannot but have inequalities of purity and impurity, perversity and correctness. (A, 38. 7a, p. 863, Letter to Cho Kibaek)

This general explanation can be pursued on a more precise level of differentiation and typology. In the following passage T'oegye pursues the qualitative differences of material force in terms of the basic polarity of the material force spectrum, the rarified, "spiritual" stuff of Heaven (basically yang) which constitutes man's psychic endowment, and the more coarse stuff of earth (basically yin) which constitutes man's physical aspect. In this context the former is referred to as *ki* (Chinese, *ch'i*—the term usually translated as "material force") and the latter as *chil* (Chinese, *chih*):

> Thus in the production of man, he is endowed with *ki* from Heaven, and Heaven's *ki* has [differences of] clarity and turbidity; he is endowed with *chil* from earth, and the *chil* of earth has [differences of] purity and impurity. Therefore one who is endowed with both the clear and the pure is the most excellent wise man; as regards heavenly principle, the most excellent wise man's knowing it is clear and his practicing it is likewise perfect. He is naturally at one with Heaven. One who is endowed with a combination of the clear *[ki]* and the impure *[chil]* or the turbid *[ki]* with the pure *[chil]* is a person of the middle sort. As regards heavenly principle, the middle person of the one kind has a surplus of knowledge but his practice is insufficient, while the other kind is insufficient in knowledge but has a surplus [of ability] for practice. At the beginning these men are [in some respects] at one with Heaven [and in others] contrary to it. One who is endowed with both turbid *[ki]* and impure *[chil]* is the most foolish person. As regards heavenly principle, the most foolish person's knowledge of it is darkened and his practice is likewise perverse. He is greatly contradictory to Heaven.[31] (*Ch'ŏnmyŏng tosŏl,* ch. 9, B, 8.19a, p. 144)

However, this does not imply any kind of determinism or fatalism; one can by diligent practice modify one's endowment. The extent to which the problem is objectively grounded in the elements of one's psychophysical constitution indicates the difficulty of the task and prepares one for long and strenuous efforts. At the same time this explanation inspires; for the first time Confucians have objectively, almost physiologically, described what makes one a sage and described how there is really a continuum between the sage and the ordinary man. Sagehood becomes an ideal at which one might actually hope to arrive—or at least not miss by much—if one approaches the task with the utmost seriousness.

Chapter 4: THE DIAGRAM OF THE GREAT LEARNING

The Great Learning,[1] *though of ancient origin, is very much a Neo-Confucian creation. It was buried in obscurity as the 42nd chapter of the voluminous compendium, the* Book of Rites, *and attracted little notice until it was taken up by the Ch'eng brothers and Chu Hsi; it subsequently became a classic in itself, its every phrase committed to memory by generation upon generation of Confucian scholars. Crucial to this development was the metaphysics of* li *originated by the Ch'eng brothers. When read in a traditional context, the* Great Learning *seems to be a rather conventional treatise on self-cultivation for rulers and noblemen; but when interpreted in the light of the philosophy of* li *it takes on an entirely new dimension of meaning, pointing out a path of self-cultivation which incorporates the new philosophy and leads to the ultimate perfection of sagehood.*

The original text of the Great Learning *as found in chapter 42 of the* Book of Rites *is undivided. Both of the Ch'eng brothers tried their hand at dividing and reordering it, but it is the text as finally arranged and annotated by Chu Hsi which became the orthodox version prescribed for Confucian students.*[2] *He divided the work into one chapter of "text," which outlines the essential steps of self-cultivation, and ten chapters of "commentary." The text he ascribed to Confucius himself, as handed down to one of his leading disciples, Tseng Tzu, with the chapters of commentary being attributed to Tseng Tzu. This ascription of authorship gave the* Great Learning *the highest possible pedigree of authority; and though it rested upon no evidence beyond the dictum of Chu Hsi himself, his authority was such that it was generally accepted.*

4 Diagram of the Great Learning

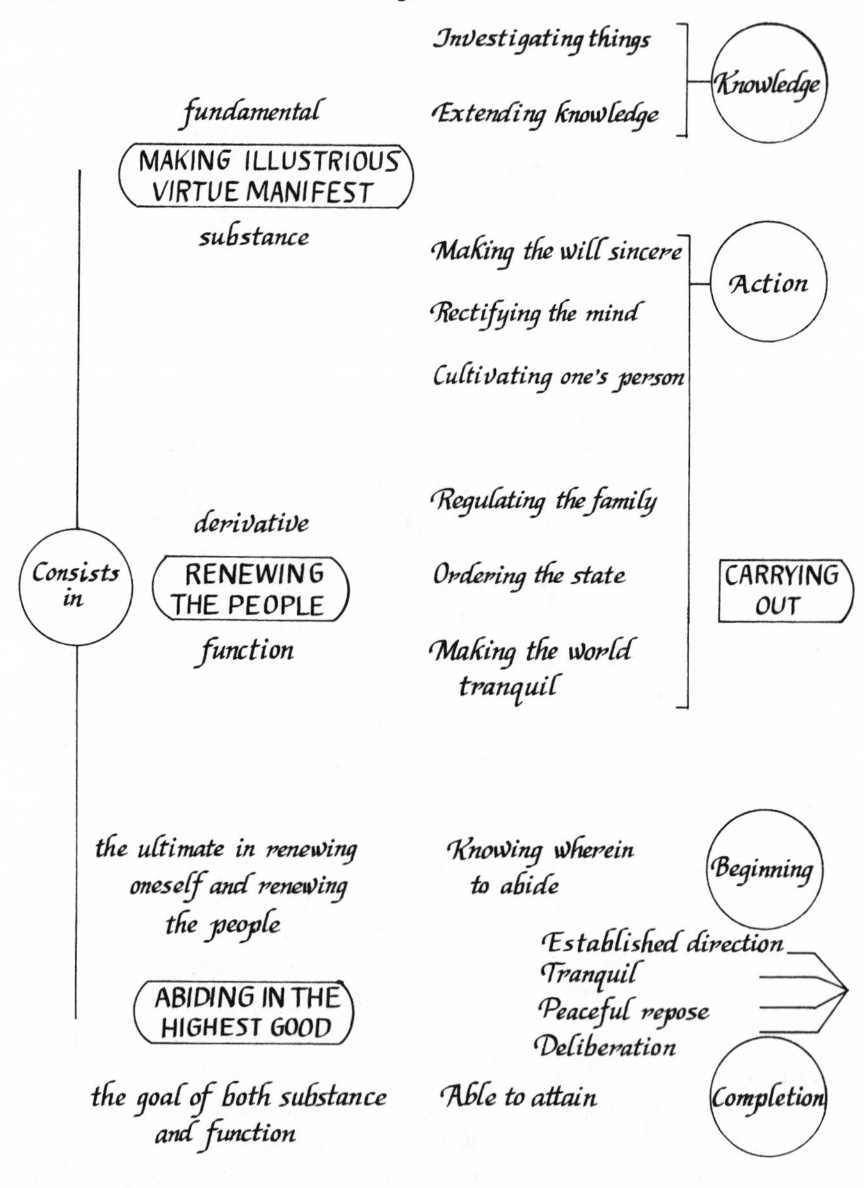

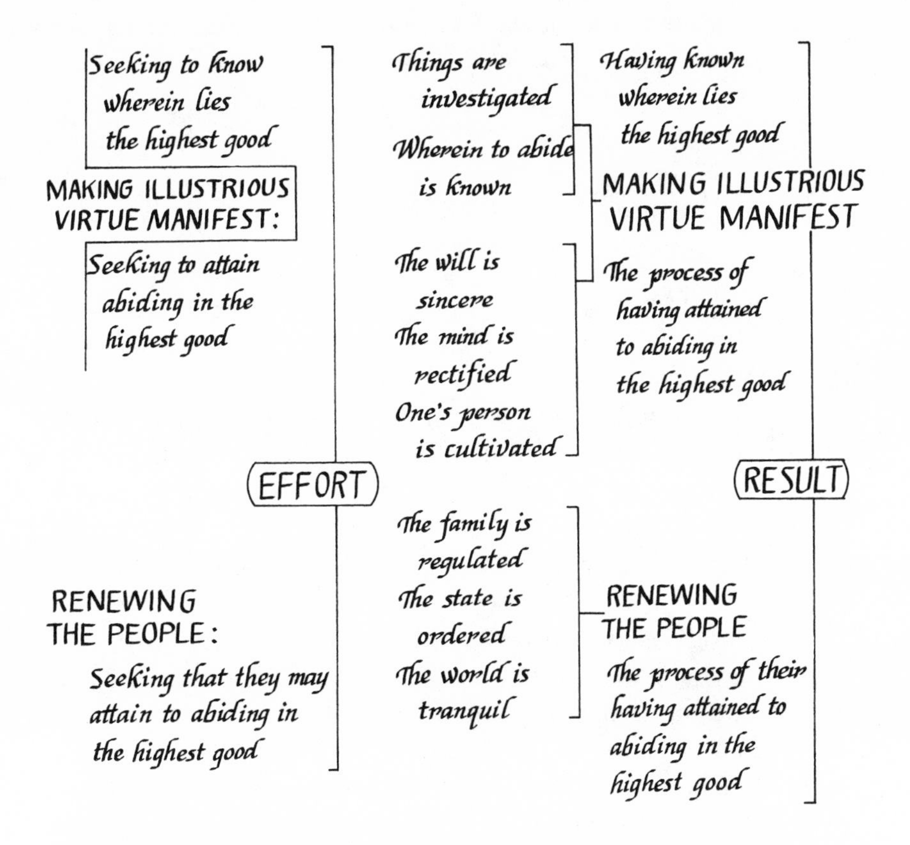

Making illustrious virtue manifest and renewing the people is the result of knowing wherein lies the ultimate good.

These four are the interconnections between knowing wherein to abide and attaining; all are spoken of as results.

Making illustrious virtue manifest and renewing the people means both oneself and the people attain to abiding in the highest good.

This chapter begins with the first section or "text" of the Great Learning, *and then takes up the discussion of mindfulness as the essential means of pursuing the practice of self-cultivation as described in the text.*

The "Text" or First Chapter of the Great Learning

The Way (Tao) of great learning consists in making illustrious virtue manifest, renewing the people, and abiding in the highest good.

Only after knowing wherein to abide can [one's will] have an established direction; only after one has an established direction can one be tranquil; only after one is tranquil can one have peaceful repose; only after one has peaceful repose can one deliberate; only after deliberation can one attain [the highest good].

Things have their roots and their ends; affairs have their beginning and their completion. Knowing what comes first and what comes last will bring one close to the Tao.

The ancients who wished to make illustrious virtue manifest throughout the world would first bring order to their states; those who wished to bring order to their states would first regulate their families; those who wished to regulate their families would first cultivate their own persons; those who wished to cultivate their persons would first rectify their minds; those who wished to rectify their minds would first make their intentions sincere; those who wished to make their intentions sincere would first extend their knowledge; the extension of knowledge consists in the investigation of things.[3]

When things are investigated, knowledge is extended[4] when knowledge is extended, the intention becomes sincere; when the intention becomes sincere, the mind is rectified; when the mind is rectified, one's person is cultivated; when one's person is cultivated, the family will be regulated; when the family is regulated, the state will be ordered; when the state is well-ordered, the world will be tranquil.

From the Son of Heaven down to the common man, all must regard cultivation of their person as the root and foundation. There has never been a case when the root is in disorder and the end is nonetheless well-ordered; there never has been a case in which that which is carefully nurtured wastes away, or that which is negligently tended flourishes.

Comments from Chu Hsi's Questions and Answers on the Great Learning

Someone asked: "How does one apply himself to the practice of mindfulness?"

Master Chu said: "Ch'eng I spoke of it as 'concentrating on one thing and not departing [from it],'[5] and again in terms of being 'well-ordered and even-minded, grave and quiet.'[6] His disciple, Hsieh [Liang-tso], explained it as 'the method of always being clear-minded and alert.'[7] In terms of Yin [T'un's] explanation, it is 'possessing one's mind in a condition of recollection and not permitting anything [to have a hold on it].[8] . . . Mindfulness is the mastery of one's entire mind and the foundation [of correctly dealing with] all affairs. If one understands this method of applying his effort, he will understand that Elementary Learning relies on this to make a beginning; if he understands how Elementary Learning relies on it for the beginning, then as for the Great Learning's necessarily relying upon it in order to achieve the completion, he will be able to see it as the one thread running through all and will have no doubts.

For once the mind is established in this condition, one may proceed with this state of mind to pursue the investigation of things and the extension of knowledge, and thereby exhaustively comprehend principle as it is present in things and affairs; this is what is meant by "honoring the good inborn qualities of one's nature and following the path of inquiry and study."[9] One may proceed with this state of mind to make his intentions sincere and rectify his mind, and thereby cultivate his person; this is what is meant by, "first establish that which is greater and the lesser will not be able to take it away."[10] One may proceed in this state of mind to regulate the family, and properly order the state, and thereby attain even to making the whole world tranquil; this is what is meant by "Cultivate your own person in order to give ease to the people;[11] make much of reverence [in your own person] and the world will enjoy tranquility."[12] All of this shows that one cannot absent himself from the practice of mindfulness for a single day. This being the case, the one word, "mindfulness," how can it but be the essence of both the beginning and the completion of sage learning![13]

T'oegye's Comments

Above is the first chapter of "the writing handed down in the Confucian school.[14] Kwŏn Kŭn,[15] who was an official in the early years of this dynasty, made the diagram of it.[16] The text of the first chapter is followed by a quotation from the *Questions and Answers on the Great Learning*'s general discussion of the meaning of Great Learning and Elementary Learning; this treatise was introduced in the text accompanying the diagram of the *Elementary Learning.*

It is not only the explanation of these two, however, which should be seen in combination; all of the eight diagrams which precede and follow them should also be seen in relation to these two diagrams. The two diagrams which precede these deal with the ultimate [framework]: seeking out the foundation, broadening and perfecting it, embodying Heaven and totally fulfilling the Tao. They present the ultimate goal and the basic foundation of Great Learning and Elementary Learning. The six diagrams that follow deal with applying one's efforts: understanding the good, making one's person sincere, exalting virtue, and broadening [the self-cultivation] project.[17] They represent the field [of application] of Great Learning and Elementary Learning, that which is to be worked upon.

And as for mindfulness, it runs throughout both the former and the latter; both in applying the effort and reaping its fruit, one must follow the work [carefully] and not let it go amiss. Therefore Master Chu explained it as he did, and these ten diagrams all take mindfulness as the essential. ([Chou Tun-i's] *Explanation of the Diagram of the Supreme Ultimate* speaks of quiescence rather than mindfulness [as the essential]; in his commentary on it Chu Hsi speaks of mindfulness in order to remedy this. [Note added by T'oegye]).

Commentary

Making Illustrious Virtue Manifest

"Illustrious virtue" is understood as the originally good nature of man, the fullness of principle with which we are naturally endowed. This nature can be obscured by the impurity of our psychophysical constitution, but it remains nonetheless intact within us; the task of the *Great Learning,* as interpreted in the Ch'eng-Chu school, is to describe how, by study and practice, we may restore that nature to its fully functioning and manifest condition and thus become what we are born to be. T'oegye in the following passage presents one of the root metaphors operative in this conceptualization:

The principle with which we are endowed [as our nature] is originally one with our person, but it is circumstantially restricted by material force and obstructed by desires which consequently form layer after layer of obstruction. If in exhaustively investigating principle one is assiduous in applying his efforts, rubbing through the first layer of obstruction is extremely difficult; rubbing away the next is not as difficult as the former, and again rubbing away the next, one becomes aware that it is gradually becoming easier. The mind of moral principle continually follows and in proportion to the rubbing away process gradually becomes manifest. It is like a mirror which is originally bright but has become dimmed by repeated layers of dust and dirt. When one uses polish to clean it, at first it takes the utmost effort: one scrapes and scrubs and barely gets off one layer of dirt. How can it but be exceedingly difficult! But as one continues with a second and third polishing, the effort required gradually becomes less and the brightness gradually emerges in proportion as the dirt is removed. Nevertheless, people who are able to get beyond the exceedingly difficult stage and arrive at the gradually easier ones are certainly rare. And even more regrettably, there are some who arrive at the gradually easier stages and do not increase their effort in order to arrive at the point where the perfect brightness appears, and consequently come to a halt in their application [to this process]. (A, 37.26b, p. 848, Letter to Yi P'yŏngsuk)

The basic idea here is clear and straightforward. However there are questions related to the philosophy of principle which are not adequately addressed by this simple image. Perhaps the most basic of these has to do with whether or not principle is totally passive in this process, as the image of the mirror would suggest. This question will be taken up below in the fifth section of the Commentary.

The Investigation of Principle

The *Great Learning* traces the process of cultivation step by step back to the foundation upon which all depend: 'Those who wished to make their intentions sincere would first extend their knowledge; the extension of knowledge consists in the investigation of things." From this investigation of things, understood as the exhaustive investigation of the principles of things/affairs, everything else follows; this, then, becomes a point of crucial importance in Neo-Confucian self-cultivation in the Ch'eng-Chu school.

The investigation of principle has as its aim truth, indeed, absolute truth, but it would be a fundamental mistake to confuse the objectivity of this kind of truth with the modern scientific drive for an objective and detached kind of knowledge of things. For the essential concern is moral, and the emphasis is on the subject rather than the object as such; that is, the essential thing is self-transformation through a personal grasp, appropriation of, and realization of moral truth as the truth of one's own existence. The following passage exemplifies this process:

As for the interpretation of humanity, righteousness, propriety, and wisdom, if one only looks at their terminological meaning, though in the recitation or interpretation [of texts] one does not make the slightest error, in the end what profit is there in it? It is necessary to make the meaning of these four words one's [personal] subject matter; entering into thought on their meaning sit quietly, immerse your mind in them, and investigate them deeply, mulling them over and getting their real flavor with a personal understanding and personal examination: Humanity is in my own mind; how does it act as the character of the mind, how does it act as the principle of love, how does it act as the moral principle of a warm, harmonious, affectionate love? Righteousness is in my mind; how does it act as the moderator of the mind, how does it act as the correct conduct of affairs, how does it act as the moral principle of judgment and discrimination? With propriety and wisdom one also ought to go through the same process. For in the original substance of the nature there are just these four. Within the undivided single principle are present ten thousand functions, as if there is a certain circumstance or intentionality but actually there is no [particular] form or location. If one does not apply himself profoundly and truly accumulate [the results of] this effort for a long time, so as to have a clear view of the broad and shining wellspring and attain [the fruits of] being constantly mindful of integrity and truthfulness in speech and liberality and reverence in conduct in the course of daily life,[18] it will be almost impossible to have the strength to extend and fulfill [this nature] with its inexhaustible responsive function. (A, 37,25b-26a, p. 848, (Letter to Yi P'yŏngsuk)

Principle makes things be as they are and is also the norm for activity. One must attain a deep personal understanding of the nature of the deepest and truest reality of one's own being and the being of other things in order to respond in a manner faithful to that reality in the unlimited variety of situations that arise.

Expressions such as "immersion," "mull over and get the taste," "personally understand," and "personally experience" are constantly used in discussing the investigation of principle; they reflect the deep mental involvement and personal appropriation which are essential to this process. Another term constantly used is "ripening":

Master Yen P'ing's[19] words to Master Chu say, "This moral principle is entirely a matter of becoming ripe in one's practice in daily life."[20] What is manifested in the daily practice of activity and tranquility, speech and silence, is all a matter of heavenly principle. Only when one has become habituated to the exercise of mental self-possession and self-reflection in the context of dealing with such matters is what one knows something real; when one attains this it is true learning. The maxims of the sages and worthies are not to be considered only in the morning or during the day; during the early dawn hours when the mind is tranquil one should personally examine heavenly principle. As for one's self-reflection in the course of daily activity and what one does during the morning and the rest of the day, when one's personal embodiment of this in practice has become [fully] ripened, sage learning is a reality. (*OHN* 22a-b, B, p. 829)

Analytically there is a distinction between the investigation of principle and mindfulness, study and practice. In this passage one sees them function as an interdependent whole in which understanding is ripened in practice as constant mental self-possession makes daily life itself the context for deepening understanding, i.e., the investigation of principle. This process is complemented by what we would more ordinarily call study, that is, book learning. In this too, ripening is crucial, lest it be only reading and not true self-transformation through appropriating what is read:

[Kim Sŏngil][21] asked about the method of reading books. Master [T'oegye] said: It is only a matter of ripening. In all reading of books, although one may clearly understand the meaning of the text, if it is not ripened, as soon as it is read it is forgotten, and it is certain that one cannot preserve it in his mind-and-heart. After study one must further apply oneself to becoming thoroughly versed and ripened in it; only then will he be able to preserve it in his mind-and-heart and be thoroughly steeped in its taste. (*OHN* 1.7a, B, p. 792)

Ripening, then, is the profound personal understanding and appropriation of principle through the gradual process of deep reflection and attentive experience in daily life. As an integral part of the investigation of principle, it signifies the holistic nature of the process, which is far removed from the type of abstract mental exercise that might be suggested by the term "investigation of principle."

Finally, we might note that ripening is a natural process. T'oegye is highly critical of facile theorizing and of forcing conclusions when they do not arise naturally out of the matrix of one's total understanding. He advises the brilliant Yi I (Yulgok)[22] on the investigation of principle as follows:

In what one investigates, sometimes one meets with complexities and intricacies that using all his strength he cannot get through, or sometimes one's nature happens to have a blind spot on the matter and it is difficult to force illumination and break it open. Then one ought to set the matter aside and approach another and investigate it. In this way, investigating one way and then another, there is an accumulation which deepens and ripens; the mind naturally gradually clears and the actuality of moral principle gradually becomes manifest to one's eye. Then if one again takes up what he formerly could not successfully investigate and reflects on it, combining it for consideration and comparison with what he has already successfully investigated, while one hardly is aware of what is happening they will interact at the same time to produce enlightenment and understanding regarding what had not been investigated [successfully]. This is the flexible approach to the investigation of principle; it does not mean that when an investigation is not successful one just puts it aside [for good]. (A, 14.21a, p. 371, Letter to Yi Sukhŏn)

The Centrality of Mindfulness

The Text of the *Great Learning* which accompanies the diagram describes an orderly, step-by-step process of cultivation. This was of profound interest to Neo-Confucians, and there is an extensive literature dealing with the various steps, their interconnections and the like. But of all this, T'oegye chooses for his commentary Chu Hsi's remarks concerning mindfulness, for although the word does not appear in the text, mindfulness is considered central to the meaning of the *Great Learning.*

Chu Hsi's remarks include a number of the phrases earlier Neo-Confucians used to describe the practice of mindfulness. Their variety reflects the fact that mindfulness is, as a technical method, a Neo-Confucian discovery; thus the early thinkers each grappled with it and expressed it in their own way, or in various ways. A closer consideration of these will be postponed for the final two chapters of the *Ten Diagrams,* which take mindfulness as their express subject.

Why mindfulness is considered central should be evident from the discussion of the investigation of principle in the preceding section. Without a well-cultivated ability to recollect and focus one's mind, the process of sustained reflection and immersion of the mind would be impossible; and equally important, mindfulness is the quality of awareness which makes daily activity an occasion of continual growth and deepening in understanding, rather than just a distraction from quiet reflection or only a field for applying what is learned elsewhere. If on the one hand the investigation of principle cannot go on without mindfulness, on the other, mindfulness works to transform life into the growth process termed "investigation of principle." As T'oegye says, "Although the two are related as head and tail and are really two divisions of practice, you should certainly not concern yourself with making them separate steps. It is just necessary to take mutual advancement in both as the method" (A, 14.18b, p. 369, Letter to Yi Sukhŏn)

Principle External and Internal: Things and One's Nature

The task of "making manifest the illustrious virtue" of one's mind is intrinsically linked, in Chu Hsi's interpretation of the *Great Learning,* with the investigation of the principle of things and affairs. Principle, unitary and above forms, transcends the categories of internality and externality and thus provides the essential linkage between the interior realm of mind and nature and the external world of things and affairs:

The Teacher [T'oegye] quoted Master Chu's writing to instruct me [Yi Tŏkhong][23] saying, " 'Although the mind is the master of this single body, the emptiness and spirituality of its substance is such that it has charge over all the principles of the world; although principle is scattered in things and affairs, its subtle and marvelous function actually is not outside of the mind of a single individual. From the first it cannot be discussed in terms of [the distinctions of] inner and outer, subtle and coarse.' "[24] Adding a note [T'oegye said], "Although principle is in things, its function is actually in the mind; those who would investigate principle must first of all understand what this means." (*OHN,* 4.1a, B, p. 836)

The exact meaning of T'oegye's final remark on this important passage from Chu Hsi's *Ta-hsüeh huo wen* is cryptic, for his interpretation of the passage changed in the very last year of his life (see below, next sec.) and we do not know the date of this comment. But at least in part it addresses an issue actively discussed at this time in Korean intellectual circles: in view of the transcendent unity of principle, is there any need for an externalistic orientation in investigating it? The following passage reflects the nature of the problem and T'oegye's way of responding to it:

In terms of principle, there certainly is no distinction between the self and things, the internal and the external, the subtle and the coarse; but in terms of things, all the things and affairs of the world are actually all outside of me. How can one on the basis of the unity of principle therefore say the things and affairs of the world are all within me? It is only that the principle of every thing and affair is the principle with which my mind is endowed; it is not external because things are external, and because it is internal [it does not mean things] are internal. Therefore the former Confucians [i.e., the Ch'engs and Chu Hsi], although they say principle is in things and affairs, do not thereby neglect this [principle within the mind] and speak only of that; although they say to approach things and approach affairs [to investigate their principle], they do not thereby put aside the self and approach those [external things]. (A, 26.35a-b, p. 628, Letter to Chŏng Chajung)

The shadow of Wang Yang-ming,[25] whose school of thought was popular at this time in China, looms large here. If the mind's (nature's) endowment with principle is equated with the innate presence of all things within the mind, the role of externally oriented inquiry is undermined and the process of self-cultivation takes on an inner, subject-centered orientation in which mind is not only central, but all-inclusive. T'oegye is highly critical of Wang Yang-ming on precisely this issue:

Yang-ming is only troubled that external things restrict the mind and does not recognize that the proper norm for human conduct and the norm for things, the true and perfect principle, is the same as the principle with which the mind is originally endowed, and that engaging in study and investigating principle is certainly the means to clarify the substance of the original mind and perfect the function of the original mind. Rather he wants to get rid of all affairs and things with a thesis that takes them all and drags them into the original mind. How is this any different from Buddhist views? (A, 41.26a-b, p. 923)

For T'oegye, the ultimate unity and identity of principle explains how the investigation of principle in external matters is simultaneously a removing of the personal ignorance and self-centeredness which overlay its living presence in our natures and hinders our natural responsiveness in accord with principle. But it does not mean we are innately endowed with all the knowledge necessary; principle as our nature and the substance of the mind may be the basis of an innate tendency to recognize and respond to its diverse manifestation in things, but the stubborn externality of things means that *they* must be carefully attended to in order to fulfill what is inherent in our natures. The transcendence of principle constitutes an intrinsic interrelatedness among beings, not, as in the Buddhist case, an ultimate and absolute identity among them.

Can Principle "Approach"?

We have noted the central importance in the *Great Learning* of the phrases which in Chu Hsi's interpretation read, "the extension of knowledge consists in the investigation of things (*ko wu*, lit. 'approach things [to investigate them]'). When things are investigated (*wu ko*, lit. 'things [are] approached') knowledge is extended." Wang Yang-ming preferred to read *ko* as "rectify," which radically altered the significance of the *Great Learning.* During T'oegye's later years there was another controversy regarding these phrases; unlike the Chinese controversy, all concerned accepted Chu Hsi's basic interpretive vocabulary, but there emerged grammatical questions that entailed different views of his meaning. Of particular importance was the second phrase, *wu ko* and Chu Hsi's annotation of the phrase, which rendered literally would be "*Wu ko* means the ultimate point of the principle of things without not arrive."

Literary Chinese is uninflected, but Korean is a highly inflected language both as regards verb endings, and more important in this case, nouns, which have case endings somewhat like the nominative (subject), dative (indirect object, point toward which motion is directed), and accusative (direct object) which are found in Latin and Greek. It was common to insert Korean inflections into the reading of Chinese texts, and in some cases the choice of inflections involved critical issues of interpretation. The phrase *wu ko,* and Chu Hsi's annotation of it, was such a case.

The point of contention was whether the dative or nominative should be used. If the dative, the passage in the light of Chu Hsi's annotation would read: "When one has arrived at the ultimate point of the principle of a thing (or things) knowledge is extended." But several groups, for different reasons,[26] argued for the use of the nominative rather than the dative. This could still lead to various interpretations, but the one which was the main object of contention would read the passage as, "When the ultimate point of the principle of a thing (things) has perfectly arrived [in the mind] knowledge is extended." This interpretation was favored in particular by those who objected to the dative on the grounds that it implied an inappropriate externality in principle. T'oegye strongly argued the case for the dative, but permitted a nominative in an innocuous sense which preserved the same meaning as the dative interpretation. The following passage reflects his basic interpretation and his principal reservation regarding the alternative reading:

[Someone might] say: "Then it is enough to just use the [dative] suffix *-e;* why do you say the [nominative] suffix *-i* is also acceptable?" I say: This is the same as their usage insofar as the [nominative] suffix *-i* is the same, but its significance is different. For those who now use the nominative mean the ultimate of the principle of things of itself completely arrives in my mind. That is, it is the mistake of dragging [external things] into [the mind] and is wrong. When I use the nominative suffix *-i* I mean that the ultimate *(-i)* of the various principles has not a single aspect which has not been arrived at. Then principle as ever is itself in the thing or affair and in my investigation of it there is no aspect which has not been arrived at, that is all. Therefore

I say [the nominative suffix] is also acceptable. (A, 26.37a, p. 629, Letter to Chŏng Chajung)

That is, he senses in the nominative reading a current which would deny the external aspect of the investigation of things and move in the direction of Wang Yang-ming, and so he rejects it. In the last year of his life, however, he became convinced by evidence adduced by Ki Taesŭng[27] that the nominative reading in precisely the sense he had rejected should be accepted. In one of his last letters to Ki he writes:

The reason that formerly I stubbornly maintained my mistaken thesis is that I only knew to maintain Master Chu's explanation that principle has no feelings or intent, no calculation, no productive activity,[28] as a basis for saying that I can exhaustively arrive at the ultimate point of the principle of things, but how could principle of itself arrive at the ultimate point. . . . Recently Kim Ijŏng[29] conveyed to me the three or four items of Master Chu's sayings you had examined that treat of principles arriving, and only then did I begin to fear that my view was mistaken. . . . For Master [Chu's] explanation . . . presents this meaning as clearly as the sun and stars, but I, although I had always had a taste for these words, was not able to penetrate them to this extent.

His [Chu Hsi's] explanation says: "That whereby people pursue learning is the mind and principle, and that is all. Although the mind is the master of this single body, the emptiness and spirituality of its substance is such that it has charge over all the principles of the world; although principle is scattered in things and affairs, its subtle and marvelous function actually is not outside of the mind of a single individual. From the first it cannot be discussed in terms of [the distinctions of] inner and outer, subtle and coarse."[30] In the annotations someone asks: "Is the marvelous subtlety of the function the function of the mind or not?" Master Chu says: "Principle necessarily has its function; why must one further say this is the mind's function?"[31]

The substance of the mind is endowed with this principle; as for principle, then, there is nothing which does not have it and not a single thing in which it is not present. But nevertheless, its function is not outside of the mind of a single individual; for although principle is in things, its function actually is in the mind. When he says principle is in all things but its function actually is not outside of the mind of a single individual, there is the doubt that principle cannot of itself function and must wait upon man's mind; it seems as if one may not speak in terms of [principle] arriving of itself. But then he further says, "Principle necessarily has its function; why must one further say this is the function of the mind?" Then although its function is not outside of a man's mind, the marvelousness of its function actually consists in principle's [self] manifestation; following on what a person's mind approaches, there is nothing [of principle] which does not arrive, nothing which is not exhausted. I should only fear that in my investigation of things there is that which has not yet been approached; I should not be concerned that principle may not be able of itself to arrive [in my mind].

Thus when [the *Great Learning*] speaks of "the investigation of things (*ko wu*)," it certainly means that I exhaustively approach the ultimate point of the principle of things. But coming to its saying, *wu ko,* why may one not say it means that the ultimate point of the principle of things, following upon what I investigate, completely arrives [in my mind]. This recognizes that the matter of having no feelings or intent, no productive activity, refers to the original substance of principle, while [the fact that] it manifests itself following [upon my investigation] and completely arrives [in my mind] is a matter of principle's extremely wondrous function. Formerly I only saw the nonaction of the original substance [of principle] and did not understand its marvelous function's being able to actively manifest itself; this was dangerously close to understanding principle as something dead. Was this not an extreme departure from the truth? (A, 18.20a-21b, pp. 464-465, Letter to Ki Myŏngŏn).

In terms of T'oegye's interpretation of *wu ko,* this is a reversal of his former position. But he still emphatically affirms the necessity of investigating external things; that is, he is not siding with those who argued for this interpretation on the basis of the unity and nonexteriority of principle. His change of mind is rather based upon a passage which opens the way, in his eyes, to understanding a more active role for principle.

One notes his enthusiasm; his response is more that of someone who finally gets the go-ahead to do what he has really wanted to do, than that of someone finally backed into a corner and forced to admit he is wrong. True, T'oegye has an exceptional ability to rejoice in true insight, even at the expense of his former positions. But in this case he is really accepting a position which resonates deeply with other aspects of his thought;[32] in particular, the proposition that principle actively manifests itself to (in) the inquiring mind parallels the active role he delineates for principle in the issuance of certain feelings (the

Four Beginnings) in man's moral life (see chapter 6). What is remarkable is not that he modified his opinion, but that his scholarly caution and restraint was so strong that he resisted almost to the end a proposition which, notwithstanding the questionable inclinations of some who supported it, was attractive as a complement to his analysis of the relationship of mind, nature, and feelings.

Chapter 5: DIAGRAM OF RULES OF THE WHITE DEER HOLLOW ACADEMY

This is the last of the three chapters the Ten Diagrams *devotes to the topic of learning. The chapters on Elementary Learning and Great Learning described the continuity of the learning process from youth to adulthood; they showed how from beginning to end it is a twofold process of study and practice and emphasized the role of mindfulness as its central methodology. The Five Relationships occupy a central place in the* Elementary Learning, *while the investigation of principle and the steps of practical self-cultivation and its expansion to include all of society are developed in the* Great Learning. *This chapter uses the rules Chu Hsi established for the White Deer Hollow Academy*[1] *to show the structural integration of these themes: as presented here, the Five Relationships are not only the foundation, but the sum and substance of all learning, the object toward which all study and practice are ultimately devoted.*

In his comments, T'oegye narrates the story of Chu Hsi's refounding of the White Deer Hollow Academy and mentions the official support it had earlier received from Emperor T'ai Tsung (960–976)*. T'oegye viewed such private academies* (sŏwŏn, shu-yüan) *as ideal institutions for Neo-Confucian learning, and was anxious to see them spread in Korea; for this, he felt, official royal sanction and support were essential. Hence there is a special point in his including this material in a document he hopes will be repeatedly perused by the king. The fifth section of the Commentary will discuss T'oegye's role in obtaining royal support for private academies in Korea and the important role they subsequently came to play in Yi dynasty society.*

5 Diagram of the Rules of the White

Five Instructions		Steps of learning
Between father and son there should be affection		Broadly study
Between ruler and minister there should be righteousness		Accurately inquire
Between husband and wife there should be proper distinction		Carefully think
Between elder and younger there should be proper order		Clearly discriminate
Between friends there should be faithfulness		Earnestly practice

[Above] are the items of the Five Instructions

Yao and Shun appointed Chieh as Minister of Instruction to reverently set forth the Five Instructions, that is, these [Five Relationships]; learning is a matter of learning these and that is all. There are likewise five steps in the process of learning which are set forth [above to the right].

Deer Hollow Academy

The essentials of investigating principle

- Integrity and trustworthiness in speech; earnestness and mindfulness in deed
- Restrain anger, block desires; refer good to others, correct transgressions

The essentials of cultivating one's person

- Be correct according to what is right, and do not consider profit
- Think only of seeking the Tao, and do not calculate accomplishments

The essentials of dealing with affairs

- What you do not wish done to yourself, do not do to others
- When your activities do not succeed, reflect and seek the reason within yourself

The essentials of how to treat others

Chu Hsi's Remarks on the *Rules*[2]

In considering the purport of how the ancient sages and wise men instructed others in the pursuit of learning, I find that it was totally a matter of explaining and clarifying moral principle for the cultivation of one's person; after [such cultivation was accomplished] it was extended so that [this rectifying influence] might reach others. It was never merely a matter of concentrating on memorizing readings and devoting oneself to literary composition in order to fish for a fine reputation and get a profitable salary. As for those who study nowadays, however, it is just the reverse.

Nevertheless, the methods whereby the sages and wise men instructed others are present in the Classics; students who have a firm intention [to pursue real learning] certainly should read and become versed in them, pondering deeply and inquiring into and discerning [their meaning]. If one understands according to principle what ought to be and takes it as his personal duty that it necessarily be so, then as for being furnished with rules and restrictions, what need will he have to wait for others to set them up in order to have something to follow and observe!

Nowadays there are rules for study, but they are only superficial in their treatment of those who pursue learning, and moreover the standards they present are not necessarily what the ancients had in mind. Therefore I will not restore any such rules to this hall; rather I have selected the great fundamental principles according to which all the sages and wise men have instructed others regarding learning, arranged them as above, and put them up on the eaves [of the hall].

May you gentlemen discuss and clarify [their meaning] among yourselves, practice and keep them, and take them as your personal responsibility; then the caution and fear with which you conduct yourself in your thought, speech, and activity will certainly be more strict than these rules. But if at times this is not the case and one transgresses the bounds,[3] then he must take up these so-called rules; they certainly cannot be neglected. May you gentlemen keep them in mind!

T'oegye's Comments

The above rules were made by Master Chu to be posted for the students of the White Deer Hollow Academy. The grotto was on the southern side of K'uang-lu Mountain in the northern part of Nan-k'ang Prefecture. During the T'ang dynasty Li Po[4] (fl. c. 810) while living there in retirement raised a white deer which followed him about, and the Hollow was named accordingly. During the Southern T'ang (937–975) an academy was established there and named the National School (*Kuo-hsiang*); it always had several hundred students. Emperor T'ai Tsung (r.960–976) of the Sung dynasty showed his favor and encouraged the academy by bestowing books and giving an official rank to the head of the academy, but since then it had fallen into decay and ruin. When Master Chu was serving as Prefect of Nan-k'ang, he petitioned the court to restore it, assembled students, set up rules, and gave instruction in Neo-Confucian learning (*tao-hsüeh*).[5] Instruction in such academies subsequently flourished throughout the empire.

I have taken the items contained in the text of the rules and made this diagram of them so that one may easily see and reflect upon them. For the teachings of [the sages] Yao and Shun consisted in the Five Relationships, and the learning of the Three Dynasties was entirely a matter of manifesting proper human relationships. Therefore in the rules the investigation of principle and diligent practice are both based upon the Five Relationships. And although what is furnished in the rules and restrictions of the learning of Emperors and rulers cannot be entirely the same as for ordinary students, insofar as they are based upon proper relationships and involve the investigation of principle and diligent practice as the essence of the method of properly cultivating one's mind-and-heart, there has never been any difference. Therefore I present this diagram with the others to furnish Your Majesty morning and night with "the admonitions of the Chamber Councilors."[6]

[T'oegye's note:]
The above five diagrams are based upon the Tao of Heaven, but their application consists in manifesting proper human relationships and devoting one's effort to the cultivation of virtue.

Commentary

On the Essence of Learning

The rules Chu Hsi wrote for study had great authority; in Korea they were written on the wall of the lecture hall of the Confucian Academy (Sŏnggyŭn'gwăn), and T'oegye referred to them in directing his own students.[7] When he wrote his own rules for the Isan *sŏwŏn,* he stipulated that the Rules for the White Deer Hollow Academy be written on its walls.[8]

In T'oegye's view the great value of these rules is that they express the essence of all learning, on whatever level, in terms of its fundamental content and basic methodology. When Pak Yŏng[9] wrote a commentary on the Rules of the White Deer Hollow Academy, T'oegye criticized it on a number of precise points of interpretation, but his most fundamental reservation was that Pak saw fit to introduce into his comments a discussion of "loftier" matters dealing with the substance of the Tao, the one thread running through all, and the like. T'oegye objected that these rules are perfect already, without going into such matters:

The learning of Master Chu is replete as regards both the integral substance and the great function.[10] But in his setting up rules for those who pursue learning he particularly takes the Five Relationships as the foundation, which he extends in terms of the order of learning and finishes in terms of what is involved in earnest practice, without going as far as discussing the integral substance of the Tao as such; this likewise is the intent conveyed by the disciples of Confucius. In his way of teaching [as exemplified in these rules], the items which follow "broadly study" have to do with the extension of knowledge to the utmost, and those that follow "earnestly practice" have to do with diligent practice. He treats all the scholars of the world in terms of these two. Principle has no distinction between subtle and coarse; one begins from the coarser [understanding] and attains the subtler. Words encompass both loftier and lower levels; one studies the lower to arrive at the loftier. It is as when a flock drinks from a river and each is filled according to his capacity. There are the lofty who are sages and wise men, and the more lowly who are good scholars; all can succeed with this approach. (A, 19,25a-b, p. 479, Letter to Hwang Chunggŏ)

Particular topics are more suited to different levels of development, but even the loftiest or most profound of these, in the Confucian context, has its true significance in its bearing on one's proper conduct in relations with other human beings (i.e., the Five Relationships). Thus these rules transcend any topical discussion and are meaningful at all stages of learning and cultivation.

The five items of Chu Hsi's rules, from "broadly study" to "earnestly practice" are taken from the twentieth chapter of the *Doctrine of the Mean.* Of the four pertaining to the investigation of principle T'oegye focuses especially on the third "careful thought":

These four are the items involved in carrying knowledge to the utmost, and among the four, careful thought is by far the most weighty. What is the meaning of "thought"? It is seeking the matter out in one's own mind-and-heart and having a personal experience and grasp of it. (A, 6.43b, p. 185)

This reminds us once again that learning in this context is a spiritual project, and the essential exercise of the mind is not speculative knowledge but personal transformation through a profound personal understanding and appropriation of what is studied.

How to Read a Book

True learning is not book learning, but books are nonetheless an important resource, for it is by the written word that the truths discovered by sages and wise men are crystallized and made available for personal reappropriation by later generations. We have already seen the aspect of reading which makes it a process of spiritual transformation, but the matter has further complexities: the synthesis of the Ch'eng-Chu school is woven of many strands and based upon a classical corpus which, even in its more limited Neo-Confucian form,[11] does not speak with a single voice. Personal appropriation of this material beyond the most elementary level becomes, for the Neo-Confucian, a matter of achieving a level of insight in which discordant notes fall into place and the whole may be grasped as a polyphonic unity. This, needless to say, demands a fairly sophisticated hermeneutical process. T'oegye presents his approach as follows:

My own awkward method of reading books is this: whenever the sages and wise men speak of moral principle, when it is plain, then I follow its plainness and seek [the meaning] on that level and do not venture lightly to tie it to some hidden meaning; when it is hidden, then I follow its hiddenness and investigate it, not venturing lightly to associate it with what is plain. When it is on a shallow level, I base myself on the shallow and do not venture to bore through it and make it deep; when it is deep, then I approach it as deep and do not venture to stop at the shallow. Aspects they explain with analytical distinctions I look at as analytically distinct and do not take it as any harm to the fact of the undivided whole; what they explain in terms of an undivided whole I look at as an undivided whole and do not take it as any harm to there being analytic distinctions. I do not base myself on my private opinion and drag the left side and pull on the right in order either to join what has been analytically distinguished into an undivided whole or to separate the undivided whole to make analytic distinctions. Doing this for a long, long time, one naturally and gradually comes to see that there is a logic [underlying their sayings] with no room for disorder; one gradually perceives that the words of the sages and wise men, whatever manner of explanation they use, are each appropriate in their place and do not obstruct one another. (A, 16.42a-b, p. 422, Letter to Ki Myŏngŏn)

The fundamental assumption of an inner logic underlying diverse expressions is a hermeneutical equivalent of "principle is one but its manifestations are diverse"; it finds expression in T'oegye's confidence in the usefulness and feasibility of diagrammatic summaries (a form widely used in Korea) which are constructed on just this premise and are to be used as materials for prolonged reflective consideration along the lines suggested in this passage. His evident concern with the tension between distinctions and unity reflects the extent to which questions having to do with the dualistic monism of the philosophy of principle and material force, and the ramifications of both the distinctness and the interdependence of the two occupy his mind.[12]

The other categories of interpretation, "the plain and the hidden," "the shallow and the deep," provide for the flexibility necessary for working through authoritative passages which at times seem to contradict one another. T'oegye is sharply critical when he feels students are just pulling out verbal contradictions from readings and making questions out of them, rather than quietly thinking them through to attain real understanding. On the other hand, such tools are counterproductive if their use is not controlled by a determined intent to really understand what a given passage is getting at. The unity of principle easily leads people in the direction of superficial syntheses which miss the true fruit to be gained by a more ripened working through of the materials and their problems:

In general, there is just a single principle which runs throughout the whole world and all creatures. Therefore if one does a rough and ignorant job of combining moral principle and verbal expressions into a thesis, there is nothing which cannot be made the same, and if one drags in [passages out of context] as pointing toward one's explanation, there is nothing which is not plausible. But in the end this does not [take into account] how at the beginning this was not the original intent of the words established by the sages and wise men. It is not enough for the discovery of the real teachings of the Classics, but finally suffices only to obscure the true principle and confuse one's actual insight [into it]. This is a pervasive problem among those who study. (A, 19.31a, p. 482, Letter to Hwang Chunggŏ)

One can see in these passages how "careful thought" is central as a means of both personal appropriation and scholarly rigor in study; the two are combined, for it is the objective truth profoundly grasped which is the instrument of personal transformation.

On Neo-Confucians and Worldly Confucians

When we look back at a certain period of Chinese or Korean or Japanese history and label it and the people acting in it as "Neo-Confucian," we generally do so because of the dominance of a certain type of vision in the intellectual and spiritual world of the time which is typically reflected in the types of institutional arrangements and the kind of legitimizing rhetoric used by the society. Those who accept the intellectual framework, participate in the institutions, and use the rhetoric are ipso facto "Neo-Confucians."

The use of such generic labels is not illegitimate, but it may easily lead us to misunderstand the mentality of actual Neo-Confucians and the dynamics of their critical interaction with their society. The fact is, serious Neo-Confucians usually felt they were a minority set apart from the generality of men and the mores of the society surrounding them. Thus Chu Hsi in his remarks on his rules refers to the predominance of those who are engrossed in the pursuit of ends such as wealth and reputation, as opposed to the few who seriously pursue the kinds of ends inherent in true learning. T'oegye illustrates the same mentality in a set of exam questions on study which he gave when presiding over the civil service examinations. The following is indicative of the tenor of his set of questions:

Ah! Ah! Our land has been considered as having the heritage of Kija's instruction, [13] a country well-versed in ritual and propriety; and in addition we have a line of rulers who have one after another honored Confucians. But while the excellence of our valuing the Tao has reached such an extent, we still do not understand what it is to explain and make clear the learning of the true Tao [*tohak,* i.e., Neo-Confucianism].[14] Not only do we not understand it; we shun it. Not only do we shun it, we become angry with it. Our looking at the writings of the sages and wise men does not go beyond regarding them as material for passing the civil service examinations and getting a salary. This is having a King Wen[15] on the throne above, but no one rising [in response to his wisdom] below; this can only be a great shame for scholar-officials! (A, 41.41b, p. 931)

Neo-Confucian learning is in no way "otherworldly," but it demands the subordination of the ordinary worldly values which the majority make the framework of their lives. Although T'oegye was surrounded by fellow officials for whom the study of basic Neo-Confucian texts was a career prerequisite, he did not delude himself that many could truly understand the kind of learning project upon which his mind was set:

Worldlings all alike race along the path of honor and profit. If they succeed, they regard it as happiness; if they fail, they feel it a matter for anxiety and lamenting. The multitude are all like this. They do not understand what the wise find in the mountains and forests that they can plant themselves there and are able to forget about such values. But there is certainly something there! There is certainly something they attain! There is certainly something which they preserve and find peace in! There is certainly something which brings happiness to their hearts, but which others cannot understand as they do. I have my intent fixed on this, but have been as one wandering and lost with nowhere to go; how could I not strain toward it and thirst for it, and instead think about a few humiliating remarks that might be made?[16] (A, 10.3a-b, p. 283, Letter to Cho Kŏnjung)

Learning and the Political World

T'oegye had long experience in a political world which often had proved treacherous and even deadly to idealistic, reform-minded Neo-Confucians; he was one of the few who emerged relatively unscathed. He subscribed to the common Neo-Confucian view that learning and self-cultivation can perfect the ruler (or anyone else, for that matter) and thus lead to the transformation of society. But he was very realistic in assessing what normally happens. He tells King Sŏnjo:

Ah! Ah! If one does not begin there will certainly be no end; and if there is no end, what use will the beginning be? And in the learning of rulers, for the most part there is a beginning but no end. In the beginning they are diligent, and in the end, lax; in the beginning they are mindful, and in the end, licentious. (A, 7.46a, p. 186)

In his last interview with Sŏnjŏ, T'oegye analyzed the forces that play upon the king in bringing about the disastrous purges of upright scholar-officials as follows:

While King Myŏngjong (r. 1545–1567) was still young the powerful and wicked had their way; when one would fall another would arise, so they continued one after another to control things, and the disasters that befell the literati were more than one can bear to speak of.[17] My informing Your Majesty of these past affairs is meant to serve as a great warning for the future. From ancient times rulers at the beginning of their governing have sought out the wise and talented, accepted remonstrance, and advanced the upright who would correct their transgressions and tell them their wrongs and draw their ruler back to the right path. Therefore in everything the ruler wanted to do, according to the matter in question they would contend with him and hold fast [to their position][18] The ruler, not getting to act freely, would become very leery of them and come to feel fed up and vexed. At this point the wicked would take the opportunity to win him over. The ruler, having in mind that if he were to employ these men he would be able to do whatever he wished, would for this reason consequently join with the inferior men and the upright and superior men would be left without a handhold. (*OHN*, 3.28b-29a, B, pp. 832-833)

T'oegye did all in his power to arm the young ruler against this, delivering strong lectures on the theme of relying upon the advice of upright ministers[19] and warning against the desire to follow his personal inclinations as the root of all evil.[20]

He does not content himself, however, with simply laying the blame for these disasters upon worldly opportunists who thus ingratiate themselves with faltering rulers, grasp political power, and purge their more principled opponents. The pitfalls of the political world are not totally unforeseeable, and true, mature learning includes the wisdom to cope with the real world. T'oegye's deepest probing of the literati disasters is rather a critique aimed at the idealistic victims:

I have thought it strange that in the case of scholars in our country, if they are somewhat committed to learning and devoted to morality, for the most part they meet with disaster. Although this is [in part] because our land is small and its people illiberal, it is also due to something not yet complete in their own actions. That which I refer to as "not yet complete" is nothing other than the fact that their learning is yet imperfect while they occupy too high a position. They do not take the measure of the times but are courageous in attempting to set the world aright; this is the path by which they come to ruin. (A, 16.4b-5a, pp. 403–404)

The outstanding example of this—though there were many others—was the meteoric career of Cho Kwangjo (1482–1519),[21] in whose rise to the pinnacle of power a generation of young idealists saw the sign of an approaching golden age, only to experience yet another purge of their ranks at his fall and execution at the age of thirty-seven. T'oegye admired him greatly and deeply lamented his loss, the more so, perhaps, because it might have been otherwise:

> [T'oegye] once said: Cho Chŏngam's (i.e., Kwangjo) inborn talents were truly excellent, but the strength of his learning was not yet complete. His conduct of affairs did not escape having aspects that exceeded what was fitting, and therefore in the end he came to ruin his endeavor. If the strength of his learning had already been complete and the vessel of his virtue fully formed, and only then had he emerged and taken on the conduct of the world's affairs, what he might have accomplished would not be easy to measure. (*OHN* 5.5b-6a, B, p. 852)

What he has in mind by "learning" in such passages has nothing to do with subtle theories, but rather refers back to what we have seen in Chu Hsi's rules, which in the end make profound wisdom in the conduct of human relationships the final content of true learning. The rock upon which well-intentioned, personally upright and idealistic Korean Neo-Confucians too often foundered was pushing too hard too fast and too stubbornly, alienating others needlessly and bringing on head-on clashes with established powers.

On Private Academies in Korea

Chu Hsi's Rules for the White Deer Hollow Academy conveniently focus and summarize the essential substance and elements of learning. But if that was all T'oegye wished to accomplish, it could have been done easily in the context of the discussion of the *Elementary Learning* and the *Great Learning.* It seems likely that an additional factor influenced his decision to include these rules in the *Ten Diagrams:* they were associated with Chu Hsi's reestablishing the White Deer Hollow Academy. Throughout the *Ten Diagrams* T'oegye is concise rather than expansive, yet here he dwells on the narrative of the founding of the academy in a relatively leisurely and detailed fashion. In his mind this is more than merely a matter of the historical circumstances surrounding the rules: it is a paradigmatic action.[22]

T'oegye was, in fact, much concerned that the institution of such private academies should spread in Korea. He noted that there were over 300 such academies in Ming China, but that Korea had not yet emulated China in this regard. The first such academy was founded in Korea by Chu Sebong[23] (1495–1554) in 1542 (completed in 1543), when he was magistrate of P'unggi County in Kyŏngsang Province. It was founded in honor of An Hyang,[24] who had lived there and had first introduced Neo-Confucianism to Korea.

When T'oegye became magistrate of P'unggi in 1548, he devoted considerable attention to the White Cloud Hollow Academy (Paegŭndong sŏwŏn) founded by Chu. In 1549, shortly before he resigned, he wrote a long letter to the governor of the province in which he detailed the history of private academies in China, explained their importance, and, finally and most importantly, asked the governor to obtain direct royal approval and support, which would put the academy on a firmer footing and encourage others to imitate it:

> In my humble opinion instruction must proceed from above and reach down to the lower levels; only then will it have roots which will enable it to last and endure for a long time. Otherwise it will be like water without a spring, full in the morning and gone by evening; how could it last long! Where the higher leads the lower will certainly follow; what the king honors the whole country will become devoted to . . . If this matter is not managed with a royal decree and its name not registered in the national records, then I fear there will be no way to stop public opinion on all sides and settle people's doubts and reservations about it[25] so that [this academy] may become an effective model for the whole country and be perpetuated. (A, 9.6b, p. 263, Letter to Sim Pangbaek)

More concretely, T'oegye suggested that the king should emulate the example of Emperor T'ai-tsung of the Sung dynasty and express his support by granting a name-plaque in his own calligraphy, bestowing books, and even endowing it with fields and slaves. His suggestion was successful, and a plaque and books were bestowed by King Myŏngjong in 1550.

After this the growth of private academies was rapid. During the reign of King Myŏngjong (1545–1567) at least sixteen were founded, and Myŏngjong followed his earlier precedent and awarded books and plaques to three more. King Sŏnjo's reign (1567–1608) saw an addition of 78, of which 20 were granted the royal favors. The development peaked in the reign of King Sukjong (r.1674–1720), during which 295 academies were founded and 132 given books and plaques by the throne.[26] This brought the total number of private academies in Korea to more than 800,[27] more than doubling the number T'oegye noted in Ming dynasty China.

Serious Neo-Confucian learning focused on mindfulness as central, and while this self-possessed, recollected state of mind encompassed both active and tranquil periods, it could best be cultivated initially in a relatively quiet and secluded environment, which came to be looked upon as the ideal circumstance, if not the absolute prerequisite, for serious application to learning. T'oegye championed the private academies because he saw them as the ideal institutional counterpart of the Neo-Confucian theory of self-cultivation:

What could they get from the private academies? Why were they so honored by China? Scholars who dwell in retirement in order to pursue their resolve, the group of those who investigate the Tao and verse themselves in learning, frequently become fed up with the world's noisy wrangling and pack up their books and escape to the broad and relaxed countryside or the quiet solitude of the seashore, where they can sing and recite[verses on] the Tao of the former sage kings, or be quiet and look into the moral principle of the world in order to nurture their virtue and ripen their humanity, regarding this as their pleasure. Therefore they are pleased to go to a private academy. They see that the national academies and district schools are located within the walls of the capital or local towns; on the one hand these[schools] are encumbered with the restrictions and obstacles of school regulations, and on the other they present temptations to turn toward other things. How could their effectiveness be compared with [the private academies]! Considered in this light, it is not only scholars' pursuit of learning which is strengthened by private academies; the nation's attainment of wise and talented men [to serve in government] will certainly by this means far surpass what could be accomplished through those [national and district schools]. (A, 9.5b, p. 263, Letter to Sim Pangbaek)

The rapid spread of private academies in the ensuing century witnesses the prestige of Neo-Confucian learning and the strength of its ethos among the yangban, the elite class which sponsored such institutions; but the mere fact that there were hundreds and hundreds of private academies does not necessarily indicate that the profound devotion to learning which T'oegye associated with them had become common and widespread. Learning was the chief legitimation of these institutions, but from the beginning of the seventeenth century and perhaps earlier, they came to have multiple functions, and learning was not necessarily foremost among these. In the generation after T'oegye's, factionalism became endemic in the Korean political world, giving rise to lasting cleavages along lines of regional, lineage, political, and even intellectual differences and loyalties. The private academies served as local bases for these factions, giving them a source of cohesion and a base of local power which enabled them to survive disasters at the capital. They were both a symbol of prestige and a means by which powerful families could glorify their lineages by publishing the collected writings of their illustrious forebears[28] or by making them the object of semipublic veneration in the twice yearly sacrificial rites to exemplary Confucians, an important part of academy life.[29] As much as centers of learning they were social centers which cemented relationships and maintained the ties by which these same families perpetuated their power and authority in local communities.

As these institutions multiplied and were transformed and politicized, criticism grew apace. They were continually criticized for their factional coloring, for their being used to glorify particular lineages, for the sometimes questionable qualities of the men they honored with sacrifices, for being more devoted to partying than to learning, and even for enlisting in their sometimes extensive slave rosters commoners attempting to escape corvée labor and military duty[30] Attempts by the government to forbid establishing new academies began in 1655; these attempts became truly effective during the reign of King Yŏngjo (1724–1776), after which growth virtually stopped. During his reign some 300 were destroyed,[31] but hundreds yet remained. Finally in 1871 it was decreed that all be destroyed except for 47, most of which remain to this day.

Chapter 6: DIAGRAM OF THE SAYING "THE MIND COMBINES AND GOVERNS THE NATURE AND THE FEELINGS"

This chapter presents the basic elements of Neo-Confucian psychological theory. In this theory the metaphysical concepts that describe the universe are applied likewise to elucidate the composition and fucntioning of the human psyche. The subject is complex, but the description of the psyche has immediate bearing upon how one approaches the practical task of self-cultivation, as was exemplified in the divergence of the Ch'eng-Chu and Wang Yang-ming schools in China.

There are three diagrams in this chapter. T'oegye borrowed Diagram A from a Chinese source; it gives us a schematic presentation of the major elements of Ch'eng-Chu psychological theory. Diagrams B and C are his own work. On one level they are simply a more detailed working out of the matter summarily presented in Diagram A; but they are also a carefully formulated expression of T'oegye's final position on the issues of his famous Four-Seven Debate with Ki Taesŭng.[1]

The Four-Seven Debate was the single most important intellectual controversy of the Yi dynasty. It was carried on in lengthy correspondence between T'oegye and Ki Taesŭng from 1559 to 1566. Then in the next generation, Yi I (Yulgok) resurrected the position Ki had finally abandoned and further developed it in debate with Sŏng Hon.[2] *T'oegye and Yulgok were the foremost philosophers of the Yi dynasty, and the positions they elaborated set a distinctive intellectual agenda for following generations of Korean Neo-Confucians.*

The topic of the debate involved the precise relationship of the Four Beginnings, feelings described by Mencius as purely good,[3] *and another*

6 Diagram of "The Mind Combines and Governs Nature and Feelings"

Diagram A

The Mind as perfectly still and not active is the nature

Mind Combines and Governs Nature and Feelings

The Not-Yet Aroused State, the Nature

Receives wood's most excellent	Endowed with the li of love which is called Humanity
Receives fire's most excellent	Endowed with the li of reverence which is called Propriety
Receives metal's most excellent	Endowed with the li of the right which is called Righteousness
Receives water's most excellent	Endowed with the li of distinction which is called Wisdom
Receives earth's most excellent	Endowed with the li of truth which is called Fidelity

Is the Substance of the Mind

Governs the Nature and the Feelings"

As stirred and going
forth penetratingly
is the feelings

The Aroused State, the Feelings,

The sense of commiseration — The manifestation of Humanity

The sense of modesty and deference — The manifestation of Propriety

The sense of shame and dislike — The manifestation of Righteousness

The sense of approving and disapproving — The manifestation of Wisdom

The sense of integrity and truth — The manifestation of Fidelity

Is the Function of the Mind

Diagram B

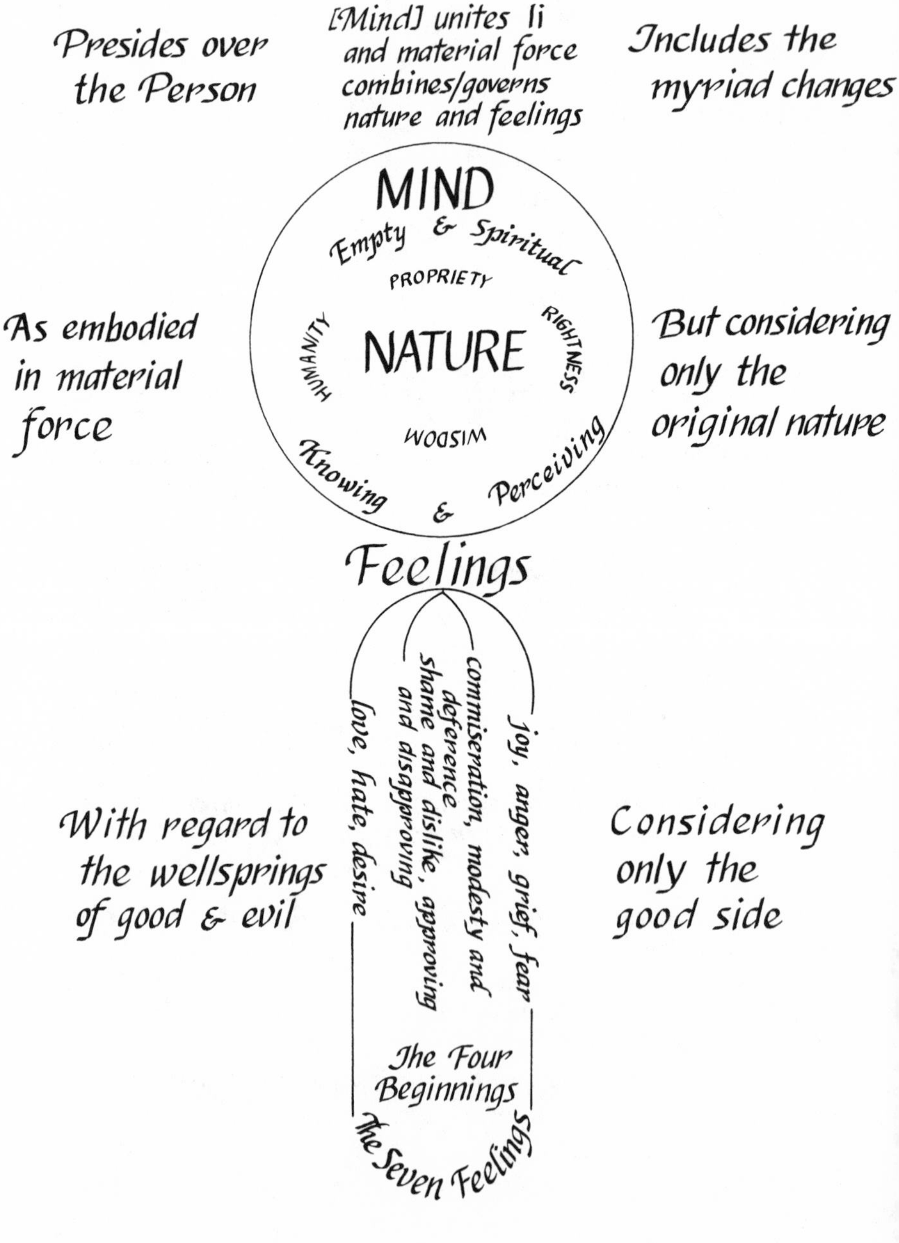

Presides over the Person

[Mind] unites li
and material force
combines/governs
nature and feelings

Includes the myriad changes

MIND

Empty & Spiritual

PROPRIETY

HUMANITY

NATURE

RIGHTNESS

WISDOM

Knowing & Perceiving

As embodied in material force

But considering only the original nature

Feelings

love, hate, desire

shame and dislike, approving and disapproving

commiseration, modesty and deference

joy, anger, grief, fear

The Four Beginnings

The Seven Feelings

With regard to the wellsprings of good & evil

Considering only the good side

Diagram C

Presides over the Person

[Mind] unites li and material force combines/governs nature and feelings

Includes the myriad changes

MIND

humanity, propriety, fidelity, rightness, wisdom

Empty

ORIGINAL

Spiritual

The Nature is fundamentally one, but on the basis of

NATURE

Being embodied in Material Force it has two names

PHYSICAL

Knowing

Perceiving

fine or coarse, good or bad

ISSUES AS

commiseration
modesty and deference
shame and dislike
approving and disapproving

Li issues and

Material Force follows

THE FOUR BEGINNINGS

desire hate love fear grief anger joy

Material Force issues

and Li mounts it

THE SEVEN FEELINGS

classical list of feelings, the Seven Feelings, which may be either good or evil.[4] *The main issue was whether or not principle and material force are involved in exactly the same way in the issuance or activation of these two kinds of feelings. If they are, the difference between these two sets of feelings is in fact only nominal. The question is technical, but it is directly related to the central issue of how one understands the relationship of principle and material force. The commentary will draw out the issues involved and show how T'oegye handled them, concluding with a discussion of the importance of this question for Ch'eng-Chu thought and its development in Korea.*

Ch'eng Fu-hsin's Discussion of Diagram A

Ch'eng Lin-yin[5] [Fu-hsin] says: The saying, "The mind combines and governs the nature and the feelings,"[6] refers to man's being born endowed with the Five Agents in their highest excellence. In their excellence, the Five Natures [i.e., humanity, propriety, etc.] are fully present; when they move, the seven feelings become manifest.[7] In general, that which combines the nature and the feelings is the mind. Thus when the mind is perfectly still and does not act, it is [in the state of] the nature, which is the substance of the mind; when it is stirred and goes forth penetratingly, it is [in the state of] feelings, which are the function of the mind.[8]

Thus Chang Tsai's saying that the mind combines and governs the nature and the feelings is indeed appropriate. The mind combines and governs the nature; thus while humanity, righteousness, propriety, and wisdom constitute the nature, there is also the expression, "The mind of humanity and righteousness."[9] The mind combines and governs the feelings; thus while compassion, shame and dislike [for evil], modesty and deference, and the sense of approval and disapproval [of right and wrong] are the feelings, there is also the expression, "the mind of compassion and the mind of shame and dislike, of modesty and deference, of approving and disapproving."[10]

If the mind does not combine and govern the nature, it will not be able to attain the perfect equilibrium which should characterize it before it is aroused and the nature will thus easily be impaired. If the mind does not combine and govern the feelings, it will not be able to attain the perfectly measured harmony [which should characterize it after it is aroused], and the feelings will easily run wild.[11]

[T'oegye's notes:]
In Ch'eng I's "Treatise on [What Yen Hui] Loved to Learn,"[12] restraining the feelings precedes rectifying the mind and nurturing the nature, while here it follows them. That is because here it is spoken of in terms of the mind combining and governing the nature and the feelings [so the discussion follows the pattern of the saying being discussed]. But if one examines the principle *(li)* involved here and discusses the matter in that light, Ch'eng I's treatise should be followed.

In [Ch'eng Fu-hsin's] diagram there were some points which were not exact, and I have slightly revised it.[13]

T'oegye's Discussion of Diagrams B and C

The first of these diagrams is the work of Ch'eng Fu-hsin, and it is accompanied by his explanation. As for the other two diagrams, I have made them myself, attempting to get to the source of what is meant by the sayings and instruction established and handed down by the sages and wise men.

DIAGRAM B

Diagram B takes up [the nature] as embodied in the endowment of material force, but singles out the original nature, that is, the nature as it is when [distorted by] no admixture of [imperfect] material force. This is what Tzu Ssu speaks of when he says the nature is the Heavenly Mandate,[14] the nature Mencius refers to when he says that the nature is [perfectly] good.[15] When Ch'eng I says that the nature is the same as *li*,[16] and when Chang Tsai speaks of the nature which is [identical with] that of Heaven and Earth,[17] it is this to which they refer.

Since the nature is here considered in this way, when it issues as feelings they likewise are considered only as good. These are what Tzu Ssu refers to as feelings which are "perfectly measured,"[18] the feelings Mencius refers to as the "Four Beginnings."[19] They are the feelings of which Ch'eng I says, "How can one term them "not good,' "[20] and of which Chu Hsi says, "That which flows forth from the nature is originally nothing but good."[21]

DIAGRAM C

Diagram C takes up the matter in terms of *li* as it is conjoined with material force. This is what Confucius referred to as the nature which is "quite similar [in men at birth],"[22] and what Ch'eng I meant when he said, "The nature is the same as material force and material force the same as nature."[23] It is what Chang Tsai calls "the physical nature,"[24] and what Chu Hsi refers to when he says, "Although it is in the midst of material force, material force is material force and the nature is the nature; they do not become mixed with one another."[25] Since the nature is considered in this way, when it issues as feelings, it is likewise said that being interdependent they may damage one another, [with the feelings becoming wrong as a result].[26]

If one considers the Four Beginnings, principle issues and material force follows in accord. Of themselves, they are purely good and without evil; only if principle's issuance is obstructed by material force before it is complete can they then degenerate into what is not good. As for the Seven feelings, material force issues and *li* "mounts" it.[27] They likewise have nothing in them which is not good; but if material forces' issuance is not properly measured and obliterates principle, they get out of control and become evil.

[The interrelation of principle and material force] being thus, Master Ch'eng [Hao] said, "If one discusses the nature but does not consider material force, it is incomplete; if one discusses material force without considering the nature, there is a lack of clarity. If one treats them as two, it is incorrect."[28] Nevertheless, this does not mean that Tzu Ssu and Mencius were "incomplete" when they spoke only with reference to principle [i.e., the original nature]. They did so only because if they had spoken of it as combined with material force they would not have been able to show the original goodness of the nature. This is the significance of the second diagram.

The essence of the matter is this: that which includes both principle and material force and combines and governs the nature and the feelings is the mind; and the moment of the nature's issuance as feelings is the subtle wellspring of the whole mind, the pivot of ten thousand transformations, the separation point of good and evil. If one who pursues learning is truly able to recollect himself through maintaining mindfulness and does not confuse principle with human desires but brings the greatest caution to bear on this matter, and if his application to the composure [of his mind] and the nurturing [of his nature] before the mind is aroused is profound and he is likewise well-versed in the exercise of reflection and discernment after it is aroused, and if he accumulates truth and is constant in his effort for a long time and does not stop, then the learning of sagehood characterized as "being discerning and undivided, holding fast the mean,"[29] and the method of cultivating the mind wherein it is composed in substance and [accurately] responsive in function, need not be sought elsewhere, but will all be attained in this.

Commentary

The first two sections of this commentary will deal mainly with matters essential to general Neo-Confucian psychological theory, which are summarized in Diagram A and its accompanying remarks. Subsequent sections of commentary will be addressed to the main issues and questions involved in the Four-Seven Debate, the conclusions of which are expressed in Diagrams B and C and their accompanying remarks.

Mind, Nature, Feelings, and Intention

Mind is the subject that possesses principle as its substance or nature, and has feelings as its function, the concrete and active manifestation of substance. Being endowed with all principle as its substance renders the mind responsive to all things in existence; actively responding in a concrete instance is a matter of feelings, which are not a distinct faculty, as in the Aristotelian analysis, but the active issuing forth of responses in the modality provided by the principle of our nature. Being concrete and particular, actual feelings are on the side of material force, though what they manifest, ideally, is principle.

The distinctive role of mind, the subject and nexus of principle and material force, is to preside over this issuance of principle in its active, material force manifestation as the feelings that arise in response to concrete situations. This presiding function is essentially expressed in terms of self-possession (mindfulness), whereby distorting elements (basically forms of self-centeredness which arise as the psychic manifestation of the imperfection or turbidity of material force) are controlled and excluded so that principle may issue forth integrally and be perfectly manifested in the character of appropriate feelings.

The typical western analysis regards man as balanced between good and evil and so makes free will, our ability to decide between them, a central issue. But the Neo-Confucian analysis focuses on the moral situation in terms of responsiveness: in the ideal order the mind's response is spontaneously perfect, but in fact it is often problematically distorted. Attention therefore centers on the means to obviate the distortion, i.e., self-possession, rather than on the role of will as the arbiter of choice. As reflected in these diagrams, the central items of concern in describing our psychological constitution are therefore nature, feelings, and mind as presiding over them; these are the essential items for understanding how a response arises.

The phenomena we associate with a separate faculty, the will, are not altogether neglected, however. Sometimes what we would call an act of the will, the intention, is treated as the function of the mind, paralleled by describing feelings as the function of the nature. This, however, could lead to a mistaken separation of mind and nature by differentiating their functions,[30] a matter T'oegye addresses as follows:

> The mind is the thing that combines principle and material force and governs and combines the nature and the feelings. Therefore it is not only the intention that issues from the mind; the issuing of the feelings is also done by the mind. Principle is without form or concreteness; as it fills and is perfectly held by the mind, it is the nature. The nature is without form or concreteness; as it is broadly manifested and issues forth as function in dependence upon the mind, it is the feelings. That which, based upon the issuing of the feelings, manages, calculates, and asserts that it must be like this or must be like that, is the intention. Since the feelings spontaneously issue forth, the former Confucians therefore described them as issuing from the nature; since the intention asserts that it must be such and such a way, they therefore described it as issuing from the mind. (A, 36.16a, p. 823, Letter to Yi Koengjung)

In the same letter T'oegye says the feelings are like a chariot and the intention like the driver's use of the chariot. The importance of the intention is thus evident. But it does not call for extensive separate treatment in this framework because structurally it parallels the feelings; that is, like the feelings, the intention is understood as an active force operative in the mind. While it does not arise spontaneously, the problems associated with it are essentially the same: the disruptive influence of self-centeredness (turbid material force) that gives rise to wrong intentions and subtle forms of self-deception. Thus in terms of self-cultivation, the intention attains its perfection of integrity or sincerity through the same process of constantly mindful application to the investigation of principle and reflective practice that brings perfection to the functioning of feelings.

The Two States of the Mind

Diagram A and its explication describe the mind as having two states, the condition before it is aroused and the condition after it is aroused.[31] This is based upon the first chapter of the *Doctrine of the Mean*: "Before pleasure, anger, sorrow, and joy are aroused it is called equilibrium; when they are aroused and attain their due measure and degree, it is called harmony." The passage itself speaks only of feelings being either aroused or not aroused. But in terms of Neo-Confucian substance-function analysis feelings were considered the active function of the mind, with the obvious corollary that when the feelings are not aroused what remains must be the tranquil substance of the mind. Thus this passage came to be understood as indicating not just two states of the feelings, but two conditions of the mind itself. This is a matter of great importance for the theory of self-cultivation; the relation of these states to actual spiritual practice, and just what may or may not pertain to each, were a perennial source of questions from students. In the following passage T'oegye gives a thorough description of the two conditions of the mind:

Man's mind has both substance and function, quiescent and aroused states, and embraces both activity and tranquility. Therefore when it is not yet stirred by something, it is quiescent and is not active; all principles are present and the mind's integral substance is perfectly possessed. When something occurs and stirs it and it goes forth penetratingly without missing the proper measure, then the mind's great function is perfectly put into action. If it is tranquil, then it is quiescent and is described as "not yet aroused." If it is active, then it is stirred and is described as "already aroused". . . .

Therefore what your letter speaks of as the condition before being engaged with something, the time when there is no arising or perishing [of thoughts, feelings, etc.], what is referred to as the condition of emptiness and spirituality, bright and with no dimness, what is called the feelings of pleasure, anger, sorrow, and joy not yet being stirred, and not yet being disturbed by thought or verbalizing, these all belong to the quiescent or tranquil condition, that is, to the condition described as "not yet aroused."

That which is described as the time when one just barely begins to think, or what is referred to as pondering, or exhaustively investigating [principle], or what is described as a time when one's thoughts are in a turmoil, or what is called responding to and dealing with affairs, all of these pertain to being stirred and [going forth] penetratingly and being active, that is, to the condition described as "already aroused." That which is described as there being in the midst of perfect tranquility the beginning of activity, does not likewise mean a condition which is already active: this is just stated with reference to there being the principle of activity, that is all. Therefore this also ought to belong to the not-yet-aroused condition.

The not-yet-aroused condition is the time for one to be cautious and fearful;[32] the already aroused condition is the time for personal watchfulness and minute self-reflection. What is referred to as applying oneself to being alert, self-possessed, and focused, or keeping charge [of oneself], this runs throughout both the not-yet-aroused and already aroused conditions and permits of no interruption; it is what is referred to as "mindfulness."

I have carefully examined your letter. Its regarding the mind before it is engaged with something as quiescent and not active, and its regarding pondering, exhaustively investigating, and responding to and dealing with affairs as belonging to the already aroused condition is acceptable. But when between these two you further put a condition of being tranquil and having a slight movement of thought that is not yet formed, and look upon it as pertaining to the not-yet-aroused condition, although what this means seems to be subtle and exact, in fact it is a great error. For if one is tranquil, then he is not yet active and this is the not-yet-aroused condition; how can there be a slightly active tranquility which can be called not yet aroused? If one engages in thought, it is already formed and this is the already aroused state; how can one have a not yet formed thought that can be called not yet aroused? (A, 19.39b-40b p. 486, Letter to Hwang Chunggŏ)

This long description makes it unmistakably clear that what in Neo-Confucian psychology is regarded as one of the two basic conditions of the mind, the not-yet-aroused condition, bespeaks not just a state of relative calm and tranquility, but a conscious and wakeful state of absolute mental quiescence. The western world would regard this as an abnormal or altered state of consciousness, the kind of thing associated with meditation practices; in the East Asian world, long familiar with Buddhist meditation, it is simply accepted as one of the two polar conditions of consciousness, a psychic manifestation of the yin-yang alternation of tranquility and activity.

This does not mean that such a condition can be dissociated from a form of meditation practice. Quite the contrary: the main practical import of this description of the two states or conditions of the mind is that for the first time it provides a systematic foundation for meditation in Confucian self-cultivation. Chu Hsi learned such meditation, called "quiet sitting," a method of "looking into the equilibruim of the mind before it is aroused," from his teacher Li T'ung. The exact place such a practice should occupy in self-cultivation was a vexatious issue that was eventually settled by the elaboration of the doctrine of mindfulness. It will be further discussed when mindfulness is taken up below in the ninth and tenth chapters.

Correspondence Between T'oegye and Ki Taesŭng on the Four-Seven Question

The statement which instigated the debate was: "The Four Beginnings are the issuance of principle; the Seven Feelings are the issuance of Material Force."[33] T'oegye heard of Ki's questioning this and quickly sent him a note toning down the extremely dualistic overtones of his original statement with a slight modification: "The issuing of the Four Beginnings is from pure principle; therefore there is none which is not good. The issuing of the Seven Feelings includes material force; therefore they have both good and evil."[34] This drew from Ki a three-page response,[35] in which he objected that basically all feelings essentially involve both principle and material force and good and evil; thus the Four Beginnings have no different status from the Seven Feelings, but rather are an expression of the Seven Feelings when they have not been distorted by material force and hence have attained their due measure and degree. What Menicus expressed as the Four Beginnings selectively attends to the good side, and although they may be said to be the issuance of pure principle since they involve no distortion, it is a mistake to contrast them with the Seven Feelings in terms of a different kind of differing relation to principle and material force, for in fact the Seven Feelings and Four Beginnings are one and the same reality.

T'oegye responded with an eight-page, more fully elaborated defense of his position;[36] he had in the meantime become more confident in its basic acceptability, for he had discovered a passage in Chu Hsi's *Yü-lei* which says simply and plainly: "The Four Beginnings are the issuance of principle; the Seven Feelings are the issuance of material force."[37] Ki Taesŭng responded with a forty-two page, paragraph-by-paragraph critique of T'oegye's letter.[38]

Ki's critique pushed T'oegye to advance his ideas and give them a more precise formulation. He sent Ki a revised copy of his earlier letter with careful notes on each corrected phrase or sentence. But more importantly, he accompanied this with forty-six pages of careful summations of and responses to Ki's points.[39] He began this with a categorical analysis in which he noted one place where he had misread Ki, four points where his own ideas or his expressions were wrong, thirteen points of agreement, eight points in which they agree on a basic level but draw different conclusions, and nine points on which there is simply no agreement.[40] Then he responded to each of the seventeen items in the last two categories in turn.

This was T'oegye's final significant discussion in the debate; although Ki wrote another lengthy and detailed reply on remaining items of disagreement,[41] T'oegye declined to respond in kind, feeling that much had been gained, the basic points investigated and laid out, and that it would not be appropriate to push for absolute and total agreement.[42] In 1566 Ki wrote a general summary statement in harmony with T'oegye's basic position,[43] which T'oegye accepted with great pleasure.

Principle and Material Force Mutually Issue the Feelings

A theory which became clearly enunciated in the course of the debate was that of "mutual issuing" *(hobal, hufa),* which came to be regarded as a hallmark of T'oegye's thought in contradistinction to that of Yulgok (Yi I), who vigorously rejected the notion. Ki Taesŭng did not argue with T'oegye concerning the expression itself, but the implications of what each understood in this expression were sharply different and at the heart of the debate. T'oegye states this theory as follows in the course of responding to Ki's objection that distinctions according to material force are appropriate in discussing the constitution of creatures, but not in discussing the feelings, which are on the level of the compound and inseparable activity of principle and material force:

> Man's entire body is produced through the conjunction of principle and material force. Therefore these two have a mutual issuance in function, and moreover their issuing is interdependent. Since they mutually issue, one can see that each has a distinctive emphasis (*so chu*); since they are interdependent, one can see that they are mutually included [in the issuance]. Since both are included, there therefore are definitely cases where they are spoken of as undivided; since each has a distinctive emphasis, there is therefore nothing impermissible in speaking of them as distinct. (A, 16.30b, p. 416, Letter to Ki Myŏngŏn)

On one level, this sets the stage for a general distinction of the two sets of feelings in terms of principle and material force, for the Four Beginnings described by Mencius are clearly meant to point to goodness, so their "distinctive emphasis" is on the side of principle, which is both normative and purely good. The Seven Feelings, which combine good and evil, are more on the side of material force, for it is the imperfection or "turbidity" of material force that accounts for evil.

This is not the heart of the issue, however. If "issuing" in the case of principle means only that it is manifested in the consequent feelings, then all proper feelings, the Four and Seven alike, issue from principle in exactly the same way, and referring to the Four Beginnings as principle does not *really* distinguish them from the Seven Feelings.

But if principle's "issuing" denotes some sort of self-manifesting activity of principle, a real distinction between the Four and Seven is possible even when the Seven are good: all that is good is certainly so termed because it is in accord with principle, but all that is in accord with principle need not be the product of principle in precisely the same way. This, then, brings us to the causal question that is at the heart of the debate and manifests the full significance of T'oegye's "mutual issuing" thesis.

The Causal Origin of the Four-Seven Distinction

In his response to T'oegye's first fully elaborated presentation of his position, Ki Taesŭng laid out the essential difference in their views as follows, beginning with a paraphrase of T'oegye's statements:

In your letter you regard the Four Beginnings as issuing from the nature composed of humanity, righteousness, propriety, and wisdom; therefore, although they are a composite of principle and material force, what is indicated in speaking of them has its distinctive emphasis on principle. In the case of the Seven Feelings, external things touch the physical form and there is movement from within, and conditioned in this way they emerge. Therefore they are not without principle, but what is indicated in speaking of them has to do with material force. *Therefore the Four Beginnings are within as pure principle and at the moment they issue forth they are not mixed with material force; the Seven Feelings are externally stirred by the physical form and their issuing is not the original substance of principle.* And so that whence the Four Beginnings and Seven Feelings arise is not the same.[44] These statements are truly what you personally have attained;[45] therefore in the whole treatise, although there are time and again various leads on the matter, the main meaning does not depart from this.

As for my foolish view, it differs from this. For human feelings are of one kind, and that whereby they are feelings definitely combines principle and material force and has both good and evil. But Mencius in approaching the marvelous composite of principle and material force, exclusively pointed to the aspect which issues from principle and is nothing but good. Tzu Ssu, in approaching the marvelous composite of principle and material force, spoke of it without discriminating; so the feelings [as he speaks of them] definitely combine principle and material force and have both good and evil: these are the Seven Feelings. Truly their approaches in discussing the matter were not the same. Nevertheless, as for those which are described as the Seven Feelings, although they involve material force, principle likewise is included. When they issue and attain their due measure and degree, they are the nature which is the Heavenly Mandate, the original substance [of principle], and are the same reality with a different name as what Mencius described as the Four Beginnings.[46]

Whether the Four Beginnings and Seven Feelings are only different names for the same reality looked at from differing perspectives, or rather truly point to some differentiation in the condition whence they arise, is a central issue that is returned to repeatedly. It is the core running through the items T'oegye cites as matters of fundamental disagreement between himself and Ki.[47] Ki Taesŭng felt that T'oegye's causal distinction between the Four and Seven was based on an overemphasis upon the questionable nature of the Seven Feelings; this leads to stressing the role of material force in their origination. But if the Seven Feelings' intrinsic connection with principle or the nature is given full recognition, and the fact that the Four Beginnings are likewise stimulated by external circumstances is also taken into account, a causal differentiation between the two is by no means as obvious as it first seemed. Ki made these arguments forcefully and at length, and T'oegye had to accept a number of his points and refine his own position in order to incorporate them. Instead of his original description of the Seven Feelings as "undecided" with regard to good and evil, he now said, as in our text (Diagram C), that "they likewise are nothing but good," and granted that they also express the original nature. The effects of Ki's arguments are clearly evident in Diagram B, where the good Seven Feelings are ranked alongside the Four Beginnings as manifestations of the original nature. That his original differentiation was not entirely abandoned, however, is also evidenced in the diagram by the way the Four Beginnings are depicted as an inner core with the Seven Feelings arranged on the outside.

T'oegye's final formulation of the relationship of the Four Beginnings and Seven Feelings appears in Diagram C. It was thus formulated by T'oegye precisely as a reworking of his initial loose differentiation of the two in terms of the degree physical form is implicated in their arising:

> Even I, likewise, do not describe the Seven Feelings as being unrelated to principle but [only] stirred and moved by the fortuitous meeting with external things. And the Four Beginnings are stirred and moved by things; they definitely are no different from the Seven Feelings in this regard. But in the case of the Four, principle issues and material force follows it; in the case of the Seven, material force issues and principle mounts it, that is all. (A, 16.32a, p. 417, Letter to Ki Myŏngŏn)

In this formulation, then, T'oegye means to do full justice to the role of principle vis-à-vis the Seven Feelings, and material force vis-à-vis the Four Beginnings. With due regard to the complementarity and interdependence of principle and material force and their mutual involvement in all feelings, he now points to a form of nontemporal priority of principle in the issuance of the Four Beginnings and of material force in the issuance of the Seven Feelings.

The Four-Seven Debate and the Understanding of Mencius

Mencius' description of the Four Beginnings is virtually synonymous with what the Ch'eng-Chu school describes as the perfectly good "original nature." Although man possesses this nature, it is concretized and active only in the context of material force; considered in this context, it is the "material nature." If the material force of the psychological endowment is turbid, like muddy water, then all that issues through the agency of this medium might be regarded as equally subject to distortion. Ki Taesŭng in fact views the situation in much this manner, arguing that in reality even the Four Beginnings are frequently distorted and so involve good and evil, just as the Seven Feelings.[48] Whatever the innate goodness of his original nature, the ordinary man is in all cases dealing with a mixed condition in which he must exercise the utmost caution and self-examination. In effect this makes Mencius' description of the Four Beginnings or original nature less an active reality upon which man builds and develops, and more an abstract ideal, a description of what man really is in the depths of his being and should strive to become in reality. T'oegye has a rather different view of Mencius:

> I characterize the Four Beginnings as likewise involving material force, the point you have repeatedly stated in the course of your discussion. . . . Even so, in your view of Mencius' explanation of the Four Beginnings, do you see it as likewise a matter of the issuance of material force? And if you see it as treating the issuance of material force, then how do you think one ought to look at what is described as "the beginning of humanity," "the beginning of righteousness, propriety, and wisdom"? If you see this as involving even a slight participation of material force, then it is not the original condition of pure heavenly principle. If you see is as a matter of pure heavenly principle, then the basis whence it issues is definitely not a mixed sort of thing like mud and water. What you mean is that humanity, righteousness, propriety, and wisdom are terms which belong to the not-yet-aroused state; therefore they are pure principle. As for the Four Beginnings, they are terms which belong to the state after [the mind] is aroused. Without material force they could not act; therefore they also involve material force, that is all. The way I would describe the Four Beginnings is that, although they are said to mount material force,[49] what Mencius was pointing out consists not in their mounting material force[50] but only in their issuing from pure principle. (A, 16,32a-b, p. 417, Letter to Ki Myŏngŏn)

Real feelings have to do with the actual world of material force, and hence with the material nature; if one is going to distinguish the Seven Feelings and Four Beginnings on this level there must be some reality, not just an abstraction, as the basis of speaking of an issuance from pure principle. This is what T'oegye expresses in his formulation of the Four Beginnings as "principle issues and material force follows it." Within the interdependent compound of principle and material force one can distinguish and differentiate kinds of feelings as originating from principle or being more intimately connected with material force.

Although all alike are feelings, all involve both principle and material force, and all may be perfectly good, there is a real, even a phenomenological difference between them:

> The reason the four [i.e., joy, anger, sorrow, and fear][51] are easily harmful to the mind is that truly what issues [intrinsically] conditioned by material force, although it is originally good, easily flows toward evil; therefore it is so, and that is all. In the case of the Four Beginnings, which issue from principle, how is there any such problem? (A, 16,37a, p. 420, Letter to Ki Myŏngŏn)

A similar differentiation also appears in the text related to Diagram C.

Looked at in terms of the interpretation of Mencius, then, Diagram B and Diagram C have more significance than might appear at first glance. Diagram B presents the doctrine of the original nature, with the added precision that the Seven Feelings when they are good also stem from and manifest the original nature. Diagram C is a presentation of the doctrine of the physical nature. But it goes beyond the common application of this doctrine as an explanation of the origin of evil, for it also explicates the existential functionality of the original nature. Even though the nature is conjoined with material force, there is a distinctive issuance of the Four Beginnings in which principle is not only manifested, but also is the point of origination. To be sure, it does so only in conjunction with material force, but not in a way that admits the distorting element of material force in the very wellspring of the origination of these feelings.

The Significance of the Four-Seven Debate

The Four-Seven Debate became a gate through which every Korean with a claim to significant Neo-Confucian learning passed. The issues involved are subtle and of a nature which admits of no final absolute determination upon which all agree; at the same time they involve fundamental questions regarding the interpretation of the relationship of principle and material force as applied not only to the feelings, but also as regards the closely related topics of the original nature and the physical nature, and the human mind and the mind of the Tao. These matters are so fundamental in the Ch'eng-Chu school that, once they were raised and became the object of broad attention, they could not just be laid aside as could the discussion of equally perplexing but more peripheral questions that became fashionable for a time and then were left behind. Thus the Four-Seven Debate decisively fixed the intellectual agenda for generations to come; the problématique that it established served as a general framework within which other questions emerged and were addressed.

Although these issues are basic, they were never raised with the same urgency in China, which instead became occupied with questions concerning the nature and the mind as rival foci in the competing Ch'eng-Chu and Lu-Wang schools of thought.[52] Korea, accepting Chu Hsi's basic description of mind as a composite of material force and principle, feelings and nature, went on to investigate the fundamental questions inherent in this description; these could be explored only by an extensive inquiry into the precise understanding of the relationship of principle and material force. The Chinese, arguing the Lu-Wang proposal that the mind itself is principle, were not led into the same kind of development of the inner problems and resources of the Ch'eng-Chu school in this fundamental area.

The Four-Seven Debate, then, established a distinctive intellectual agenda for Korean Neo-Confucianism. In so doing, one might suggest, it contributed in no small way to a closely related and distinctive feature of Korean Neo-Confucianism: its exclusive devotion to the Ch'eng-Chu school and the absence of any significant role of Wang Yang-ming's thought in Yi dynasty intellectual life, in spite of its great popularity in China. Once embarked upon this inquiry, the Korean intellectual world had little place for Wang Yang-ming; his thought was not so much a furthering of these questions as it was an invitation to abandon them for a quite different alternative. One might also go beyond the intellectual level as such to further consider that the intellectual debate was very soon socially grounded, both in terms of regional and factional loyalties and in the less palpable terms of prestige, recognition for "learning" accorded to those who could handle these issues with competence. There was no similar social reward or gratification for the study of Wang Yang-ming.

But on a more profound level than this, there is a way in which the Four-Seven Debate, and particularly the ideas developed by T'oegye, made Wang's thought less compelling and attractive. The Lu-Wang school, by equating principle directly with the mind rather than with the nature, gave full expression to the dynamic, active side of the original goodness of human nature as discussed by Mencius. The Ch'eng-Chu school preserved Mencius' teaching in its doctrine of the perfectly good original nature, but in the context of the correlated doctrine of the imperfection of the physical nature (the nature as existentially embodied in material force), there was the danger, as we have seen, that the goodness spoken of by Mencius might be reduced to more an analytic intellectual affirmation than an existential reality. T'oegye's differentiation of the Four Beginnings from the Seven Feelings, however, establishes an existential functionality for the original goodness of human nature, and at the same time remains fully within the context of the Ch'eng-Chu school and leaves the doctrine of the material nature fundamentally intact.

While the underlying problématique of T'oegye's thought is quite different from that of the Lu-Wang school, with regard to Mencius, who occupies a key place in both discussions, they do cover the same ground, albeit with widely different results. Once this discussion was established in the Korean intellectual world, the Lu-Wang school's treatment of Mencius might well be dismissed in favor of a more fine-grained analysis that remained fully within the authoritative Ch'eng-Chu tradition. Wang Yang-ming was disregarded not only because Korean minds were occupied by other things, but because with these developments there was little intellectual need for the alternative he presented.

Chapter 7: DIAGRAM OF THE EXPLANATION OF HUMANITY

From the earliest times, jen, *humanity, has been the virtue of all virtues in the Confucian tradition. Confucius used the term to signify the highest perfection, the epitome of all human excellence. The good as such is indefinable, but it is inexhaustibly describable; thus one finds in the* Analects *many and varied descriptions of what is involved in* jen, *but no definition.*

*Mencius says, "*Jen *is to be human," that is, it is the full perfection of the human being as such. The form of the Chinese character* jen *itself reflects what this means, for it is a composite of the characters for "man" and "two," i.e., two persons together. In other words,* jen *is the quality of relating to other persons in a proper, fully human manner, a description that reflects the Confucian conviction that the highest human excellence is cultivated in and manifested by the quality of interpersonal relationships. But it was the saying of Confucius that* jen *is "loving others"[1] and Mencius' description of* jen *as the quality that grows out of the innate human feeling of commiseration with the suffering of others[2] that set the tone for much of the later Confucian tradition:* jen *came to be interpreted mainly in terms of warm human fellow-feeling, or "love" in its nonsexual sense.*

Thus jen *is frequently translated as "benevolence," "love," "human-heartedness," or "humanity." "Humanity" is perhaps the rendition best suited to the Neo-Confucian context, for it conveys the notion of the fullest human perfection and at the same time connotes the kind of warm feelings associated with* jen; *both of these are vital to the Neo-Confucian treatment of* jen.

The Neo-Confucians preserved this heritage concerning jen. *But their philosophy of principle now explicated a vision of the ultimate unity of*

7 Diagram of the Explanation of

HUMANITY – *is the mind of Heaven and Earth whereby they produce and give life to creatures and this is what*

MAN

receives as his own MIND

Origination, penetration, benefitting, steadfastness

these are the mind of Heaven and Earth

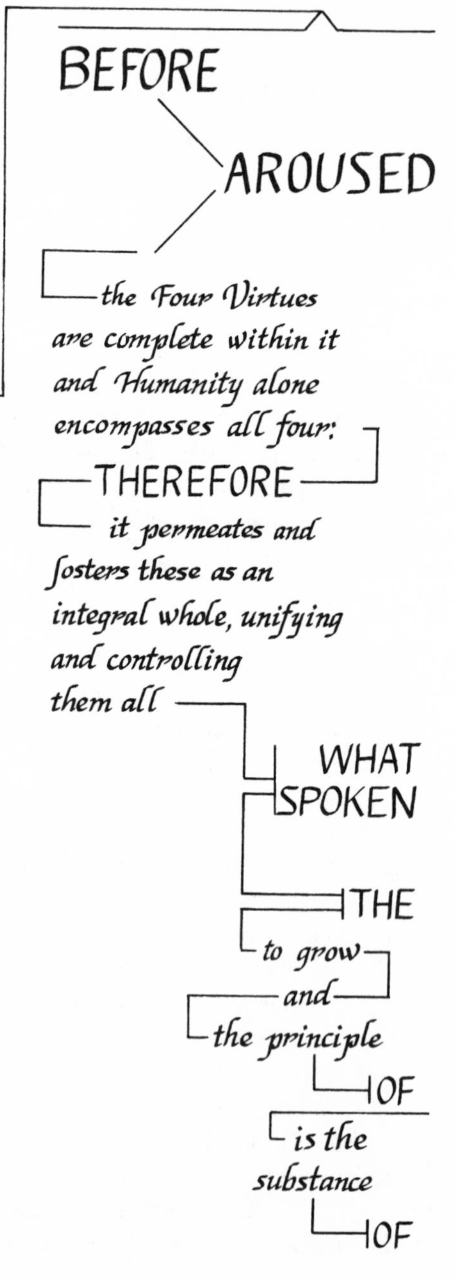

Humanity (Jen)

AFTER

Interacts
the Four Beginnings are manifested and commiseration runs throughout all four;
THEREFORE
it entirely flows throughout and permeates all of them and comprehends them all
IS
OF AS
the feelings of
NATURE
and
the manifestation
LOVE
is the function
HUMANITY

SPEAKING
generically, the condition before the mind is aroused
specifically, humanity
IS SUBSTANCE
the condition after it is aroused
commiseration
IS FUNCTION

IMPARTIALITY
is that whereby one embodies humanity as in the saying, "To overcome oneself and return to propriety is to be humane."
For if one is impartial then he will be humane; if he is humane, he will be LOVING
FILIAL PIETY and RESPECTFULNESS
are functions [of humanity] and
ALTRUISM is the means whereby it is extended to others
As for CONSCIOUS AWARENESS it is what is involved in the exercise of wisdom.

man and the universe, and a new description of man's inner life had developed from the application of the categories of substance and function to describe the relationship of the nature and the feelings in the life of the mind-and-heart. This new framework invited a new inquiry into the meaning of jen: *how can* jen *be thought of as a cosmic quality in which man participates; what does it mean to say that* jen *is the substance of the mind? Addressing such questions brought a profound new development in the way of understanding* jen *that moved decisively beyond traditional formulations.*

The materials presented in this chapter, Chu Hsi's "Treatise on Jen"[3] *and his "Diagram of the Explanation of Jen"*[4] *represent the height of this development. In them we find Chu Hsi's synthesis of the ideas of his predecessors and his criticism of developments that he felt were inadequate. His synthesis not only related and organized earlier ideas, but moved beyond them in terms of his own formulation of* jen *as "the character of the mind and the principle of love."*[5] *The "Treatise" was the product of some ten years' debate and reformulation; he nonetheless felt it lacked clarity concerning substance and function, a lack that he remedied with the later "Diagram," which is schematized in terms of these categories and their psychological correlative, the not-yet-aroused and aroused states of the mind.*[6] *This chapter presents first the text of the diagram, and then a somewhat abridged text of the "Treatise."*

Text of the Diagram

Master Chu says: "Humanity is the mind of Heaven and Earth whereby they produce and give life to creatures,"[7] and this is what man receives as his own mind. Before [this mind] is aroused, the four virtues are complete within it, and humanity alone encompasses all four; thus it permeates and fosters these virtues as an integral whole, unifying and controlling them all. What is spoken of as "the nature to grow"[8] and the principle of love is the substance of humanity.

When [the mind] is aroused and interacts [with things],

the Four Beginnings are manifested and commiseration alone runs throughout all four; thus it entirely flows throughout and permeates all of them, and comprehends them all. What is spoken of as the feelings of the nature and the manifestation of love is the function of humanity.

Speaking generically, the condition before [the mind] is aroused is that of substance, and the condition after it is aroused is that of function. Speaking specifically, humanity is substance and commiseration is function. Impartiality is that whereby one embodies humanity, as illustrated in the saying [of Confucius], "To overcome oneself and return to propriety is to be humane."[9] For if one is impartial, then he will be humane; if he is humane, he will be loving. Filial piety and respectfulness are functions [of humanity], and altruism is the means whereby it is extended to others [in practice].[10] As for [the equation of humanity with] conscious awareness, [consciousness] is what is involved in the exercise of wisdom.[11]

Chu Hsi's "Treatise on *Jen*"[12]

And again he says: The mind of Heaven and Earth has four characteristics: they are origination, flourishing, benefiting, and firmness, and origination runs throughout all.[13] As they move in rotation, we have the cycle of spring, summer, fall, and winter, and the generative force of spring runs throughout all. Therefore in the mind of man there are likewise four characteristics: they are humanity, righteousness, propriety, and wisdom, and humanity encompasses them all. When these issue forth as function, they become the feelings: they are love, respect, a sense of what is proper, and a sense which distinguishes [right and wrong], and commiseration runs throughout all of these. . . .

For humanity's constituting the Tao consists in the fact that the mind [i.e., disposition] of Heaven and Earth to produce and give life to creatures is present in everything. Before the feelings are aroused, this [disposition] is already integrally present as substance, and when they are aroused its function is inexhaustible. If one can in truth embody and preserve it, [he will find that] the wellspring of all good and the foundation of all activity is entirely present within it. This is why the teaching of the Confucian school always urges those who would pursue learning to seek after humanity with unflagging diligence.

In the words [of Confucius] there is the saying, "To overcome oneself and return to propriety is to be humane."[14] This means that if one is able to overcome and expel all of one's self-centeredness and return to the principle of Heaven, then the substance of this mind [i.e., humanity] will be present everywhere and the function of this mind will be always operative.

[Confucius] again has said, "When dwelling at home be respectful; when handling affairs be mindful; in your relationships with others be loyal."[15] This is how one preserves this mind. Again it is said, "Be filial in serving parents," "Be respectful in serving elder brothers,"[16] and "Be altruistic in dealing with others."[17] This is how this mind is put into practice. . . .

But what is this mind [of which we speak]? In Heaven and Earth it is the inexhaustible disposition to produce and give life to creatures; in men it is the warm love for others and the disposition to benefit all creatures. It encompasses the four virtues and runs throughout the Four Beginnings.

Someone said: "Master Ch'eng [I] said, 'Love is a feeling and humanity is the nature; thus one may not regard humanity as love.'[18] In view of what you have said, is this incorrect?"

I said: Such is not the case. What Master Ch'eng said[19] has to do with applying the term humanity to the active manifestation of love, while in my discussion I apply the term to the principle of love. For when it comes to the feelings and the nature, although their spheres are not the same, nonetheless they communicate as an interconnected system of veins, each having its own place; how could they ever be separated and cut off as if having nothing to do with one another! I am distressed nowadays that students just recite the words of Master Ch'eng without seeking out their intention, and so come to speak of humanity as something distinctly separate from love. I have discussed this with the particular intention of clarifying his meaning; in regarding [what I have said] as differing from Master Ch'eng's explanation, is it not you who are mistaken?

Another question: "Among the disciples of the Ch'eng [brothers], there are some who take all things being as one with oneself as the substance of humanity,[20] and also some who interpret humanity in terms of the mind's having conscious awareness;[21] are all these incorrect?"

I said: Saying that all things are one with oneself can serve to manifest the fact that with humanity there is nothing one does not love, but it is not the actual manner in which humanity is considered as substance. Speaking of the mind's possessing conscious awareness can manifest the fact that humanity encompasses wisdom, but it is not the reality from which humanity is so termed. This is apparent if one considers Confucius' reply to the question of Tzu Kung about broadly confering benefits upon the people and saving the whole country,[22] and Ch'eng I's saying that one cannot interpret humanity in terms of consciousness.[23] How can you try to discuss humanity on this basis!. . . .

T'oegye's Comments

The above explanation of humanity is that given by Chu Hsi, and he also made the diagram to go with it. In explaining the Tao of humanity there is nothing more which could be said. The commentary section of the *Great Learning* says, "One who is a [true] ruler abides in humanity."[24] If Your Majesty wishes to seek out what the ancient Emperors and Rulers handed down concerning the wondrous manner in which the mind embodies humanity, its meaning is exhaustively presented here.

Commentary

The Universe as a Single Body

In our discussion of the *Western Inscription* in chapter 2, we saw how the unity between man and cosmos was introduced as a new and powerful foundation for Confucian ethics. Chang Tsai used the image of the universe as a single family sharing a single nature and physical being; hence he discussed *jen* in terms of the familial virtue, filial piety. The Ch'eng brothers went on to develop the concept of humanity in terms of each person's integral unity with all other creatures as members of a single body. Medical texts had used the term *pu-jen* (not-*jen*) as a technical expression for paralysis. In a well-known and influential passage, Ch'eng Hao picked this up and used it to discuss *jen* in the context of the body image:

> Books on medicine speak of the paralysis of the four limbs as "not-*jen*." This expression is an excellent description. The man of humanity regards Heaven and Earth and all creatures as a single body; there is nothing that is not himself. Having recognized [all things] as himself, where will there be anything to which [his humanity] does not reach? But if something is not a part of the self, then it naturally is unrelated with the self. As in the case of the paralysis of the four limbs, since the vital force has ceased to run through them, they no longer belong to the self. Therefore to broadly benefit and assist all is the function of a sage.[25]

In his "Treatise on Jen," Chu Hsi carefully criticizes the one-body idea; not that he disagrees with the idea as such, but it is inadequate as an expression of the real substance of *jen*. His criticism is directed particularly at Yang Shih, who explicitly equates them: "Question: As for all things being one with oneself, is that the substance of humanity? [Yang Shih] said: It is."[26]

Chu Hsi's orientation is practical; he wants an expression of *jen* which has to do with the actual reality of the mind. If one takes the one-body idea as the literal reality of the mind, it becomes a

Buddhistic monism. If not that, then the idea needs further development and explication in order to become practical. Thus in the final paragraph of the "Treatise on Jen," which has been omitted by T'oegye, he says: "Furthermore, to talk about *jen* in general terms of the unity of things and the self will lead people to be vague, confused, neglectful, and make no effort to be alert. The bad effect—and there has been—may be to consider other things as oneself."[27]

A substitute for the one-body idea, as Wing-tsit Chan has noted,[28] is to be found in the notion of impartiality expressed in the "Diagram". "Impartiality" means not just equal treatment, as in the English usage, but refers in the Confucian context especially to not differentiating between oneself and others, an idea closely akin to the one-body idea, but more immediate and practical. Chu Hsi's friend, Chang Shih,[29] wished to directly equate impartiality with the substance of *jen*. Chu Hsi admits there is an intimate connection, but argues that taking impartiality as the substance of *jen* would in effect obscure the actual meaning of *jen* as a characteristic of the nature and an inherent source of love.[30] He explicates his view of the matter as follows:

> *Jen* is just the principle of love. All men have it, but sometimes they are not impartial and hence among those they should love there are some they do not. If one is impartial, then he looks upon Heaven and Earth and all creatures as forming a single body and there is nothing he does not love. But as for the principle of love, it is a principle men naturally and originally possess; it is not necessary that they first be as a single body with Heaven and Earth and all creatures and only then possess it.[31]

Thus Chu Hsi in his "Treatise" and "Diagram" treats impartiality as the fundamental condition for the proper manifestation of *jen* as an all-encompassing love. As the famous saying of Confucius puts it, to become humane one should "overcome oneself and return to propriety";[32] this overcoming of one's self-centeredness is, indeed, fundamental in the practical approach to cultivating in oneself the loving concern for others which manifests the humanity which comprises our nature. But the condition for its proper manifestation is not itself the substance of *jen*, the true source from which this loving concern issues forth.

Jen *as the Generative Life-Force*

The *Book of Changes* says, "To produce and give life is the great virtue of Heaven and Earth,"[33] and the comments on the *fu* ("return") hexagram, which symbolizes the initial movement of the life force in spring, say: "In *fu* one sees the mind of Heaven and Earth."[34] Humanity, as we have seen, was long correlated with origination, the issuance of life in spring. But though the stage was thus set, it was not until Neo-Confucian developments made plausible a literal connection between the generative, vital force of life and *jen* that we move from correlations to direct equations such as that which stands at the head of Chu Hsi's *Diagram:* "Humanity is the mind of Heaven and Earth whereby they produce and give life to generate creatures and this is what man receives as his own mind."

Jen is both the virtue of proper relationships and a quality inherent in the mind. The Ch'eng brothers were important sources for ideas relating the vital, generative force of the universe to both these aspects of *jen*. With regard to the relational aspect, the passage of Ch'eng Hao that deals with paralysis (see above, first section) was an extremely important contribution, for it went beyond the generality of speaking of one-body to specify the flow of the vital force as the operative factor of unity. Chu Hsi elaborated this as follows:

For saying that "humanity is the mind of Heaven and Earth whereby they produce and give life to creatures and this is what men and other creatures receive as their mind," means that Heaven and Earth and man and all things alike possess this mind, and its force (*te*) has always run throughout all. Thus although Heaven and Earth and man and other creatures each are different, nevertheless in reality there is, as it were, a single circulatory system running through them. Therefore if one personally realizes this mind and can preserve and foster it, there is nothing that the principle of the mind does not reach and one naturally loves everything. But if one's capacities are small and [this mind] is beclouded by selfish desires, then its flowing forth is cut off and there are those to whom one's love does not reach. Therefore those who can bear seeing others suffer and are without commiseration are just blocked up by selfishness and have not yet recognized the principle of their mind that runs through the self, Heaven and Earth, and all creatures. Thus the essence of seeking humanity is simply a matter of not losing one's original mind.[35]

Impartiality, as we have seen, unblocks this vital flow, but the flow itself is the dynamic manifestation of our humanity. While this expresses the relational aspect of humanity, humanity as "the principle of love," we must turn to another image for a description of humanity as the actual substance of the individual mind, "the character (*te*) of the mind."[36]

It was Ch'eng I who provided this image. In the course of attempting to clarify how humanity is the substance of the mind, related to but not identical with its function, a student asked: "Is it like the seed of grain which must await the yang force to grow?" Ch'eng I responded: "No. The yang force's activation rather would be the feelings. The mind is like the seed of grain; its nature to grow is humanity."[37] This is a new departure in the discussion of *jen,* drawing for the first time on a hitherto unrelated meaning of the character *jen* as a "kernal" or "seed." Chu Hsi reflects on it as follows:

Further, I have considered the matter in terms of I-ch'uan (Ch'eng I)'s explanation of the seed of grain: the mind is like the seed of grain, its nature to grow is humanity, and the activation of the yang force is the feelings. For what is called "the nature to grow" is the substance of humanity; its activation is the function of humanity. As for broadly benefiting and assisting all, this is the grain's bearing fruit and so it reaches men with its benefit."[38]

The image of the seed with its inner nature to grow is effective because it provides a way to link the understanding of the substance of the mind with the vital generative force of Heaven and Earth, and at the same time preserves the distinction between active function and quiescent substance. The seed which is not yet sprouting nonetheless encloses a very real generative vitality, its "nature to grow"; there is a clear difference between a live seed and something dead. *Jen* as the substance of the mind is much more than a mere empty potency; it is the inner animation of the mind that makes it not physically but morally alive and responsive to other beings.

Thus in the "Treatise" and "Diagram" there is a quite literal continuity in the pairing of *jen* with the generative, originating character of spring. *Jen's* encompassing all the virtues likewise is transformed; the traditional language of all virtue being a manifestation of humanity is now interpreted in terms of *jen* as the inner vitality of all the virtues, and one must read the traditional parallels with the seasons in a much more literal sense. In his "Jade Mountain Lecture," Chu Hsi expressed it as follows:

The word *jen* signifies a vitality *(sheng)* that totally penetrates and pervasively flows through the midst of the four [virtues]: *Jen* is definitely the original substance of humanity; righteousness is *jen*'s judicious ordinance; propriety is *jen*'s appropriate adorning; wisdom is *jen*'s discrimination. It truly is like the vital force of spring which runs throughout the four seasons: spring is the generation of vitality; summer is the growth of vitality; autumn is the reaping [of the fruits of] vitality; winter is the storing up of vitality."[39]

Wing-tsit Chan sums up this aspect of *jen* well: "Put differently, *jen* as a general virtue is not merely the sum total of all virtues, but the generative force that makes virtues real, social, and dynamic. In the broadest sense, it is the process of production itself."[40]

Jen *as Consciousness: A Bypath*

The final sentence of the "Diagram" negates the outright equation of *jen* with conscious awareness. The last portion of the "Treatise" likewise criticizes the equation of humanity and consciousness. The criticism was evoked by Hsieh Liang-tso.[41] We have seen how Chu Hsi picked up on the flow of vital force as the key insight in Ch'eng Hao's passage describing paralysis as "not-*jen*"; the same image can also suggest that "not-*jen*" is somehow a matter of a severing of consciousness, which no longer pervades the whole body. Hsieh developed this aspect of the image:

When the mind has consciousness of something, it is called *jen*. If one is *jen* his mind is one with things. The fruit of plants, trees, and the five grains are referred to as *jen*; they are so named because they are alive. Being alive, there is consciousness. The paralysis of the four limbs is referred to as "not-*jen*"; it is so named because of the absence of consciousness. If there is no consciousness, it is dead.[42]

On one level there is a close parallel here with *jen* as a generative, vital force: the comparison of the shrunken, unhealthy consciousness of the ego-centered person and the impaired sensibility of the paralytic holds true whether one interprets it in terms of an obstruction of vitality or of consciousness. But if one is literal and serious in understanding *jen* as consciousness, problems arise: on the one hand the emphasis upon a unitive consciousness sounds Buddhistic;[43] on the other, only certain forms of consciousness, such as the spontaneous alarm at seeing a child about to fall into a well, can be called *jen.*[44] And most fundamentally, consciousness as such belongs more directly to knowing than to love, and so is the particular function of wisdom, pertaining to *jen* only insofar as *jen* is the all-encompassing animating force of all the virtues which constitute human nature.[45]

In fact, the element of useful insight in the equation of *jen* with consciousness is likewise preserved in considering *jen* as the vital generative power operative in wisdom; this prepares us to recognize the role of loving concern in certain forms of knowledge without the necessity of equating all knowing with loving. Thus Chu Hsi rejected this interpretation and focused instead on *jen* as a vital, generative force, "the nature to grow," a formulation that may mark a new development but is nonetheless also deeply rooted in traditional Confucian thought.

T'oegye and the Question of Jen

Since *jen* is the virtue of virtues in the Confucian tradition and the understanding of it underwent important development in the course of Neo-Confucian reflection, it is completely understandable that T'oegye includes the major exposition of the topic, Chu Hsi's "Treatise on *Jen*," in his *Ten Diagrams*. But the *Ten Dia-*

grams was intended, in the first instance, as a work for the instruction of the king, and in that context the cosmic view of *jen* elaborated here has a special meaning for the understanding of kingship and government. T'oegye discusses this as follows in a memorial to King Sŏnjo:

> I venture to say that the great virtue of Heaven and Earth is to produce and give life. Between Heaven and Earth there is a dense multitude of living creatures; whether they be animals or plants, large or small, they are all compassionately covered and loved by Heaven. How much more is this the case when it comes to the likes of us humans, who are the most spiritual and are as the mind of Heaven and Earth! Although Heaven has this mind, it is not able itself to manifest it, but must especially favor the most sagacious, wise, and excellent, one whose virtue can unite spirits and men, and make him ruler, entrusting him with the duty of looking after [the people] in order to put its humane and loving governance into practice. (A, 6.34a, p. 190)

Apart from such practical exhortations and routine mentions of the centrality and importance of *jen,* however, there seems to be very little discussion of the understanding of *jen* in T'oegye's works. Chu Hsi's "Treatise" and "Diagram" present his final position on questions such as the substance and function of *jen, jen* as the character of the mind and the principle of love, and the relationship of *jen* to impartiality, propriety, and altruism; they also critically review other ideas regarding *jen.* These issues involve complexities and subtleties typical of the sort that are the subject of endless interchanges between Neo-Confucian teachers and students. But T'oegye's voluminous correspondence contains almost no significant discussion of these matters. The few passing references I have been able to find have not offered a basis for elaborating a commentary on this chapter out of T'oegye's own works.[46]

T'oegye was certainly well aware of not only the "Treatise" and "Diagram," but also the whole discussion and debate out of which they emerged. This is evidenced by his *Chu sŏ chŏryo,* a selection of about one-third of Chu Hsi's letters, which includes a judicious selection of portions of Chu Hsi's most important correspondence relating to the "Treatise."[47] To what extent he used Chu Hsi's discussion of *jen* in his teaching is unclear. It does seem evident, however, that in the intellectual world of his time the topic as developed in the "Treatise" and "Diagram" was not problematic. In over 2,000 pages of T'oegye's letters I have found only one minor question directly relating to this material, and T'oegye settles it in two lines.[48]

What conclusions one may draw from this is uncertain. Perhaps it reflects the success of Chu Hsi's analysis and formulation of the meaning of *jen.* Out of the welter of classical descriptions of *jen* he wrought a complex but very precise and systematic analysis in terms of the substance-function structure of the mind-and-heart; he also critically reviewed the new avenues explored by earlier Neo-Confucians and brought these developments to a sharp focus in his formulation of *jen* as the principle of love and the character of the mind. The reasoning which supports his position is presented with clarity, consistency, and precision in his correspondence, particularly in his letters to Chang Shih.[49] If one accepts his basic premises, there are no obvious loose ends or contradictory expressions to be cleared up in Chu Hsi's final explication of *jen.*

This does not mean that the full meaning of the "Treatise" and "Diagram" is simple and easy to understand; they have a history and inner rational which must be examined and carefully considered. But other major aspects of the Ch'eng-Chu school of thought, such as the relationship of activity and quiet or study and practice with regard to self-cultivation, or the relationship of principle and material force with regard to understanding the cosmos and the human psyche, involve dialectical tensions that result in differing and sometimes apparently contradictory statements being made from varied perspectives. These provided Koreans obvious material for questions, debate, and further development. As for Chu Hsi's discussion of *jen,* perhaps we can take the comment with which T'oegye concludes this chapter at face value: "In explaining the Tao of humanity there is nothing more which could be said."

Chapter 8: DIAGRAM OF THE STUDY OF THE MIND

From his youth Chen Te-hsiu's Classic of the Mind-and-Heart[1] was one of the most important and formative influences on T'oegye. In the supplemented and annotated edition that circulated widely in Korea and was used by T'oegye, the Hsin-ching fu-chu (Simgyŏng puju),[2] this diagram and its explanatory text are inserted immediately before the first chapter with the following note: "This diagram of Mr. Ch'eng [Fu-hsin][3] exhausts the wonders of the study of the mind-and-heart, and what it discusses likewise suffices to manifest the essence of the study of the mind and heart."[4] Thus it serves as both an introduction and summation to the Classic of the Mind-and-Heart. T'oegye, who remarks that he has always "loved this diagram,"[5] uses it here in a similar fashion, making it an introduction to and summation of Neo-Confucian ascetical doctrine, the method of cultivating one's mind-and-heart, which is the central concern of the Classic.

In China the term "study of the mind-and-heart (hsin-hsüeh)" became, in the Ming dynasty (1368–1644), a designation for the Lu-Wang school of thought, pointing to that school's emphasis on the direct cultivation of the innate goodness of the mind, in contrast to the Ch'eng-Chu school, which insisted that the investigation of principle is essential since understanding is analytically prior to practice. The Ch'eng-Chu school thus became characterized as "the study of principle."

This development has somewhat obscured the fact that the study of the mind-and-heart is likewise central in the Ch'eng-Chu school. Chen Te-hsiu's Classic of the Mind-and-Heart and Ch'eng Fu-hsin's "Diagram of the Study of the Mind-and-Heart" both witness the vigor with which *this aspect of Chu Hsi's teaching was developed during the Yüan dynasty (1279–1368).*[6] *T'oegye's constant emphasis upon the centrality of mindfulness is a faithful reflection of Chu Hsi, but it is also an unmistakable reflection of the influence of Chen's* Classic, *which played such a central role in his early and middle years and formed his mind before he had the opportunity for his later immersion in Chu Hsi's own works.*

Ch'eng Fu-hsin's Explanation of the Diagram[7]

Ch'eng Lin-yin [Fu-hsin] says: "The 'mind of the infant'[8] is the 'naturally good mind'[9] before it has been disturbed by human desires; the 'human mind'[10] is the mind that has been awakened to desire. The 'mind of the great man'[11] is the 'original mind'[12] which is perfectly endowed with moral principle; the 'mind of the Tao'[13] is the mind that has been awakened to moral principle."

This does not mean that there are two kinds of mind; but since in fact man is produced through the material force that gives one physical form, no one can be without the "human mind"; and [at the same time] origination [as a human being] is from the nature, which is the Mandate [of Heaven], and this is what is referred to as the "mind of the Tao."

[The lower half of the diagram], from "be discerning and undivided, select [the good] and hold to it firmly,"[14] on down, is concerned with the efforts to block [selfish] human desires and to preserve the principle of Heaven [which is our nature.] [On the left-hand side] from "watchful when alone,"[15] on down are the efforts addressed to blocking [selfish] human desires. In this it is necessary to reach the stage described as "the mind is not moved";[16] then "Wealth and high position will not be able to corrupt him, poverty and low estate will not be able to move him, and majesty and force will not be able to bend him."[17] At

8 Diagram of the Study of the Mind

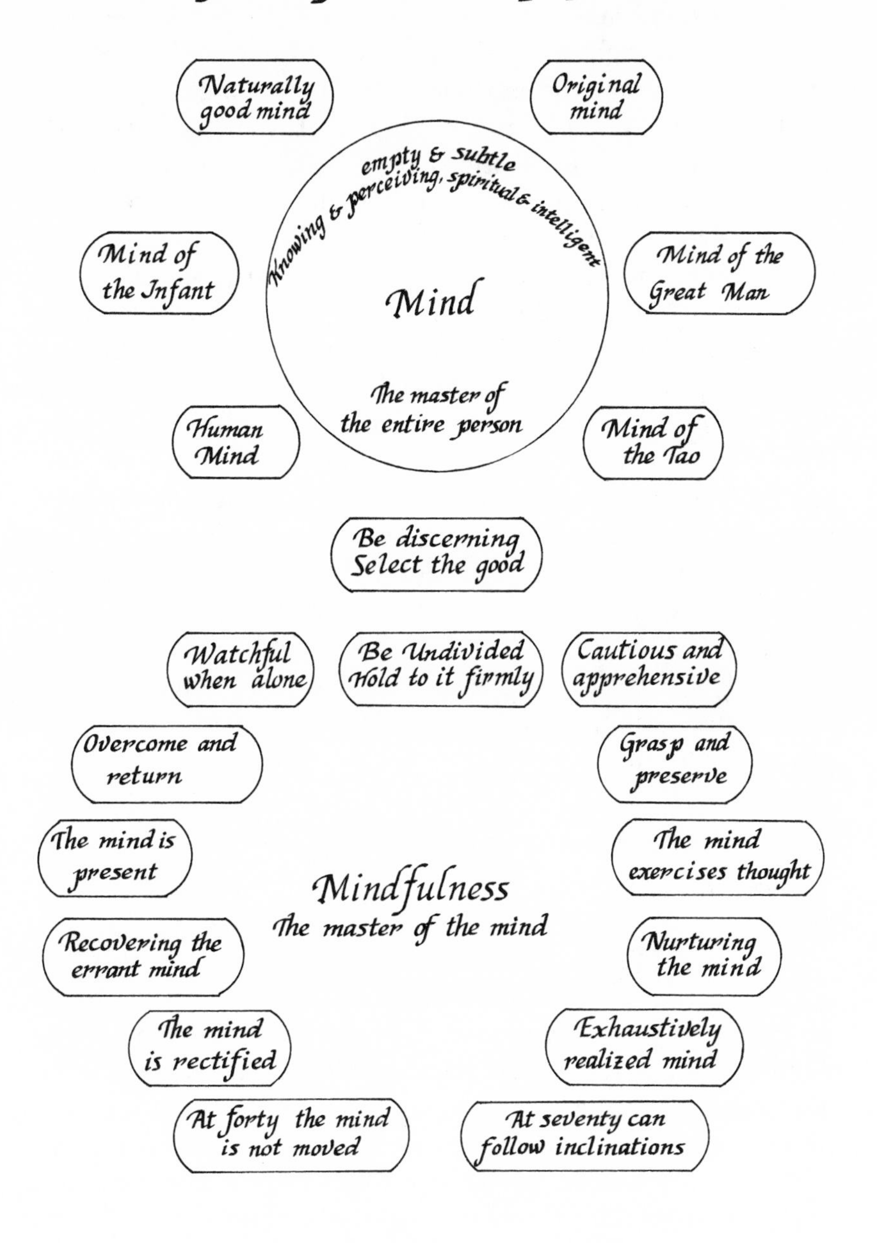

this stage one can see his tao has become lustrous and his virtue has been established.

[On the right-hand side], from "cautious and apprehensive,"[18] on down are the efforts regarding preserving the principle of Heaven. In this it is necessary to reach the stage described as "can follow one's inclinations";[19] then the mind will be identical with its substance and desires identical with function, and that substance is the Tao and that function is righteousness. One's speech will accord with the norm and [the actions] of one's person will accord with the proper standard. At this stage one can see he may "apprehend without exercising deliberate thought, hit upon what is right with no deliberate effort."[20]

In sum, the essence of applying one's efforts is nothing other than a matter of not departing from constant mindfulness, for the mind is the master of the entire person and mindfulness is the master of the mind. If one who pursues learning will but thoroughly master what is meant by "focusing on one thing without departing from it,"[21] "being properly ordered and controlled, grave and quiet,"[22] and "recollecting the mind and making it always awake and alert,"[23] his practice will be utterly perfect and complete, and entering the condition of sagehood likewise will not be difficult.

T'oegye's Comments

Ch'eng Lin-yin collected together the terms in which the sages and wise men have discussed the study of the mind and made the above diagram of them. His categorically distinguishing and arranging them in corresponding pairs is complex but not tiresome, for by this means he shows that the system of the mind-and-heart in sage learning is likewise complex, and one must apply diligent effort to all these aspects.

[The lower half of the diagram] is arranged in an order that proceeds from the top to the bottom; it is meant as a schematic presentation [of the process of self-cultivation] simply in terms of what is shallower and what more profound, what is less mature and what more mature. Since this is its approach, it does not mean to depict the stages and steps of the process in the temporal order of prior and posterior, as [does the *Great Learning* in speaking of] extending knowledge to the utmost, making the will sincere, rectifying the mind, and cultivating one's person.[24]

But someone[25] might doubt: "Since you say it is a schematic arrangement, 'recovering the errant mind'[26] is the very first step in applying one's efforts, so it should not be placed after "the mind is present.' "[27]

I would suggest that if one speaks of "recovering the lost mind" in the more shallow sense, it certainly comes as the very first step in applying one's efforts [to self-cultivation]; but if one speaks of it in a more profound and ultimate sense, if for even the slightest moment a single thought deviates a tiny bit, it also may be termed an "errant mind." Such was the case when Yen Hui was described as not being able to avoid deviating [from the perfect observance of humanity] after a period of three months.[28] If one cannot entirely be without deviation, any deviance is a slip into an errant condition; when Yen Hui made the least mistake he could immediately recognize it, and having recognized it would not repeat it,[29] and this also may be classed as "recovering the errant mind." Therefore the order of Ch'eng's diagram is as it is.

Mr. Ch'eng's courtesy name was Tzu-hsien, and he was from Hsin-an. He dwelt in retirement and did not take office; the correctness of his conduct was extremely perfect. From youth to old age he exhaustively studied the Classics and gained a profound understanding of them. He was the author of the *Diagrams of the Sentences of the Four Books,* in three *kwŏn* (*chüan*).

When Emperor Jen-tsung [r. 1311–1320] of the Yüan dynasty, due to a special recommendation, summoned him and intended to employ him as an official, Tzu-hsien did not wish to comply. He was made a provincial erudite (*hsiang-chün po-shih*), but resigned his position and returned home. Such was the kind of man he was;[30] how could he have failed to understand [concerning "recovering the errant mind"] and made a mistake!

Commentary

On Reading the Diagram

We have seen that one aspect of the investigation of principle is the patient play of the mind over the diversity of the authoritative sources, trying to see how each speaks with its own voice and exposes an aspect of the topic, while final insight comes through comprehending their interrelationship as multiple facets of a single whole. The diagramatic form, so popular in Korea, is an instrument well suited to this approach. The object of diagrammatic schematization is not rapid and simplified learning but rather the structured presentation of a body of complex, interrelated material as an aid to sustained reflection. This is clear in T'oegye's advice on reading the upper part of this diagram:

One must see in it the kind of thing the mind is: in the midst of its undifferentiated integral substance it is divided up like this in accord with the ways it is manifested or the aspects one attends to. The various kinds of terminological headings are meant to make one who pursues learning base himself upon these terms and seek out their meaning and intent. If for a long time one mulls them over and savors the taste [of each] with a personal understanding, then all the principles will coalesce, and in this is found the integral substance of the mind. (A, 23.28a, p. 561, Letter to Cho Sagyŏng)

What T'oegye understands as the "meaning and intent" of the terms and their arrangement in the upper portion of the diagram is presented in the following passage:

The six types of mind arranged above, below, and to the right and left of the "mind" circle simply describe how there is a particular point to each of the ways the sages and wise men talk about the mind. It is like this: because of its fundamental (*ponyŏn, pen-jan*) goodness it is called the "naturally good mind"; because of its original possession (*ponyu, pen-yu*) of goodness it is called the "original mind"; as being simple and without any artificiality, and nothing more, it is called the "mind of the infant"; as simple and without any artificiality and being able to comprehend all changes totally, it is called the "mind of the great man"; being produced through the psychophysical component it is called the "human mind"; and having its origin in the Mandate which constitutes the nature, it is called the "mind of the Tao."[31] Since the "naturally good mind" and the "original mind" have very similar types of meaning they are placed in correlation to each other at the top on the left and right; the "mind of the infant" and "mind of the great man," and the "human mind" and the "mind of the Tao," because their fundamental terminology involves a mutual contrast, are arranged in pairs to the left and right of the middle and bottom respectively. (A, 14.35b, p. 378, Letter to Yi Sukhŏn)

The Human Mind and the Mind of the Tao

Two of the pairs of terms regarding the mind in the upper half of the diagram come from Mencius, as well as six of the twelve items in the lower half of the diagram. This reflects his importance for the Neo-Confucian theory of the mind-and-heart, a topic which he discussed more than any other classical author. But the explication of this terminology also shows that his primary concern was to establish the fundamental goodness of human nature. Chang Tsai, some 1,300 years later, finally provided Confucians with a doctrine that could explicate an intrinsic source of aberrant tendencies within man without thereby vitiating the fundamental and vital fact of goodness at the core of human nature that Mencius was so concerned to defend: this was the doctrine of the physical nature. This development called for an authoritative classical source and terminology that would reflect not only the innate goodness, but also the problematic side of human dispositions. It was found in a passage in the *Book of Documents*: "The human mind is insecure, the mind of the Tao is subtle; be discerning, be undivided [One]. Hold fast the Mean!"[32]

This passage, as is evident in the diagram, became the keystone of the understanding of the mind in the Ch'eng-Chu school: the "mind of the Tao" embodies the innate goodness of human nature spoken of by Mencius and enshrined philosophically in the doctrine that equates human nature with principle, while the "human mind" is taken as a manifestation of the physical nature, Chang Tsai's explication of evil.

The *Classic of the Mind-and-Heart* is a compendium of quotations. Not surprisingly, it begins with this passage on the mind of the Tao and the human mind, and this is immediately interpreted by a quotation from Chu Hsi:

The empty spirituality[33] and consciousness of the mind-and-heart are one and undivided. But there is a difference between the human mind and the mind of the Tao since some aspects arise through the individuality [or selfishness] of the physical form while some originate in the rectitude of the Mandate that is the nature, and the consequent type of consciousness is not the same. Therefore the one is perilous and insecure and the other is wondrously subtle and difficult to perceive. Nevertheless, there is no one who does not have physical form, and so even the most wise cannot be without the human mind; likewise there is no one who does not possess this nature, and so even the stupidest person cannot be without the mind of the Tao. These two are mixed together within the mind-and-heart, and if one does not know how to control them the perilous will become even more perilous and the subtle will become even more subtle and in the end the impartiality of the principle of Heaven will not be able to overcome the selfishness of human desire. If one is discerning he will discriminate between these two and not let them get mixed. If one is undivided he will maintain the rectitude of the original mind and not become separated from it.[34]

This passage, which comes from Chu Hsi's introduction to the *Doctrine of the Mean,* is the most important single interpretation of the rather vague words of the *Book of Documents.* One notes that in spite of the affirmation of the fundamental goodness of human nature—the mind of the Tao—the tone is exceedingly reserved and highly aware of the weakness or moral peril which attends our psychophysical endowment, manifested as the human mind. DeBary has characterized this well as a moral "rigorism,"[35] it is an uneasy partner with the more affirmative Mencian heritage.

It would be easy, from Chu Hsi's words above, to slip into an attitude that virtually equates the psychophysical endowment or "physical nature," and the "human mind," its manifestation, with selfishness (*sa*). However the observation that even the wisest, that is, the sage, also has a "human mind," is a warning that the equation cannot be that simple. T'oegye notes that the disciples of the Ch'eng brothers understood the "human mind" as selfishness, and that Chu Hsi at first followed them in this but later corrected it.[36] He observes that *sa* may mean not "selfish," but "private," i.e., pertaining to the individuality of human existence, which is a consequence of physicality; it is in this sense that one should understand the "human mind."[37] Thus he carefully distinguishes between equating the human mind with selfishness and saying that it is the basis from which one may easily slip into selfishness:

The human mind is the foundation of [selfish] human desires. Human desires are the flow of the human mind; they arise from the mind as physically conditioned. The sage likewise cannot but have [the human mind]; therefore one can only call it the human mind and cannot directly consider it as human desire. Nevertheless human desires in fact proceed from it; therefore I say it is the foundation of human desires. The mind ensnared by greed is the condition of the ordinary man who acts contrary to Heaven; therefore it is termed "human desire" and called something other than "human mind." This leads one to understand that such is not the original condition of the human mind; therefore I say it is the "flow" of the human mind. Thus the human mind is prior and human desires come later; the former is correct and the latter is evil.[38] (A, 40.9b-10a, p. 897, Letter to Nephew [Yi] Yŏnggyo)

This careful analysis gives full recognition to the fundamental soundness of man, including his physicality and the desires that may appropriately follow from it. But it also recognizes the tendency for the fact of individuality to flow into the aberration of self-centeredness; the more turbid one's psychophysical endowment, the more entrapped one becomes in individuality and the less able one is to live by the community of principle.

The Essence of Cultivating the Mind-and-Heart

The approach to the cultivation of the mind-and-heart is conceptualized in terms of the polarity of the mind of the Tao and the human mind. T'oegye sums it up as follows:

In general, although the study of the mind-and-heart is complex, one can sum up its essence as nothing other than blocking [self-centered] human desires and preserving the principle of Heaven, just these two and that is all. . . . All the matters that are involved in blocking human desires should be categorized on the side of the human mind, and all that pertain to preserving the principle of Heaven should be categorized on the side of the mind of the Tao . . . The intent of Ch'eng Lin-yin's "Diagram of the Study of the Mind-and-Heart" is truly like this. (A, 37.28b, p. 849, Letter to Yi P'yŏngsuk)

The subtlety of the mind of the Tao implies that it may easily be obscured, and the perilousness of the human mind signifies the ease with which it may slide into self-centeredness. Clearly this leads to a kind of moral rigorism. But the categorizing of moral self-cultivation is bipolar: something good to be preserved and nurtured, and something potentially negative to be guarded against and blocked off. As deBary has observed, this makes Neo-Confucian moralism something quite different from the more exclusively negative focus of western Puritanism.[39]

The division of the stages of moral growth according to the mind of the Tao and the human mind basically separates the purely positive from that which implies a negativity to be brought under control. To complete the picture, it is further necessary to see cultivation in terms of the cultivation of the mind in its two states, before it is aroused (substance, the nature) and after it is aroused (function, the feelings). It was not possible to incorporate this dimension directly into the diagram, for both the mind of the Tao and the human mind are technically *manifestations* of the composition of the mind rather than actual components, and thus belong on the "after it is aroused" side. Nonetheless, there is a general symmetry between the diagram's distinction of preserving the principle of Heaven and blocking human desires and cultivating the mind in its quiet and active states respectively: blocking human desires clearly belongs to the active state of the mind, while preserving principle looks to the quiet union of the mind with principle (nature, substance) and the undivided, consistent maintenance of this principle as the mind moves forth into activity. When viewed within this framework, one might further observe, what emerges as of critical importance is not so much either the quiet or the active states of the mind as such, but rather the point of interchange between the two, the subtle incipience (*ki, chi*) of activity in which lie the seeds of what is to follow.

From this perspective, then, one can understand why mindfulness assumes a central importance in this diagram. Equally applicable to the quiet and active states of the mind, it also presides over the transition and is in fact the essence of cultivating the mind-and-heart. T'oegye says:

As for man's receiving the Mandate from Heaven, he is endowed with the principles of the four virtues, and that which is the master of his person is the mind. That which is stirred within by things and follows the subtle incipience (*ki, chi*) of good and evil as the function of the mind is the feelings and the intention. Therefore the superior man, when this mind is quiet, unfailingly preserves and nurtures it to maintain its substance; when the feelings and intentions issue forth, he unfailingly exercises self-reflection and discernment in order to rectify its function.

Nonetheless, the principle of this mind is so vast it cannot be concretely laid hold of, so boundless it cannot be limited. If there is not mindfulness to make it undivided, how will one be able to preserve its nature and establish its substance! The issuance of this mind is subtle, as difficult to discern as the most minute particle; it is insecure, as perilous as treading [the edge of] a deep pit. If there is not mindfulness to make it undivided, then again, how will one be able to rectify its subtle incipient activation (*ki, chi*) and perfect its function!

Therefore the superior man's way of learning is this: when the mind is not yet aroused, he unfailingly takes mindfulness as primary and applies himself to the preservation and nurture of the mind; when the mind has been aroused, he likewise unfailingly takes mindfulness as primary and applies himself to reflection and discernment. This is how mindfulness is the means by which both the beginning and the end of learning is accomplished; it runs throughout both substance and function [i.e., quiescence and activity]. (*Ch'ŏnmyŏng tosŏl*, ch. 10, B, 8.20a-b, p. 144)

One notes the special importance here of the "subtle incipient activation" (*ki, chi*), the almost imperceptible arising of currents in the mind which grow into full-fledged forces of good and evil. The subtle incipient activation is logically schematized as the incipience of activation after quiescence, but in a more general sense there is also such incipience whenever our ever-changing context calls forth new feelings and reactions. The constant emphasis upon mindfulness, a calm, recollected, self-possessed state of mind, bespeaks a resolve to bring these subtle beginnings under conscious, discerning control. There is an inverse proportionality at work in this, for at this level evil is most easily blocked and controlled, but the highest and most demanding mental discipline is required to exercise discernment at such a subtle level. The general moral observation that "the human mind is perilous" is thus paired with an analysis of the genesis of mental conditions, and together these point to the rigorous kind of mentally oriented moral cultivation that may be summarized by the single expression, "constant mindfulness."

The Placement of this Diagram

In the original order of the *Ten Diagrams*, this chapter preceded the chapter on Chu Hsi's "Treatise on Jen." Yi I (Yulgok) wrote to T'oegye suggesting that their positions should be reversed, and T'oegye, observing that he had already been thinking about that, readily agreed.[40] Unfortunately, neither letter mentions any reason for the desirability of such a change. Nonetheless, there is a difference made by the order that made it an object of concern for them, and it is appropriate to consider what that difference might be, even in the absence of direct evidence as to what T'oegye and Yulgok had in mind.

The sixth chapter describes the structure and constitution of the mind, and the present chapter introduces the correlative approach to self-cultivation. A chapter dealing with *jen,* the epitome of all virtue, might logically follow these as a depiction of the highest achievement in Confucian self-cultivation. This was in fact T'oegye's original arrangement. It has, however, the drawback of interrupting the close connection between this chapter and the two final chapters, which are devoted to the discussion of mindfulness, introduced here as the essence of self-cultivation.

But the "Treatise on Jen" is not only a discussion of *jen;* it is also a description of the mind that explains its fundamental character or substance as an integral continuation of the inner nature and dynamism of the whole universe. In this perspective, it is related to the structural considerations of the sixth chapter and serves as a fitting prelude to the discussion of the cultivation of the mind begun in this chapter. This is T'oegye's final arrangement.

The *Ten Diagrams* attempts to present a comprehensive vision of existence and elaborate its consequences for the way we form ourselves and carry on our daily life. In such a work, questions of a proper and coherent order of presentation have ramifications in which more is at stake than just logical coherence. What comes first has a direct bearing on the understanding of what follows. Thus changing the position of the "Treatise on Jen" makes it not just the final goal of all self-cultivation, but a basic commentary on the nature of the mind and the universe, a window through which to view the task of self-cultivation. This chapter approaches the concrete world of moral cultivation and cannot but show the mind with its forces divided between currents representing the original goodness of man's nature and the self-centered proclivities which attend our physical, individual existence. This side of Chu Hsi's thought was developed into what became, at times, an excessive rigorism tinged with a negative, suspicious attitude toward human feelings.[41] Earnest moral concern and high seriousness were present in this, but one senses a loss of the grand, positive, overall vision which characterizes Chu Hsi's thought as a whole. The rearranging of these chapters places the discussion of moral self-cultivation and its natural emphasis on the need for constant watchfulness and mindfulness in the clear overarching perspective of the "Treatise on Jen," and thus preserves the delicate balance of cautious optimism which is the Mencian heritage of the Ch'eng-Chu school.

Chapter 9: DIAGRAM OF THE ADMONITION FOR MINDFULNESS STUDIO

Mindfulness stands at the heart of Chu Hsi's teaching as it is understood by T'oegye, and in this chapter T'oegye presents the text which served as his own source of inspiration, constant reflection, and self-examination. Describing his early formation, he says: "The Explanation of the Diagram of the Supreme Ultimate in the Hsing-li ta-ch'üan gave me a start [in learning]; the Admonition for Mindfulness Studio was the matter for my practice."[1] In later years the Admonition was pasted to the wall of his study as a constant reminder; in this he was following the example of Chu Hsi, who composed the Admonition and put it on the wall of his study.

As the comments in this chapter indicate, the Admonition approaches mindfulness topically, presenting its various applications to activity and quiet, to external deportment and internal attitudes. In addition to the text in the last chüan of the Hsing-li ta-ch'üan where T'oegye first encountered it, the Admonition appears in the ChuTzu ch'üan-shu, 85, and in the final chüan of the Classic of the Mind-and-Heart. The text as presented here follows a variant reading found in the Classic,[2] and most of the comments T'oegye appends to it likewise appear there. Thus this chapter, as well as the one which precedes it, directly reflects the continual influence of Chen Te-hsiu's Classic on T'oegye's thought.

9 Diagram of the Admonition for Mindfulness Studio

Properly order your clothing and cap; make your gaze reverent.
Recollect your mind abiding as if you were present before the Lord on High.

The appearance of the feet must be as if they were heavy; the disposition of the hands must be respectful.
First select the ground and then tread; twist and turn [your way] through the antmounds.

When you go abroad behave to everyone as if you were meeting an important guest; preside over affairs as if presiding over a sacrifice.
Always cautious and fearful, never venture to slacken.

Stop up your mouth like the opening of a bottle; guard your intentions as you would a city wall.
Always reverent and sincere, never treat anything frivolously.

TRANQUILITY
ACTION
WITHOUT OFFENSE

EXTERIOR
INTERIOR
MUTUALLY CORRECTING

Attending to affairs in this manner

Mind

CONCENTRATION ON ONE

Because of two do not divide your mind into two;
Because of three do not divide your mind into three.
Let your mind be undivided
As it watches over the myriad changes

WITHOUT DEPARTING

When attending to something to the west, do not go east;
When attending to something to the north, do not go south.
When you encounter some affair, attend only to it;
Do not set off about something else.

is called maintaining mindfulness.

IF FALTER

If one should falter for a single moment, selfish desire will put forth 10,000 shoots; one will be hot when there is no fire, cold when there is no ice.

IF A DISPARITY

If there is a hair's breadth disparity, Heaven and Earth will change their places, the Three Guidelines will perish and the Nine Laws will be wiped out.

Oh, little ones, ponder this!
Be mindful!
Let the Ink Minister take this admonition and convey it to your Lord Mind.

The Admonition for Mindfulness Studio

Properly order your clothing and cap and make your gaze reverent;[3] recollect your mind and make it abide, as if you were present before the Lord on High.[4] The appearance of the feet must be as if they were heavy, the disposition of the hands respectful. First select the ground and then tread; twist and turn [your way] through the antmounds.[5]

When you go abroad, behave to everyone as if you were meeting an important guest; preside over affairs as if presiding at a sacrifice.[6] Always cautious and fearful,[7] never venture to slacken. Stop up your mouth like the opening of a bottle, and guard your intentions as you would a city wall. Always reverent and sincere,[8] never venture to treat anything frivolously.

When attending to something to the west, do not go east; when attending to something to the north, do not go south. When you encounter some affair attend only to it; do not set off about something else. Because of two [matters to be dealt with] do not divide your mind into two; because of three do not divide your mind into three. Let your mind be undivided[9] as it watches over the myriad changes. Attending to affairs in this manner is called maintaining mindfulness. Both action and tranquility should be without offense; one's exterior and interior should mutually rectify one another.

If one should falter for a single moment, selfish desire will put forth ten thousand shoots;[10] one will be hot when there is no fire, cold when there is no ice.[11] If there is a hair's breadth disparity [from what is right] Heaven and Earth will change their places;[12] the Three Guidelines will perish and the Nine Laws will be wiped out.[13]

Ah, little ones, ponder this! Be mindful! Let the Ink Minister take this admonition and convey it to your Lord Mind!

Comments of Chu Hsi and Others

Chu Hsi says: "If a circle is to be proper, its curve must be round and in accord with the norm provided by the compass; if a square is to be proper, its angles must be square and in accord with the norm provided by a square. 'Antmounds' refers to the mounds made by ants; there is an old saying which speaks of mounting a horse and twisting and turning [one's way] through the antmounds. This refers to the fact that the path lying between the antmounds is tortuous and narrow; thus it is a difficult feat to mount one's horse and twist and turn, threading a path through them without breaking one's gait."[14]

"Stopping up one's mouth like the opening of a bottle means not saying anything recklessly. Guarding one's intention as one would the wall of a city means preventing any depravity from entering."[15]

And again he says: "One who would be mindful must focus his attention on one thing. If at first there is one matter and another is added, then [one's mind becomes divided] into two, for that makes two matters. If originally there is one matter and two are added, then [the mind becomes divided] into three, for that makes three matters."[16] Faltering for a single moment refers to the temporal aspect; 'a hair's breadth disparity' is said in terms of the matter itself."[17]

Wu Lin-ch'uan[18] says: "The *Admonition* consists of ten sections of four lines each. The first section says that in tranquility one should be without offense, and the second that in action one should be without offense. The third speaks of the correctness of one's external [deportment], and the fourth of the correctness of one's interior [dispositions]. The fifth speaks of how, when the mind is proper, it will fully reach to the matter in hand [without being sidetracked], while the sixth speaks of concentrating on one thing [at a time] in dealing with affairs.

The seventh sentence is a general conclusion to the first six. The eighth describes the ills which attend upon not succeeding in being 'without departing' and the ninth describes the ills that follow from not being able to 'concentrate on one [thing].' The tenth sentence is a general conclusion to the entire work."[19]

Chen Te-hsiu[20] says: "There is nothing more that could be said about the meaning of mindfulness. Those whose wills are firmly set upon pursuing sage learning ought to become thoroughly versed in this and go over it repeatedly."[21]

T'oegye's Remarks

Master Chu, in his own prefatory remarks to the above *Admonition* says: "After reading the *Admonition on Concentrating on One Thing,* by Chang Ching-fu [Shih],[22] I took its general purport and made this *Admonition for Mindfulness Studio* and put it on the wall of my study as a reminder for myself."[23] And again: "This is a topical treatment of mindfulness, so the exposition is made from a number of standpoints."[24]

I would suggest that this exposition of the topics offers a good foundation for the actual practice [of mindfulness]. Wang Lu-chai (Po)[25] of Chin-hua arranged the topics to make a diagram and achieved this kind of clear and well-ordered presentation in which everything finds its proper place. One should personally experience and get a taste of its meaning, cautioning oneself and using it for self-reflection in the course of daily life and in whatever comes to mind. If one assimilates it in this way, he will never doubt but that "mindfulness constitutes the beginning and the end of sage learning."[26]

Commentary

The Centrality of Mind and Its Cultivation

The centrality of the mind-and-heart in self-cultivation is graphically evident in this diagram. T'oegye discusses the importance of the mind and the essentials of its cultivation as follows:

The mind is the foundation of all affairs and the nature is the origin of all good; therefore when the former Confucians discussed learning they unfailingly regarded "recovering the errant mind"[27] and "nurturing the virtuous nature"[28] as the very first thing to which one must apply oneself as the means whereby one fulfills his fundamental constitution. This they regarded as the foundation for fulfilling the Tao and developing the full extent of one's virtue; as for the essence of the way to apply one's effort, what need is there to seek it in anything else!

Likewise it is said: "Concentrate on one thing without departing [from it],"[29] "Be cautious, be apprehensive."[30] The application of concentrating on one thing runs throughout both the active and quiet states, while the field of caution and apprehension is entirely in the not-yet-aroused state. Neither of these can be omitted. And regulating the exterior in order to nurture the interior is an even more urgent matter. Therefore instructions such as the "Three Self-examinations,"[31] the "Three Things Valued,"[32] and the "Four Things Not Done"[33] all concern responding [to affairs] and dealing [with others]; this likewise is what is meant by nurturing one's fundamental constitution. If one does not approach it in this fashion and one-sidedly emphasizes applying himself to just the mind, it is rare not to fall into Buddhist views. (A, 16.6b-7a, pp. 404–405, Letter to Ki Myŏngŏn)

In this passage three aspects of the cultivation of the mind-and-heart emerge: (1) maintaining a concentrated, self-possessed state of mind ("concentrate on one thing without departing"); (2) a reverential dimension ("be cautious, be apprehensive"); (3) beginning by regulating the external in order to cultivate the internal. These aspects also are evident in Chu Hsi's *Admonition for Mindfulness Studio.* We shall discuss each in turn, beginning with the third.

Mindfulness through Propriety: Beginning from the External

Traditional Confucianism had simply taken the whole person as the object of self-cultivation. It approached this through a relatively common-sense, externalistic methodology which stressed forming a good character through self-discipline and the inculcation of good habits, with the disciplined observance of the rules of propriety serving as a major means to this end. When Buddhism entered East Asia, it brought with it a new focus on the inner life of the mind, and its sophisticated meditative techniques for the transformation of consciousness made Confucian methodology look embarrassingly simple and superficial by contrast. When the Neo-Confucian movement finally revitalized the Confucian tradition after centuries of Buddhist predominance, it is not surprising that it was characterized by a new awareness of man's interiority, now taking the mind-and-heart as the central object of self-cultivation and elaborating the doctrine of mindfulness as the appropriate and essential methodology. The Neo-Confucians had learned much from the Buddhists.

Maxims of the traditional propriety, such as the "Four Things Not Done," however, continued to have a serious place in self-cultivation. Chu Hsi's *Admonition* begins, one notes, not with the inner life of consciousness but with dress, demeanor, physical comportment, and one's attitude in dealing with others. But this external self-discipline is now given an explicitly internal orientation: "Regulate the external in order to nurture the interior," as T'oegye puts it. Many passages emphasize this as the most concrete and practical approach to regulating the mind-and-heart. T'oegye says:

I have heard that the ancients, wishing to preserve the mind-and-heart that is without form or shadow, would unfailingly apply themselves to that which has form and shadow that could be relied upon and maintained. This is what the "Four Things Not Done" and the "Three Things Valued" of Yen Hui and Tseng Tzu are. Therefore in his letter replying to He Shu-ching Master Chu says: "From the level of Yen Hui or Tseng Tzu[34] on down, it is necessary to apply one's practice to matters such as one's seeing and listening, one's speech and demeanor one's way of expressing oneself. For man's mind has no form and its coming and going is not fixed; one must preserve and settle it in accord with an established norm, then of themselves both the inner and outer will become steady. This is the absolute essence of day-to-day practice. If you examine it in this light, you will realize that the inner and outer have never been separated, and what is described as being serious, properly ordered, controlled, and grave, is truly the means by which one preserves one's mind-and-heart."[35] . . . One may not split the inner and the outer into two separate matters and regard the outer as coarse, shallow, and easy to do, while regarding the inner as subtle and mysterious and a practice difficult to attain. (A, 29,12a-b, p. 682, Letter to Kim Ijŏng)

While the above passage emphasizes the practicality of this kind of approach, it is also clear that the practicality is conjoined with a value orientation expressed in terms of avoiding a Buddhistic devaluation of the external in attending to the internal. Confucian self-cultivation has as its final goal not some kind of personal, inner enlightenment, but the proper conduct of human relationships and government. Neo-Confucians enlarged that tradition by introducing a more personal, inner dimension to self-cultivation that held the promise of a kind of personal fulfillment or awakening: one could become a sage. But Confucian sagehood could never be divorced from the external perfection of man as a social being, and true to this tradition the Ch'eng-Chu school makes every effort to hold the internal and external together as two aspects of a single unity. Proper deportment in dress, speech, and conduct are not only useful stratagems for controlling the mind, but important values in themselves. Thus underlying the stress on this approach is an ultimate Confucian concern for the external world of human society and the proper conduct of human relationships. This is the distinctively Confucian dimension of the cultivation of the mind-and-heart. As T'oegye said above (see previous sec.): "If one does not approach it in this fashion and one-sidedly emphasizes applying himself to just the mind, it is rare not to fall into Buddhist views."

As the theory of mindfulness developed, a number of different descriptions of it emerged; some of these were more externalistic, others more directly descriptive of a state or condition of the mind. If mindfulness entailed some kind of altered state of consciousness, one might see a progression from external to internal practice in these descriptions, but such is not the case. Thus T'oegye sees the externalistic approach as not only most concrete and practical, but as encompassing what is signified by more internally oriented descriptions:

Now, in seeking where to begin applying your effort, you should take Master Ch'eng's "properly ordered and controlled, grave and quiet"[36] saying as the first matter. If you practice it for a long time and are not neglectful, you will personally experience that you have not been deceived by his saying that "then the mind will become single and will not offend by wrong or depraved thoughts."[37] If your exterior is grave and quiet and your mind within is single, then what is referred to as "Focus on one thing; do not depart,"[38] what is described as "The mind is recollected and does not allow a single thing [to have hold on it]"[39] and what is called "always being bright and alert"[40] will all be included in it without having to depend on a separate particular form of practice for each item. (A, 29.13a-b, p. 683, Letter to Kim Ijŏng)

A final matter of importance for T'oegye in making the externalistic approach primary has to do with the delicate balance between neglecting to make enough effort and going too far, artificially forcing oneself or "helping [the corn] grow" by pulling on it, as described by Mencius.[41] Especially with regards to a mind-oriented cultivation, forcing could be disastrous, but some effort is obviously necessary. T'oegye himself ruined his health as a young man by excesses in this regard and never fully recovered it. T'oegye feels that the external approach, which admits of simple and concrete norms, offers an important advantage in this respect:

[Yi Tŏkhong][42] said: The explanations of mindfulness are multiple; how can I avoid being ensnared in the problem of being either negligent or artificially helping [it grow]?

[T'oegye] said: Although there are many explanations, none are more to the point than those of Ch'eng [I], Hsieh [Liang-tso], Yin [T'un], and Chu [Hsi]. But among those who pursue learning, some wish to apply themselves to practicing "always being bright and alert," others to "not allowing a single thing [to have hold on their minds]";[43] thus they set their minds in advance on seeking [a particular condition] or they go about trying to manage [the mind] a particular way. It is very rare that this does not give rise to the problem of "pulling up the shoots [to help them grow]"[44] But if one, not wishing to "help it grow," does not use even a little deliberateness, it is likewise rare that this does not end up with the situation of neglecting the work and not doing the weeding.

For beginning students nothing is better than devoting one's practice to being "properly ordered and controlled, grave and quiet."[45] In this there is no place for searching after [a particular mental condition] or trying to manage [the mind] in a particular way; it is just a matter of establishing oneself in accord with the fixed norm (lit. "square, compass, and ink-line"), being "cautious and watchful in the hidden, secluded places [where you are not observed],"[46] and not allowing the mind-and-heart to get away the least bit.[47] Then, after practicing this for a long time, one naturally becomes "always bright and alert," one naturally does "not allow a single thing [to have hold on the mind]"—and this without the least problem regarding being negligent or helping [it grow]. (*OHN*, 1.14b-15a, B, pp. 795–796)

In conclusion, we might note that while T'oegye thus emphasizes the externalistic approach to mindfulness, he by no means excludes a more internalistic, even meditative, approach. The passages we have seen have dealt mainly with how to begin to approach mindfulness. For beginners the external approach is relatively easier and safer, and insures a proper value orientation. But for the more advanced, the cultivation of a deep inward quiet through meditation also has its place. This will be taken up in the discussion of the next chapter.

Mindfulness as Recollection and Self-Possession

While attending to external propriety may be the most effective or secure method of approaching mindfulness, the essence of mindfulness is rather a matter of a constantly maintained state of mental recollection and self-possession, a state in which one may quietly focus on the matter at hand. This is what such definitions as "always bright and alert," "the mind is recollected and not a single thing is allowed [to have a hold on it]," or "Concentrate on one thing;

do not depart,"[48] are trying to formulate. The last of these, which appears at the center of our diagram, became a favorite description of mindfulness in the Ch'eng-Chu school; although it is a description of a mental state, at the same time it is more like the externalistic approach discussed above in being specific and concrete and immediately practicable.

The ability to concentrate upon the matter at hand is an obvious condition for both the investigation of principle and responsiveness to principle embodied in the affairs with which one must deal. But T'oegye explains that this single-minded focus cannot become an end in itself:

> [In your letter] you say that when you are thinking of one thing and something else presents itself, you try to avoid relaxing [your attention] to consider it. This likewise is a matter of the mind's not having two [simultaneous] functions and is fitting with respect to applying oneself to "concentrating on one thing." Nevertheless, if one explains it one-sidedly like this, I fear it will also prove to have aspects which obstruct principle. . . . If the mind meets a certain matter to which it ought to respond and does not respond, then it is being obstinately insensitive and fails to exercise its proper office. If one deals in this way with the ten thousand changes, how will one be able to attain due measure and degree! . . . If when one meets a number of affairs which come up together he attends at one moment to the left, at the next to the right, once to that, once to this, how could they be properly considered when all mixed up like that. They are to be considered in turn and dealt with in turn; it is just a matter of the mind's self-mastery being present and preeminent as the governing principle *(kang)* of the multitude of affairs. Then the subtle wellsprings of the affair at hand will finally appear, the four limbs will be silently instructed, and none of the intricacies of the matter will be missed. (A, 28.17b-18a, p. 660, Letter to Kim Tonsŏ)

Mindfulness as the ability to quietly focus the mind is different from simply becoming engrossed or absorbed in a situation, a case in which the object possesses the mind and becomes an obstacle to dealing appropriately with the flow of changing events. The mind must focus on a situation in order to think it through and handle it correctly, but the power of concentration must be rooted not in the attraction of the object, but in the mind's self-possession, which frees it from the hold of any object and hence from the power of any object to inappropriately distract it. T'oegye praises a description of "concentrating on one thing" sent him by Yi I (Yulgok) for bringing out these nuances:

Your discussion of the meaning of "concentrating on one thing without departing" and "dealing responsively with the ten thousand changes" is very good. Your quoting Master Chu's "Following the matter [at hand] one responds as appropriate; the mind fundamentally is not predisposed to have any particular thing [as its object]," and Mister Fang's "The midst [of the mind] is empty, but there is a master there," makes it even more precise.[49] (A, 14,24b, p. 372, Letter to Yi Sukhŏn)

Ultimately it is this empty self-mastery of the mind which makes possible the quiet concentration on the matter at hand. "Empty" in this context means not only the absence of any particular object, but more fundamentally, the absence of factors which predispose one to particular objects, that is, the absence of self-centered desires for personal gain, reputation, and the like which give things a hold over the mind. In this respect, mindfulness goes beyond mere mental self-discipline, for the perfection of this kind of self-mastery demands a high level of moral cultivation.

Mindfulness as Reverence

Chu Hsi's *Admonition for Mindfulness Studio* says, "Recollect your mind and make it abide, as if you were present before the Lord on High . . . When you go abroad, behave to everyone as if you were meeting an important guest; preside over affairs as if presiding at a sacrifice." The term *kyŏng (ching),* which we have been translating as "mindfulness," more traditionally meant rather "reverence." While the translation of *kyŏng/ching* as "mindfulness" brings out the technical Neo-Confucian understanding of it as a method of constant mental self-possession and single-mindedness, these passages in the *Admonition* are a reminder that the traditional sense of the term also remains. In fact, not only does reverence remain as an aspect of mindfulness; one might well say that it is the inner soul or animating force which inspires the methodological practice of mindfulness. If "mindfulness" bespeaks the method, "reverence" bespeaks the fundamental attitude, the motivation which is the deeper meaning of the method.

Neo-Confucians easily alternated the language of principle and ancient concepts of divine governance to emphasize the ultimate seriousness of cultivating the mind-and-heart and attending with mindful reverence to daily affairs. T'oegye exhorts King Sŏnjo:

> Thus the *Book of Odes* speaks of reverence for the Tao of Heaven, saying: "Reverence it, reverence it! Heaven is lustrous, its Mandate is not easy! Do not say it is lofty and high above; ascending and descending, it watches daily over your affairs."[50] For with regard to the issuing forth of the principle of Heaven, there is nothing in which it is not present and no time that it is not so. If in one's daily conduct there is a slight deviance from the principle of Heaven and one slips into following [selfish] human desire, this is not how one reverences Heaven. . . . The oversight of Heaven is bright and perceptive; how can it but be feared! Therefore the *Odes* again says: "Fear the majesty of Heaven; at all times maintain [your awe]."[51] . . . This is the nature of the principle of reverencing and fearing Heaven. Likewise Mencius says: "Preserving one's mind and nurturing one's nature is the way to serve Heaven."[52] The Tao of serving Heaven is just a matter of preserving and nurturing the mind and the nature and that is all. (*OHN*, 3.23a-b, B, p. 830)

The ancient *Book of Odes* frequently referred to a personal, transcendent Being who watches over and governs the affairs of men. By the time of Confucius, however, this belief was already evolving into less personalistic concepts such as Heaven or the Tao. The object of religious reverence and awe was not abandoned and lost in this process, but rather rendered immanent as a governing or directive agency within the universe itself. The Neo-Confucian formulation of the philosophy of principle or the Supreme Ultimate was the heir of this process. Principle is immanent within the things of the world, the affairs of human society, and in man's own nature, but it does not thereby become mundane; rather it indicates that within the mundane which itself demands our ultimate seriousness and reverence.

The ordinariness of daily life, however, easily dulls the awareness of the ultimacy incorporated therein. As a corrective, Neo-Confucians at times self-consciously used the archaic, more overtly religious language of the *Book of Odes* to renew the proper sense of that in which they were engaged. One of T'oegye's favorite passages in the *Classic of the Mind-and-Heart* illustrates this clearly:

> The *Book of Odes* says: "The Lord on High watches over you; do not be of two minds." And again it says: "Do not be of two minds, do not be negligent; the Lord on High watches over you."[53]

This is followed with the comment:

> In my humble opinion, what is meant by this ode is such that, although its immediate reference is to attacking [the evil king] Chou, nevertheless when one who pursues learning (chants these verses), in the course of daily life there is a shivering feeling, as if the Lord on High were actually watching over him; then how can this but be of great help in his keeping out depravity and fostering sincerity. Or again, there are those who see what is right but are not necessarily courageous in doing it, or because of considerations of benefit and harm, gain and loss, divide their minds. These likewise should learn to taste these words in order to become more determined.[54]

These remarks distil the essence of the sense of reverence and seriousness, the "fear of the Lord" which is the inner spirit of mindfulness. The "as if" is no hindrance: the "shivering feeling" of reverent awe is as appropriate to a life lived in the immanent presence of the Supreme Ultimate or principle as it is to being in the presence of the Lord on High. Thus for a man like T'oegye this passage hits just the right note: "I have a deep love for its words; every time I recite and savor them I am moved more than I can say."[55]

Chapter 10: DIAGRAM OF THE ADMONITION ON "RISING EARLY AND RETIRING LATE"

The Admonition on "Rising Early and Retiring Late"[1] *depicts the practice of mindfulness in the context of the fluctuating rhythm of the daily routine. Because of this temporal framework, T'oegye chose it as an ideal complement to the more topical treatment of mindfulness presented in chapter 9. It is also ideal as the conclusion of a work structured to present the inner articulation of the thought of the Ch'eng-Chu school: the* Ten Diagrams *began with the metaphysical framework, continued with discussions of learning, the constitution and cultivation of the mind-and-heart, and now culminates with a description of daily life, the ultimate concern to which all this is directed.*

In earlier chapters we have considered the role of the investigation of principle and maintaining constant mindfulness in the process of self-cultivation. This chapter, by describing a well-lived day, gives us a concrete picture of the life-style that is the ideal embodiment of this kind of self-cultivation. Accounts of T'oegye's own life when he finally managed to escape from holding office bear a close resemblance to what is presented here, and in 1560 he wrote: "The Admonition on 'Rising Early and Retiring Late' *fully expresses the way of pursuing learning. Although I have not been able personally to carry it out [fully], it is what I wish to practice."*[2]

10 Diagram of the Admonition on "Rising Early and Retiring Late"

When the cock crows and you awake,
thoughts gradually increase their pace;
at this time how can one but compose
himself and bring order to them.
Sometimes reflect on your past faults;
at others follow out what has been
newly apprehended.
With proper order and sequence,
lucidly ponder this matter in silence,

The foundation being thus established,
as day breaks, rise, brush your teeth,
comb your hair, and don your robes and cap.
Then sitting erect, compose your body
and recollect your mind, making it
as luminous as the rising sun.
Become solemn and silent, ordered and
even, empty and lucid, still and undivided.

AWAKE EARLY

RISE AT DAWN

Then open your books and enter the
presence of the sages and wise men;

Nurture [your mind] in the
restorative atmosphere of
night; after Steadfastness
there is a return to Origination

When some matter arises, respond
to it; then you may experience

Confucius is seated, Yen Hui
and Tseng Tzu attend before
and behind.
Personally and reverently attend
to the words of the sage Master,
Carefully going over and
reconsidering the questions and
discussions of the disciples,
settle them [in your own mind].

READ BOOKS

Mindfulness

RESPOND TO AFFAIRS

[What you have been learning]
in actual practice. The clear
Mandate will shine forth; keep
your attention constantly upon it.
When the matter has been responded
to and is finished, then be as you
were before, with your mind clear
and calm. Recollect your spirit
and dispel distracting thoughts.

Be mindful of the
matter at hand,
Industrious day
and night.

INDUSTRIOUS DURING DAY

Over the cyclic alteration of activity
and quiet, the mind alone presides;
It should be possessed in quiet and
discerning in activity.
Do not allow it to become divided
into two or three.
In the time left over from reading,
from time to time take a swim
to relax your mind and to refresh
and nourish your feelings and nature.

COMBINING NIGHT AND DAY

ALERT AT NIGHT

As the sun sets one tends to slacken,
and a dull spirit easily comes upon one.
Purify, refresh, order and settle yourself,
reinvigorating your mind.
When the night is late, go to bed, [lying]
with your hands at your sides and
your feet together.
Do not let your mind wander in thought,
but make it return to abide [in repose].

Text of the Admonition

When the cock crows and you awake, thoughts gradually increase their pace; at this time how can one but compose himself and bring order to them. Sometimes reflect on your past faults; at others follow out what has been newly apprehended. With proper order and sequence, lucidly ponder this matter in silence.

The foundation being thus established, as day breaks, rise, brush your teeth, comb your hair, and don your robes and cap. Then, sitting erect, compose your body and recollect your mind, making it as luminous as the rising sun; become solemn and silent, ordered and even, empty and lucid, still and undivided.

Then open your books and enter the presence of the sages and wise men; Confucius is seated, Yen Hui and Tseng Tzu[3] attend before and behind. Personally and reverently attend to the words of the sage Master; carefully going over and reconsidering the questions and discussions of the disciples, settle them [in your own mind].

When some matter arises, respond to it; then you may experience [what you have been learning] in actual practice. The clear Mandate will shine forth; keep your attention constantly upon it. When the matter has been responded to and is finished, be as you were before, with your mind clear and calm. Recollect your spirit and dispel distracting thoughts.

Over the cyclic alternation of activity and quiet, the mind alone presides; it should be possessed in quiet and discerning in activity. Do not allow it to become divided into two or three. In the time left over from reading, from time to time take a swim to relax your mind and refresh and nourish your feelings and nature.

As the sun sets one tends to slacken and a dull spirit easily comes upon one; purify, refresh, order, and settle yourself, reinvigorating your mind. When the night is far gone, go to bed, lying with your hands at your sides and your feet together; do not let your mind wander in thought, but make it return to abide [in repose]. Nurture it in the restorative atmosphere of the night;[4] after Steadfastness there is a return to Origination.[5]

Be mindful of the matter at hand, industrious day and night.

T'oegye's Comments

The above *Admonition* was composed by Ch'en Mao-ch'ing (Po)[6] of Nan-t'ang as a self-reminder. When Wang Lu-chai [Po][7] of Chin-hwa was master of the Shang-ts'ai Academy in T'ai-chou, he emphasized this [admonition] as the basis for his instruction, and had all of the students recite it, become thoroughly versed in it, and follow it in practice.

I have ventured to imitate Wang's diagram of the *Admonition for Mindfulness Studio* and made this diagram to correspond with that one. The *Admonition for Mindfulness Studio* presented the various topics to which one applies himself [in the practice of mindfulness], and so the diagram of it is arranged topically. This admonition presents the application [of mindfulness] according to the different periods of the day, so its diagram is arranged according to temporal divisions.

Indeed, the uninterrupted flow of the Tao throughout the affairs of daily life is such that there is nowhere one can go that it is not present; thus there is not a single foot of ground in which principle is absent. What place is there that one may cease his diligence? And [the Tao] does not pause for the least instant; thus there is not a moment's time in which principle is absent. What time is there that one must not apply himself? Therefore Tzu Ssu has said: "As for the Tao, one may not depart from it for the least moment; if one could depart from it, it would not be the Tao. Thus the superior man is careful and cautious even when he is not seen, fearful and anxious even when he is not heard."[8] And again: "Nothing is more visible than what is concealed, nothing more manifest than what is subtle; therefore the superior man is cautious when he is alone."[9]

This is how, in harmony with the alternation of quiet and activity and in accord with the time and the place, one carries to the utmost the complementary practices of preserving and nurturing [one's innate, good dispositions in quiescence] and exercising reflection and discernment [in activity]. When one is finally able to conduct himself in this manner, there will be no topic which is neglected, and so there will not be "a hair's breadth disparity"; there will be no time of day which is not attended to, so one will not "falter for a single moment."[10] One must advance in both respects in unison; in this lies the essence of becoming a sage.

[T'oegye's note:]
The above five diagrams are based on considerations of the mind and the nature; their essential theme is the exercise of diligence in cultivating oneself in the course of daily life, and esteem for the practice of mindfulness and reverent fear.

Commentary

This chapter presents mindfulness as practiced in the course of a daily routine characterized by an alternating rhythm of quietness and activity. Quietness and activity represent not only the ebb and flow of events, but, as we have seen, fundamental conditions of the mind, each of which must have its appropriate cultivation through mindfulness. Our comments, then, will first address various aspects of self-cultivation through mindfulness as it applies to these two conditions, a matter which was a constant source of questions for young Neo-Confucians as they embarked upon serious practice.

The General Context: the Moral Life as Response

If, as is common in the West, the moral life is conceived of primarily as a question of deciding between and doing either good or evil, attention is naturally directed toward the exercise of judgment and will, the decisive and directive functions of the moral subject. In the Confucian tradition, however, the moral question is primarily framed as one of appropriately responding to a situation; this leads to a focus on what distorts or hinders the appropriate response, and results in a mode of self-cultivation designed to minimize or remove the distorting factor. In this context self, or self-centeredness, emerges as the principal problem. The philosophy of principle set up a framework for self-cultivation which de jure solved this problem in terms of the transcendent unity of principle, the one, all-embracing normative pattern which transcends the distinction of self and other. T'oegye says:

Although there are ten thousand differentiations among things, principle is one. Because principle is one, the nature has no distinction between inner and outer. The means by which the mind-and-heart of the superior man is able to be vast and empty in exercising all-embracing impartiality is that he is able to make his nature integral and so be without the distinction of inner and outer [i.e., self and nonself]. The means by which he is able to respond appropriately to something that presents itself is that he follows the oneness of principle with no distinction between this or that. If one only understands that things are external and does not understand that principle has no distinction between this or that, this is to distinguish principle and things as if they were two; this is certainly impermissible. Or if one only understands that things are not external but does not recognize principle as the standard, this means that there will be no mastery within and things will finally seize control; this likewise is impermissible. The superior man understands that there is no distinction between inner and outer in the nature, and in his response to things he uniformly follows principle. Therefore although he continually deals with external things, such things can cause no hindrance to the self; [within] he is limpid with nothing [having a hold on him] and so his nature is settled. (A, 13.16a-b, p. 353)

That is, dealing with affairs is problematic only insofar as self-centered desires give things a hold over the mind, which causes disturbance, confusion, and inappropriate responses. Accordingly the ideal condition of the mind is presented in terms appropriate to its perfect responsiveness:

[Yi] Tŏkhong asked: As for not a single thing being permitted [to have a hold] within the mind-and-heart, does that mean that even such a thing as a norm of what is appropriate likewise should not be permitted?

[T'oegye] said: No, that's not it. The integral substance of the mind is perfectly empty and perfectly still, like a clear mirror that reflects things. When something presents itself one responds to it but it does not clog up [the mind]; when it goes, one is as previously, empty and clear. If [the mind] becomes fixated with something it is like a mirror soiled with mud; it is entirely unable to attain its empty, clear, quiet, undivided condition. (*OHN* 1.14a, B, p. 795)

Buddhists were fond of the mirror image as a description of a selfless consciousness untouched by the phenomena reflected in it, but here the point of the image is totally Confucian: quiet, emptiness of self or any fixed object, and clarity are not ends in themselves, but mental qualities that make one perfectly responsive to the ever-changing situations encountered by one involved in the affairs of the world. Mindfulness is the practice by which such qualities are cultivated.

Making Quiet the Primary Thing

Looking at the mind as a basis of response easily leads to the view of the mind as essentially empty and quiet when not responding, as we have seen above. A distinctive Neo-Confucian development was the systematic expression of this view in terms of two interrelated states or conditions of the mind: quiescence (substance) and activity (function).

As the basis of response, the quiet state has a certain analytic priority. Chou Tun-i emphasized quietness as primary, and Ch'eng Hao instructed his students in a meditation method known as "quiet-sitting" (*ching-tso, chŏngjwa.*) Ch'eng I admired the spirit of seriousness and discipine in this practice, but also was concerned lest this quietness become a countervalue to activity and take on a Buddhist rather than a Confucian cast; thus he introduced the doctrine of mindfulness.

As applied to the quiet state, what is entailed in the practice of mindfulness may be virtually identical with quiet-sitting; the important difference is that mindfulness was explicitly formulated as a practice that encompasses both quiet and activity and gives priority and preference to neither. One is quiet when it is time for quiet, active when it is time to be active, and that is all. It was Chu Hsi, who had himself been trained in the quiet-sitting tradition by his teacher Li' T'ung, who most clearly formulated the mindfulness doctrine in such a way as to balance one-sidedness in either direction.

"Balance" can also mean tension, however, and there was clearly scope within the mindfulness doctrine for widely differing life-styles vis-à-vis the place of activity and quiet. T'oegye approached the question of quiet and inwardness with caution due to its proximity to Buddhism; we have seen his emphasis on external propriety as a fundamental and reliable approach to cultivating mindfulness. But in his view quietness occupies a fundamental and important place; mindfulness is a doctrine to ensure balance, but not to undermine that place:

The purport of making quiet the primary thing has been spoken of by Confucius, Mencius, Chou [Tun-i], and the Ch'engs; in the school of Kuei-shan [Yang Shih] what was passed on as the essential key until it reached Hui-am [Chu Hsi] likewise consisted in this. How much more is it so since it is the medicine which fits your particular problem! But if one makes a single slip in this matter he will fall into Zen. Therefore Master Ch'eng [I] and Master Chu also have a thesis about employing mindfulness rather than quietness. This was because they feared people would mistakenly slip into [Zen] and so they put forth this explanation to save them; it was not that they regarded making quiet the primary thing as impermissible. Nevertheless one likewise should not get fed up with the complexity of broad study and restraining oneself with propriety, and exclusively devote oneself to concentrating on quietness. (A, 28.29b-30a, p. 666, Letter to Kim Ijŏng)

Mindfulness, then, is a broad-gauge doctrine that ensures balance; it encompasses and goes beyond quiet-sitting, but does not supplant that practice. T'oegye had the highest respect for Li T'ung and his teaching regarding self-cultivation, and he accepted the deliberate, disciplined approach to cultivating quietness entailed in quiet-sitting:

[Kim Sŏngil] asked about Master Yen-p'ing [Li T'ung]'s theory of quiet-sitting.

Master [T'oegye] said: Only after [practicing] quiet-sitting can one's mind and body become recollected and moral principles finally all come together and be anchored. If one's form and bones are heedlessly relaxed and without restraint, then the body and mind are darkened and disordered and moral principle no longer has a place to which to gather and be anchored. Therefore Kao-t'ing [Chu Hsi] quiet-sat facing Master Yen-p'ing for an entire day, and after he had parted from him likewise did so on his own.

[Further] question: How about if one has the problem of feeling constrained in quiet-sitting?

Master [T'oegye] said: If this body made of flesh and blood has been entirely without restraint from its youth, and then in a single morning one suddenly wants to quiet-sit and be recollected, how can there but be the problem of feeling constrained? It is necessary to steadfastly endure a very painful period during which there is no feeling of lively animation; then after a long period of years of practice one finally will no longer have the problem of feeling constrained. If one dislikes constraint and expects to do this with natural spontaneity, this is what pertains to the state of sages and wise men whose entire body follows what is ordained with reverence and serenity; it is not something that is possible for a beginning student. In general the problem of feeling constrained is in fact due to one's continually wanting to steal some relaxation while one's practice of maintaining mindfulness is not yet perfect. If the mind is bright and alert and not slack and unrestrained, then the entire body naturally becomes recollected and composed and follows what is ordained. (*OHN* 1.16b-17a, B, pp. 796–797)

Quiet, objectless consciousness is a unitive, integrating experience that takes on different meaning and different experiential significance in different philosophic or religious frameworks. In the above passage, T'oegye's phrase, "moral principles all come together and are anchored," indicates its meaning in the Neo-Confucian context. In activity the mind pursues and concentrates on this or that matter, or principle in this or that manifestation; in quietness, there is a coalescing and unification that transcends what may be spoken or expressed, but is nonetheless intimately related to the particularity of what is experienced and understood in the active state. The relationship of activity and quiescence thus understood is an experiential reiteration of the philosophical dictum, "principle is one but manifested diversely." The gathering together of principle reflects the transcendent unity and nonspecificity of the Supreme Ultimate, the sum of all principle which is also the substance of the mind. "Nurturing the nature in quietness" is an experience of this all-embracing unity; but the Supreme Ultimate as real and concrete value is nothing apart from its diversified manifestation in the beings and affairs of the real world, and this likewise must be the final reference point and value of quietness.

Spontaneity and Naturalness

Neo-Confucians accepted the tradition that commonly described the sage as spontaneously perfect: his response to every situation would be invariably correct with no need for deliberation or thought. The key to this perfection, it was agreed, was the fact that in the sage there is no self-will. Activity is physically the activity of the self or person, but there is no self-centeredness disjoining the person from the Tao or principle, and so actions are spontaneously in accord with the norm.

With such assumptions regarding the nature of the ideal condition, the temptation was to construe spontaneity not only as an attribute of the perfect state, but as a means to its attainment. The mind in quiescence is in perfect unity with principle, its substance; if in moving into activity one could avoid deliberation, a function of the self, would not activity of itself become perfect? The doctrine of mindfulness counters this Taoistic approach; it makes unremitting self-possession and attentiveness, not spontaneity, the key to self-cultivation. T'oegye says:

In general, the way one should pursue learning does not take into account the presence or absence of affairs [to be dealt with] or the presence or absence of intention; one should only regard mindfulness as the primary thing and then neither activity nor quiescence will miss the norm. Before thoughts have arisen the substance of the mind will be empty and clear and its fundament deep and pure; after thoughts have arisen moral principle will be clearly manifest and [selfish] desire will recede and be cut off. The problem of a confused and disordered [state of mind] will gradually diminish in proportion as one accumulates [practice] and comes closer to becoming fully accomplished. This is the essential method. But now if one does not concern himself with this and instead regards the spontaneous arising of thoughts as one deals with affairs and interacts with others as what is permissible, then he will want to be absolutely without thought when there is no affair to be dealt with. If one regards having [deliberate] intentions and thoughts as a hindrance to the mind, this means one would have to be like a sage who has no [deliberate] intentions or thoughts; then there would be no hindrance to the mind. Wanting to cut off thoughts is close to [Taoist] sitting in forgetfulness; being without [deliberate] intention or thought, furthermore, is not something that one who is less than a great wise man can approach. I fear this is all wrong. What's more, as for what has been said about there being a self-centered intent as soon as there is [deliberate] thought, that is certainly true if one is speaking with regard to someone whose original nature has been ensnared and submerged. But if one considers it in terms of moral principle, how can the arising of self-centered intentions be considered the fault of [deliberate] thought? Mencius says, "The office of the mind is to think. If one thinks one apprehends [what is right]; if one does not exercise thought, he does not attain it."[11] . . . This means that the arising of self-centered intentions in ordinary people is in fact due to their not exercising thought. (A, 28.17a-b, p. 660, Letter to Kim Tonsŏ)

According to the Ch'eng-Chu school the no-thought/spontaneous-response paradigm of cultivation fails to take into account the ordinary person's imperfect psychophysical endowment, the "physical nature." The physical nature has no role in the quiescent state, but exercises a potentially disruptive function as soon as there is activity. Its imperfection is manifested both as self-centered inclinations and lack of clear knowledge; these can be remedied only by long and strenuous application to the discipline of mindfulness and the investigation of principle. Thus constant self-possession and alertness is paired with study and reflection in this chapter's presentation of an ideal daily routine.

Because of the objectively rooted imperfection of the physical nature, then, reflection, deliberation, and self-possession are required. Pure spontaneity does not mean pure perfection. But on the other hand, principle or the Tao is not just an abstract norm, but a reality operative within us and in the world around us. Self-cultivation is in one respect a process of overcoming oneself, but it is also and more ultimately a matter of becoming truly natural:

The substance of the Tao flowingly operates in the course of one's daily dealing with affairs and interacting with others without a moment's cessation or pause; therefore "[the mind] must be occupied and one cannot be heedless."[12] It does not permit the least bit of manipulation; therefore "one must not look for results or help it grow."[13] Only then will the mind-and-heart be one with principle and the [function of the] substance of the Tao be faultless and without obstruction. (A, 25.37a, p. 609, Letter to Chŏng Chajung)

This perspective balances the critique of spontaneity. Diligent self-restraint and reflection are necessary, but on a deeper level the mind-and-heart is naturally quiet and properly responsive. A gentle, quiet, and protracted corrective tendency will allow these qualities to emerge; a deliberate, aggressive attempt to subdue the mind-and-heart will only cause problems. In the following passage, T'oegye reviews and answers the question of a student having difficulty finding the proper balance:

> [Your letter says]: "Formerly in teaching how to practice maintaining mindfulness you [i.e., T'oegye] said if there is an intention to seize and hold [the mind] it will become burdened and disturbed. As I think it over again nowadays, in times of quietness sometimes it is possible for [the mind] to be possessed of itself with no need for me to try to seize and hold it. But when it comes to activity, if I do not make efforts to seize and hold it, it wanders far afield and is not settled and fixed. How is this? In general, my old habits have not yet been gotten rid of, so it is difficult for the new efforts to take hold. If I strain my mind and employ effort, it is close to being doable, but when external things approach I always experience the problem of hunting after the happiness of my mind-and-heart, which turns me about and soaks in, until finally I do not myself recognize it as wrong. If one wishes to scrape away the old habits to strengthen the new work, what way is there to make this possible?"
>
> How can a beginning student be able to have the strength to deal with the active aspect without an intent to seize and hold [the mind]? But it is absolutely impermissible to be excessively intent and be too urgent in holding it; one should just apply oneself to a timely practice which falls between not exercising a deliberate intent and not not exercising a deliberate intent. When one has practiced this for a long time and is thoroughly versed in it he will gradually see that activity and quiet become as one. My meaning is that truly one cannot expect rapid results which are arrived at overnight. How much more so in a case like yours where one is entangled in old habits; how can it but be extremely fearful! Nevertheless, this likewise is just a matter of earnestly fixing one's intention, diligently practicing, concentrating on mindfulness, clarifying principle, and repressing and reforming [old habits]. (A, 31.1a-b, p. 720, Letter to U Kyŏngsŏn)

The Ch'eng-Chu school of thought constantly emphasized the need for earnest and diligent practice over a long period of time. Taken alone, such exhortations seem to present self-cultivation as an extremely arduous process of continual and strenous exertion. Concrete advice such as the above, however, puts this in a somewhat different light. The length of time reflects not so much the difficulty as the quiet, patient, almost indeliberate nature of "earnest and diligent practice." One does not storm the gates of heaven; natural processes are constant but gradual in effecting their results. The assurance that the desired goal is in line with the innermost tendencies of nature is the Neo-Confucian's surety that over a sufficient period of time this gentle but continuous effort will bear fruit.

An Alternative Lifestyle

The *Admonition on "Rising Early and Retiring Late"* depicts a daily routine of quiet-sitting, reflection, and scholarly pursuits, interrupted only occasionally by the need to attend to some other affair. It is not the life of a busy government official, but of a scholar living in relative retirement from the affairs of the world—the life T'oegye longed for and finally achieved in the last decades of his life. The routine described here is the natural expression of the type of self-cultivation we have been considering. In theory it might be possible to pursue the investigation of principle and maintain constant mindfulness in virtually any kind of life situation, but in fact this type of self-cultivation could hardly be pursued by a busy official unless he were already deeply grounded in it by prior training in a more secluded and quiet environment.

Traditionally there was but one ideal Confucian lifestyle: that of an official career in government. Self-cultivation had been regarded as the preparation for that career. But, as we have seen, the Neo-Confucian movement deepened the inner dimensions of self-cultivation, arriving at a full cultivation of the mind-and-heart that could rival the profundity of Buddhist asceticism. And like its Buddhist rival, this new Confucian self-cultivation could constitute a total way of life. The new style of life related ambivalently to office holding: like traditional self-cultivation, it could be thought of as an ideal preparation for an official career, but it could also be considered as an attractive and worthy alternative to such a career. In either case, new and distinctive tensions were involved.

T'oegye's young friend and correspondent in the Four-Seven Debate, Ki Taesŭng, passed the civil service examinations and was on the threshold of a promising career; but instead he wished to pursue a life of quiet retirement, study, and self-cultivation and wrote to T'oegye for advice. T'oegye observed that he had already gone too far: had he made this choice earlier in his career it would have worked out, but now there is no chance the government would permit him to live in retirement. Then he warned:

> But if you once make a slip with regard to what I have said, you will fall into being content with common practice and fitting in with convention, following the ignoble way of the world in every respect. One must without fail constantly maintain a firm intention that cannot be wrested away, a spirit that cannot be bent, a discernment that cannot be clouded, and a strength of learning that is tempered and hardened as days and months pass; only then will you perhaps be able to stand firm and not be taken up and overturned by worldly fame, profit, and majesty. If not, what you now have a taste for will become insipid and you will not be able to attain it; it will "get harder as you bore into it"[14] and you will not be able to enter in. If you allow a slight gap you will not be able to avoid your mind becoming lazy, your intention becoming lax, and your thoughts being turned about. The worldly notion of what constitutes profit and loss, disaster or blessing, consequently acts as a pressure and threat that gradually dissolves and melts [one's original resolve]; thus there are few who do not change from the ends they initially served and come to regard accommodation with the world as acceptable and turning their backs on the Tao for the pursuit of gain as the most profitable course. This is the most fearful thing of all. (A, 16.6a-b, p. 404)

The value conflict spoken of here is to a certain extent a common theme in Confucian writings of whatever period, and the negative aspect has undoubtedly been heightened by T'oegye's personal experience. But there is a difference in T'oegye's frame of reference: he speaks not just of negative forces, but of a total environment characterized by such forces. It is "the world" in the sense of the term as used by ascetics of virtually all religious traditions in speaking of the common way of life in contrast to their own special and pure way of life and spiritual cultivation. It is a viewpoint that arises from different and contrasting types of life that may be entered upon or left; to be "in the world," is in this perspective a choice, since an alternative is possible.

Life in retirement was not totally cut off from "the world," however; a deliberate rejection of society could be viewed by Confucians only as an aberration. Rather a life of scholarly retirement and self-cultivation was viewed as the ideal preparation for life in the world as well as an alternative to such a life. The point was not to produce delicate spiritual flowers that could survive only in a pure environment:

> [Yi] Tŏkhong asked: Confucius said: "Do not have friends who are not as good as yourself."[15] Does that mean that if someone is not better than oneself one should have absolutely nothing to do with him?
>
> [T'oegye] said: Ordinary people's feelings are that they like having as friends those who are not better than themselves and dislike having friends who are better. Therefore the Sage spoke in this way; he did not mean one should have absolutely nothing to do with them. If one wishes wholly to select only the good as friends, this likewise is one-sided."
>
> [Tŏkhong] said: But as for having to do with evil men, how about being swept away and falling to their level?
>
> [T'oegye] said: If good, one emulates it; if bad, one emends it. That way everyone is my teacher. If you are swept away and fall to their level, for what have you been pursuing learning? (*OHN*, 3.3a-b, B, p. 820)

From Confucius onwards the orthodox Confucian view was that the foundation for office holding must be sound character formation. Neo-Confucian self-cultivation practices were ideally suited to that end. But the emergence of this type of self-cultivation aggravated a long-standing Confucian tension regarding the chief institutionalized means of recruitment to office, the civil service examination system. The basic problem was that moral cultivation could not be measured by objective examination; such examinations could assess only such matters as literary skill, familiarity (memorization) with the classics and their orthodox interpretation, etc. Not only could "real learning" not be tested, but preparation for such examinations involved a time commitment, methodology, and cast of mind that were often perceived as antithetical to the demands of self-cultivation or "real learning" in Neo-Confucian terms. One section of T'oegye's recorded conversations (*Ŏnhaengnok*) is entitled, "On the Corruption of the Examinations." What is meant is not that the examination system was itself corrupt, but that its influence tended to corrupt those who submitted themselves to the process. The following illustrates T'oegye's sentiments:

I [Chŏng Sasŏng] was sitting in attendance in the study. The Teacher [T'oegye] said to those assembled there: "The meaning of the Confucian school is of itself something apart. Proficiency in literary skills is not Confucian; passing the civil service examinations is not Confucian." Then he sighed and said: "In the world a great number of men of excellent ability become completely absorbed in conventional studies. Who is there that is able to succeed in liberating himself from the mortar-bowl of the examinations!" (*OHN*, 5.11a, B, p. 855)

If committed Neo-Confucian scholars felt the exam system ground up men of great potential, parents and relatives concerned with the worldly fortunes of their families felt the problem from the opposite direction. They were not pleased to see their promising young men absorbed in a form of learning that had little direct connection with conventional careers and worldly success. Proponents of the new learning of the mind-and-heart such as T'oegye were under pressure to focus on more immediately "relevant" kinds of teaching:

Our Teacher [T'oegye] also said: "Fathers and elder brothers nowadays always regard expounding the *Classic of the Mind-and-Heart* and the *Reflection on Things at Hand* as wrong and criticize their sons and younger brothers [for engaging in such studies]. Scholars likewise are intimidated by public opinion and few expound this learning. In my lecturing on the *Classic of the Mind-and-Heart* I feel a certain uneasiness, but I am unwilling to put aside our kind of learning and lecture on other texts." (*OHN*, 5.18b-19a, B, pp. 858–859)

There was, then, a very imperfect fit between the Neo-Confucian pursuit of learning and self-cultivation as described in the *Ten Diagrams*, and the institutionalized criteria of achievement related to government careers. This warns us that in reflecting upon the "Neo-

Confucian society" of Yi dynasty Korea it is important to distinguish between Neo-Confucianism as an institutionalized ideology and Neo-Confucianism as a way of life. As an ideology it furnished the entire elite class with a shared vocabulary and a common conceptual framework that served to order and legitimate their world. But as a way of life it marked out a distinctive and demanding path of spiritual cultivation that was pursued by a self-conscious minority who were often at odds with the mundane values and systems accepted by their fellows.

Appendix on Terminology

Language is both formed by and informs particular views of the world. Where those views are markedly different, as in the case of traditional East Asia and the western world, it is not surprising that concepts and the terms in which they are embodied pose difficulties for the translator. Just as western missionaries agonized over how to translate "God" into classical Chinese, translators of eastern thought cudgel their minds to discover adequate—or at least not misleading—renditions of basic Chinese terminology. The more fundamental the concept, it seems, the more resistant it is to translation. This appendix will discuss a few important philosophical terms that require special explanation if their English rendition is to be understood. Presented in alphabetical order (Korean pronounciation, Chinese in parenthesis) they are: (1) *ch'e-yong* (*t'i-yung*); (2) *ki* (*ch'i*); (3) *kyŏng* (*ching*); (4) *li*; (5) *sim* (*hsin*); (6) *to* (*tao*).

CH'E-YONG *(T'I-YUNG)*

Ch'e and *yong* in common parlance mean "body" and "use," but in philosophical discourse they take on a technical meaning and are commonly translated as "substance" and "function," respectively. "Substance," however, should not be confused with the meaning the term commonly has in western philosophy. The correlated categories of substance and function are broadly and flexibly applied to analyze situations in which some sort of prior-posterior, fundamental-derivative relationship is present. Feet and walking, or a tree and bearing fruit, are simple examples of substance-function relationships. Here one may easily see the connection between the prephilosophic meanings ("body," "use") and their adaptation as philosophical terms.

The more serious philosophical use of these categories, however, has as its background the tendency to see that which is active, manifest, and phenomenal, as stemming from that which is nonactive, nonmanifest, and nonphenomenal: the Tao is the more ultimate, changeless, and shapeless reality underlying and manifested in the myriad changing forms and activities of the phenomenal world. One of the most important Neo-Confucian uses of the substance-function categories is the description of man's nature as substance and feelings as function. The nature is *li,* the inner pattern or disposition of our being, while the feelings are the manifestation of this inner disposition in activity. Humanity (*jen*), for example, is a component of human nature, and instances of love, affection, and compassion for others are its active manifestation: humanity is substance, love is function.

KYŎNG (CHING)

The basic classical meaning of *kyŏng* was "reverence." It could either apply to inner dispositions or describe external appearances, as in a "reverent demeanor," etc. As Neo-Confucians focused their attention in a new way on the cultivation of the inner life of the mind-and-heart, *kyŏng* was transformed into a technical term to designate the essential practice of this kind of cultivation. Thus, although it could be cultivated through attention to proper demeanor, posture, dress and the like, *kyŏng* in Neo-Confucian discourse essentially refers to a particular inner state of mind.

As a form of mental or spiritual discipline, the Neo-Confucian *kyŏng* might still be best understood as systemizing the inward elements involved in reverence. In the presence of an object of great reverence, one is serious and self-possessed, attentive at once to the object and to one's personal deportment. The Neo-Confucian *kyŏng* is essentially a self-possessed, recollected state of mind. It is the opposite of being ruled by desires, which give external objects mastery over one's person; hence it is serene self-possession. It is likewise the opposite of a distracted and wandering frame of mind; hence it is manifested in a focused attention when there is an object to be attended to, and a quiet, unified mind when no such activity is called for. This latter condition is closely related to a Neo-Confucian meditative discipline called "quiet-sitting." Further, it is serious and composed; *kyŏng* is not opposed to laughter and lightheartedness when these are appropriate, but it is contrary to frivolity and heedlessness. Here we return to the original meaning of the term: the animating force of this rigorous mental discipline is a fundamentally reverent disposition that recognizes that everywhere and always we are involved in something ultimate. Big or small, heavy or light, every circumstance is finally a matter of *li*, "principle."

A number of translations have been suggested for this term. A.C. Graham uses "composure," which brings out the inner recollection and self-possession, but somewhat neglects the attentiveness to affairs that is an important aspect of *kyŏng*. "Attentiveness" and "concentration" reflects metal focus but not the inward self-possession. Wing-tsit Chan follws Bruce in prefering "seriousness," and through him "seriousness," or sometimes "reverential seriousness," have become fairly common translations. In common English usage, however, seriousness bespeaks mainly a kind of earnestness. While this is indeed fundamental to *kyŏng*, it does not necessarily reflect the kind of mental recollection and inward self-possession at the core of this discipline. There were many earnest and serious young Neo-Confucians who had great difficulty maintaining the focused and recollected state of mind signified by *kyŏng*.

My own preference as a translation for *kyŏng* is "mindfulness." The term clearly opposes mental dissipation, distraction, or heedlessness. It has the connotations of caution and carefulness that figure prominently in Neo-Confucian discussions of *kyŏng*, and is a natural component of a reverent disposition. Although it is more commonly used with an object (one is mindful of something), it can also describe the poised and collected state of mind when there is no particular object present. The term is also etymologically consistent with the

Neo-Confucian description of *kyŏng* as the condition in which the mind is "full" with its own self-mastery.

In both denotation and connotation, then, "mindfulness" seems a good translation for *kyŏng.* A disadvantage is that "mindfulness" is also used for certain forms of Buddhist meditation; *kyŏng* was not derived from Buddhist practices and no such implication is intended in adopting a similar translation. In my judgment the advantages of the term outweigh this disadvantage.

KI (CH'I)

Ki originally signified steam or vapor, and thence the various vapors or forces of the atmosphere responsible for the weather. Identified as well with the breath of living things, it came also to signify the principle of vitality itself, often associated with either breath or blood, and was extended to include likewise the force manifested in physical strength or strong emotions.

As philosophers came to think of the concrete universe as formed by some kind of process of condensation, *ki* became the term for the basic stuff of the universe, that out of which everything that exists is formed. In its most subtle or rarefied *(yŏng, ling)* condition it possesses "wondrous" or "spiritual" (*sin, shen*) modes of activity, while in its more coarse or turbid condition it has the form and the limitations of physical matter. Thus *ki* encompasses what we would call "spirits," and beings such as man (and to a lesser degree animals and plants) that have "spiritual" capacities, as well as material beings. Although terms such as *yŏng* and *sin* often must be translated as "spirit" or "spiritual," no spirit/matter dichotomy of the western type is implied.

Ki, then, is the stuff out of which beings are formed; it accounts for differentiation and individuation. But the attributes of movement, force, or energy evident in its nonphilosophic usage likewise remain prominent: it is not only the concretizing, but also the energizing element of all beings. All forms of mental and physical activity relate to *ki,* the matter-energy of all things. The conventional translation followed in this book, "material force," is intended to reflect both the concretizing and energizing aspects of *ki.*

LI

Li is unquestionably the most important single term in Neo-Confucian discourse. Its original meaning had to do with order or putting things in order; thence it comes to signify the patterning or structure that underlines and brings about order. In its patterning or structuring aspect *li* is responsible for making things be as they are and act as they do; in this respect Neo-Confucians equate *li* with the inherent nature of each and every being. As the inner nature of each thing, or holistically of the entire universe, *li* is regarded as both formative and normative. These two functions are closely interrelated: that which is at the source of the formation and particular mode of activity of the various beings also stands over them as the norm of what is appropriate to their being and activity. Finally, as an extension of its formative and normative aspects, *li* can also be equated with the ultimate Truth, since the accurate apprehension of anything, from particular items and situations to the whole of existence, is a matter of apprehending *li*.

While *li* is the inherent nature and norm of particular beings, from another perspective it may be regarded as a single underlying pattern that embraces all beings as a harmonious whole and serves as the norm for their appropriate interaction. In this respect *li* is comprehensive and unitary as well as particular and diverse, an idea Neo-Confucians expressed in the formula: "*Li* is one, but manifested diversely." A living human body offers a useful paradigm of this. It ultimately has a single principle or pattern of operation, but this is manifested in the diverse operations of the various parts of the body. In a close-up perspective the finger has one pattern of operation, the heart another: each has its own *li*. But a broader perspective transcends this particularity, for a finger and heart are misunderstood if they are seen as disconnected realities. Ultimately the finger presupposes the heart, the heart presupposes fingers: they are but diverse aspects of the single patterned unity of an organic whole. The universe itself is just such an organic whole, and ultimately there is just one *li* or pattern manifested diversely in the many beings that are its component parts.

With the term *li* as its unifying thread, Neo-Confucian discourse flows effortlessly from metaphysical discussion to considerations of morality and questions of ascetical practice. A variety of translations ("pattern," "structure," "norm," "value," "truth," etc.) would serve to bring out the nuance of *li* appropriate to these different contexts, but such variety would also obscure the continuity that is at the heart of the system. If *li* is to be translated at all, the consistency of a single term is highly desirable.

The most widely used translation of *li* is "principle." No other term comes as close to combining the formative and normative aspects of *li*, for there are principles of structure and function as well as principles of moral conduct. The function of *li* as a metaphysical component of existence and its unitary nature are aspects of *li* that would not be readily associated with "principle" but familiarity with Neo-Confucian thought can easily remedy that.

A more subtle and less easily remedied problem is the fact that *li* and principle belong to quite different epistemological traditions. In particular, *li* has nothing of the notion of abstract universality that is a strong connotation of principle; the universality of *li* is one of constancy and omnipresence, not abstraction. The Neo-Confucian emphasis on the investigation and comprehension of moral principle (*li*) was not, as the translation might suggest, a quest for universally valid propositions that could be prudently *applied* to particular cases; rather, it aimed at developing an educated and profound sensitivity to constant moral values as a basis for recognizing the appropriate course in the complex value configuration of each situation. The epistemology is intuitionist, more geared to the development of a sense of values than the elaboration of a coherent and consistent set of "principles."

Thus it is only with reservation that I have decided to follow the convention and translate *li* as "principle." Along with "principle," the untranslated *li* will also occur frequently as a reminder that the translation is not altogether adequate.

SIM (HSIN)

Sim designates the heart, but in the East Asian tradition the heart is the seat of thought as well as feeling. Thus the single term encompasses what is meant by the English "mind" as well as "heart." In a given context one or the other aspect may take precedence, but in general the Neo-Confucian approach is holistic, little attempt being made to strictly separate intellect and feeling. Study, or "the investigation of principle," for example, certainly aims at developing accurate understanding, but real understanding is assumed to involve an appropriate affective response as well as an intellectual grasp of the matter.

The most adequate translation of *sim,* then, is "mind-and-heart." This, however, is rather cumbersome, and in many passages dealing with matters such as learning and mental self-possession I have simply translated it as "mind." This is alternated with "mind-and-heart," both as context may demand, and also to avoid having the text take on an overly intellectualistic cast.

TO (TAO)

"Tao" is one of the most fundamental and widely used terms in East Asian thought. Literally it means the "way" or "path." One travels a path to get somewhere; to be off the path, not in accord with the Tao, means one does not get where one should. Thus Tao can take on a normative aspect: not just a path, but "the right path" or course one should follow. From being the path traversed, Tao also came to signify the course of things, the "way" things happen, and that which governs the way they happen. The phenomena of nature are generally cyclic and repetitive: the four seasons revolve and living creatures continually repeat the same pattern of birth, growth, propagation, and death. Thus the Tao may be seen not just as the particular way things happen, but as a constant underlying pattern or structure guiding the ever-changing but ever-the-same transformations of the universe, on all its levels. There is only one Tao, a single pattern variously manifested in the interrelated constant phenomena of the natural world and the moral constituents of human nature.

"Tao" and *li* (principle) obviously have much in common, and in many contexts Neo-Confucians can use them interchangeably. It is less philosophic content than tendencies of linguistic usage that differentiates these terms. One may speak of the Tao of a ruler, the Tao of a wife, the Tao of filial piety, etc., but the distinctive strength of the term is its aptness to be used in a nonspecific, comprehensive sense: one speaks of "the Tao." Although *li* can also signify the single all-embracing and normative pattern, it is more apt to be used to discuss specific instances or aspects of that pattern.

The term "Tao" has become familiar to the western intellectual community, and since it carries metaphysical and moral connotations not necessarily associated with "way," its close English equivalent, I have left the term untranslated.

Notes

Translator's Preface

1. The *naejip* or "inner collection" in 49 fascicles was the earliest collection of T'oegye's writings. It was later supplemented by a *pyoljip* (separate collection), *waejip* (outer collection), and *sokjip* (supplementary collection). The *pyoljip* and *waejip* each only one fascicle, are appended to volume 1 of the *Chŏnsŏ*. The more important *sokjip*, in 8 fascicles, is contained in the second volume.

Introduction

1. For a discussion of these early cosmological schools, see Feng Yu-lan, *A History of Chinese Philosophy*, vol. 1, pp. 159–169.

2. This is discussed in chapter 6 below; the title of the chapter, "The mind combines and governs the nature and the feelings, "is itself a quotation from Chang.

3. These are the *Lun-yü chi-chu* (Collected Commentaries on the *Analects*,) the *Meng Tzu chi-chu* (Collected Commentaries on the *Mencius*), the *Ta-hsüeh chang-chü* (Commentary on the *Great Learning*), and the *Chung-yung chang-chü* (Commentary on the *Doctrine of the Mean*).

4. His courtesy name was Yŏngsuk, and his honorific name was Mogŭn. He studied Neo-Confucianism in China from 1348–1351, and returned again in 1354, when he placed first and second in the two final stages of the civil service exam. He enjoyed great favor with Koryŏ's King Kongmin (r.1351–1374) and was responsible for the legal institution of the three-year mourning period in Korea. Yi was famed as the foremost Neo-Confucian scholar of the times and also as an outstanding poet and literary stylist. In the last decades of the dynasty he was the leader of the conservative Koryŏ-loyalist group.

5. His courtesy name was Talga, and his honorific name was P'oŭn. An outstanding scholar and man of letters, he rendered important service on several missions to China during the early years of the new Ming dynasty. His attempts to prevent Yi Sŏnggye's founding of a new dynasty led to his assassination in 1392, but his reputation was utilized by the new dynasty, which made him a symbol of loyalty.

Although there is no record of his scholarship, his reputation continued to grow, and on the basis of his moral character, strong stance against Buddhism, and direct contact with China, he came to be regarded as the true father of Korean Neo-Confucianism and his tablet was placed in Korea's Confucian Shrine.

6. Kwŏn's courtesy name was Kawŏn, and his honorific name was Yangch'on. He was one of Yi Saek's leading disciples. Although he opposed the dynastic change, he eventually accepted office and in the first decades of the new dynasty was regarded as the foremost scholar of the time. His *Iphak tosŏl* (Diagrammatic Explanations for Beginners) is one of the earliest Korean treatises on Neo-Confucian thought.

7. His courtesy name was Chongji, and his honorific name was Sambong. He was a disciple of Yi Saek. Coming from an obscure background, he rose to become the real power behind the throne as the chief merit subject of the new dynasty, until he and his group were suddenly purged as the result of the first succession struggle of the Yi dynasty in 1398. His writings, the *Sim ki i py'ŏn* (Essay on the Mind, Vital Force, and Principle) and the *P'ulssi chappyŏn* (Various Arguments Against the Buddhists), are, along with the *Iphak tosŏl* (see note 7), the sole examples of early Korean Neo-Confucian intellectualism. Both are anti-Buddhist tracts that attack Buddhism on intellectual grounds, the first and most important works of this nature in Korea.

8. For an excellent account of early attempts to use ritual norms and institutions as a means to transform Korean society, see Martina Deuchler, "Neo-Confucianism: The Impulse for Social Action in Early Yi Korea."

9. For a detailed account of the first three purges, see Edward W. Wagner, *The Literati Purges: Political Conflict in Early Yi Korea.*

10. The *Sahŏnbu,* the *Saganwŏn,* and the *Hongmun'gwan,* respectively. Here, as elsewhere, I have followed the translation of government posts and offices established by Wagner, comprehensively listed in *Literati Purges,* Appendix A, pp. 125–133.

11. Village Contracts (*hyangyak, hsiang-yüeh*) are said to have been originated in China by Lu Ta-chün (1031–1082), but it was Chu Hsi who further developed and championed this institution. They were pacts made by local communities and enforced through community-based organizations designed to order conduct in the various aspects of village life, with Confucian morality and values furnishing the essential structure and content.

12. The *Sillok* is the official daily record of the operations of the government.

13. *Sillok,* 1517.8.7, as tr. by Wagner, *Literati Purges,* p. 90.

14. Most of the following account is taken from T'oegye's *Chronological Biography* (*yŏnbo, nien-fu*) found in *T'oegye chŏnso* (hereafter, *TGCS*), B, pp. 553–620.

15. *Yangban,* lit. "the two divisions,"is the term that designates Korea's elite or aristocratic class. The term itself is derived from the two types of government officials, the civil and the military.

16. *TGCS,* A, 10.2b, p. 282, Letter to Cho Kŏnjung.

17. In 1592 and again in 1597 Korea was devastated by large-scale Japanese invasions that were finally beaten off only with the assistance of Ming armies.

18. *Ŏnhaengnok* (hereafter, *OHN*), 6.18a, B, p. 872 (Pak Sun).

19. *OHN*, 6.15a, *TGCS*, B, p. 871 (Chŏng Yuil).

20. This is the reason his disciple Kim Sŏngil offers for T'oegye's precipitous departure (*OHN*, 3.12a, *TGCS*, B, p. 824); although it is not mentioned elsewhere, it is a plausible explanation of an act otherwise quite at odds with T'oegye's character.

21. *OHN*, 1.2a, *TGCS*, B, p. 789.

22. Chen's courtesy name was Ching-yüan and his honorific name was Hsi-shan. He was one of the key figures in the transmission of Chu Hsi's learning. His best known work, the *Ta-hsüeh yen-i* (Extended Meaning of the *Great Learning*, became a constant fixture in the education of rulers in China and Korea. For an excellent discussion of Chen Te-hsiu, the *Extended Meaning,* and the *Classic of the Mind-and-Heart,* see. Wm. Theodore deBary, *Neo-Confucian Orthodoxy and the Learning of the Mind-and-Heart,* pp. 67–126.

23. The *Hsin-ching fu-chu* was published in China in 1492. Within the next 70 years three editions were published in Korea, attesting its popularity on the peninsula. For a study of T'oegye and this work, including its prior and later publication history, see Yun Pyŏngt'ae, "T'oegeywa Simgyŏng puju," (T'oegye and the *Hsin-ching fu-chu,* and "Simpyŏng puju yuhuron ponŭi kanbon" (The Publication of Editions of the *Hsin-ching fu-chu* with T'oegye's Epilogue).

24. For a discussion of this term, see the Appendix on Terminology.

25. *Hsin-ching fu-chu,* 4.28b.

26. The *Hsing-li ta-ch'üan* was the product of a large compilation project carried out under imperial auspices directed by Hu Kuang (1370–1418). First published in 1415, the Ming emperor had it presented to the Korean ruler in 1426.

27. *OHN,* 1.1b, *TGCS,* B, p. 789.

28. *OHN,* 1.5a, *TGCS,* B, p. 791.

29. See his remarks in his preface to his recension of Chu Hsi's letters, the *Chu sŏ chŏryo, TGCS,* A, 423a-b, p. 939.

30. *Ihak t'ongnok,* table of contents (*mongnok*) 3a, *TGCS,* B, p. 250.

31. The "Chŏnsŭmnok nonbyŏn " (Critique of Wang Yang-ming's *Ch'uan-hsi lu*), *TGCS,* A, 41.23b-35b, pp. 922–925, and the "Paeksasigyo chŏnsumnok ch'ojŏn insŏ kihu" (Postscript to Conveyed Copy of Ch'en Po-sha's *Shih-chiao* and Wang Yang-ming's *Ch'uan-hsi lu*), *TGCS,* A, 41.29b-35a, pp. 925–928.

32. Ki's courtesy name was Myŏngŏn and his honorific name was Kobong. He passed the civil service examinations in 1558. One of the best minds and most broadly and deeply learned of his generation, he became a leading exponent of *sarim* concerns at court. He served as Headmaster fo the Confucian Academy and Censor General, but his promising career was cut short by illness and he died just two years after T'oegye.

33. *TGCS,* B, pp. 151–190.

34. See below, chapter 5, T'oegye's Comments.

35. *T'ung shu,* chapter 20.

36. This structure is indicated by T'oegye in annotations at the end of chapter 5 and chapter 10.

37. T'oegye presents this view in his remarks at the end of chapter 4.
38. See his remarks at the end of chapter 4.

Address Presenting the *Ten Diagrams on Sage Learning* to King Sŏnjo

1. *P'anjungch'ubusa,* a Junior First Rank position. The Office of Ministers Without Portfolio was the highest ranking military agency. It was an honorary sinecure position frequently assigned to high-ranking civil officials no longer serving actively in government.

2. *Analects,* 17:17: "Heaven does not speak, but [in accord with it] the four seasons proceed in their course and the hundred living things are produced. Yet Heaven does not speak!" This saying has been an important reference point in the Confucian tradition, for Confucians have generally taken a nonanthropomorphic, naturalistic view of the Ultimate and the mode in which its governance operated. "Heaven" is the most common term for referring to an ultimate seat or source of governing in the universe, while "Tao" is used when this governing is thought of as happening according to an under-lying, directive pattern inherent in all things. Heaven governs not by legislative *fiat,* but by the inherent pattern (Tao) of the universe.

3. The River Diagram was believed to have been carried out of the Yellow River on the back of a "dragon horse," during the reign of the legendary Emperor Fu hsi, while the Lo Writing came from the Lo River on the back of a tortoise in the time of the legendary Emperor Yü. They were supposed to have been transmitted to King Wen, the founder of the Chou dynasty, who elaborated Fu Hsi's eight trigrams into the 64 hexagrams and accompanying texts which are the core of the *Book of Changes.* Subsequently lost, they were "rediscovered" during the Former Han dynasty (206 B.C–25 A.D.), a time when apocrypha and prognostication texts enjoyed a wide currency.

4. These are idealized legendary and semilegendary figures from the earliest period of Chinese history and prehistory; their reigns represented the ideal of wisdom and proper government. For Confucians the most important of these are the Sage Emperors Yao (2357?–2256? B.C.)and Shun (2255?–2206? B.C.), and King Wen (1184?–1135?B.C.) and the Duke of Chou (c. 1110?). The latter two belong to the historical Chou dynasty (1122?–256 B.C.), the early period of which was idealized and taken as a model by Confucians. The account of the reigns of these Sage Emperors and Wise Rulers is to be found in the *Book of Documents,* one of the earliest Confucian Classics (English tr. by James Legge, *The Chinese Classics,* vol. 3).

5. *Kuo Yü* (Narratives of the States), Ch'u, A:6. Commentators do not agree regarding the precise meaning of the various ancient offices referred to here, so the translation is uncertain.

6. This practice, with a similar list of objects, is described in the "Wu-wang chien tsu" chapter of the *Ta Tai li-chi* (Book of Rites of the Elder Tai).

7. The *T'ien-ch'iu chin-chien lu* (Golden Mirror Record of a Thousand Autumns) was presented to the emperor on his birthday in 736 by Chang Chiu-ling (673–740). It was customary on such occasions for officials to present precious gifts such as golden mirrors; Chang instead presented this compilation of historical examples of good and bad government.

8. The *Wu-i t'u*. Sung Ching (662–737) was noted for combining inflexible sternness with remarkable benignity. *Wu-i*, "without idleness," is the title of *Book of Documents*, 5:15, a chapter in which the Duke of Chou lectures the young ruler on this evil. Sung made a diagram of the chapter and presented it to the emperor.

9. Li Te-yü (787–849) served under six emperors of the T'ang dynasty, leading a checkered career which took him from the heights of power to banishment to distant parts of the empire and back again. The *Tan-i liu-chen* (Six Maxims of the Crimson Screen) was addressed to the Emperor Ching-tsung, whose extravagances Li staunchly opposed. The "crimson screen" of the title refers to the screen which stood behind the emperor in his audience chamber.

10. On Chen Te-hsiu, see Introduction, note 22. The *Pin-fung ch'i-yüeh t'u* (Diagram of the Seventh-Month Ode of the Odes of Pin) is based upon *Book of Odes*, #154. The Seventh-Month Ode, so-named for its first line, narrates the various sorts of agricultural labors of the common people throughout the course of the year.

11. The responsibility was not T'oegye's alone; a broad spectrum of some 22 officials held concurrent appointments to the Office of Royal Lectures (*kyŏngyŏn*, lit. "Classic-mat"). They met, ideally, three times daily with the king. The nominal task of these meetings was, as the title suggests, the exegesis and interpretation of classical texts, but these were also applied, sermon style, to the affairs and questions of the day, and the ensuing discussions could range broadly. Thus this was a major forum not only for formal instruction, but the presentation of views on current issues and for remonstrance as well. Cf. Edward Wagner, *The Literati Purges*, p. 16. For a discussion of the origin of this institution and its function in relation to the instruction of rulers, see deBary, *Neo-Confucian Orthodoxy*, pp. 29–30; 35–37.

12. This saying of Chang Tsai is the heart of the Ch'eng-Chu School's psychological theory and is discussed in chapter 6. T'oegye's "two small diagrams" summarize his most original contribution to Neo-Confucian thought and mark the point where Korean Neo-Confucianism begins on the course of its own distinctive and characteristic intellectual development. On Ch'eng Fu-hsin, see below, ch. 2, n. 32.

13. These diagrams are: ch. 3, Elementary Learning; ch. 5, Rules of the White Deer Hollow Academy; ch. 10, Admonition on Rising Early and Retiring Late.

14. This suggestion was promptly acted upon and both the screen and handbook were made. There are a number of references to the *Ten Diagrams* in T'oegye's correspondence with other scholars during the next two years, indicating that the work was almost immediately in circulation in the scholarly community.

15. *Mencius*, 6A:15.

16. *Book of Documents*, 5:4.5. The "Grand Plan" is said to have been given

by Chi Tzu (Kor. "Kija") to King Wu at the beginning of the Chou dynasty. As one of the earliest comprehensive schematizations of the rudiments of an ideal, civilized government, it was an important reference point for later Confucians. But for Koreans this reference had special meaning because Chi Tzu was said to have fled to Korea rather than serve under a new dynasty after having served under its predecessor, the Shang. The legend of his founding a Chinese civilization on the Korean Peninsula attracted the special attention of Yi dynasty Neo-Confucians, who could thus claim to be restoring their country's most ancient and legitimate heritage.

17. The "emptiness" (*hŏ, hsü*) of the mind indicates that it is intrinsically free of ego-centeredness; it is, in its ideal condition, "empty" of any selfish desires or impulses. It is "spiritual" (*yŏng, ling*) in its wondrous ability to encompass and penetrate all things; no dichotomy of spirit/matter in the western sense is implied. For further discussion, see Appendix on Terminology under *ki* (*ch'i*).

18. See Appendix on Terminology.

19. *Analects*, 2:15.

20. *Mencius*, 3A:1.

21. On mindfulness (*kyŏng, ching*), see Appendix on Terminology. T'oegye makes this the central theme of the *Ten Diagrams*. The psychological theory regarding "inner" and "outer" is explained in chapter 6. Chapters 8-10 take up the subject of mindfulness at length.

22. A paraphrase of *Doctrine of the Mean*, ch. 1.

23. A reference to *Mencius* 6A:8, which describes how the calm atmosphere of the early predawn hours works to restore human nature to its originally good condition just as the vital force of nature works in the night to restore damaged vegetation.

24. I am unable to locate these references.

25. *Mencius*, 4B:14.

26. *Mencius*, 4A:27.

27. *Analects*, 6:7. Yen Hui was Confucius' favorite and foremost disciple. He died while still very young, a loss Confucius greatly mourned.

28. This is taken from Chu Hsi's annotation of *Analects*, 15:11.

29. *Analects*, 4:15: when Confucius said that there is a single thread running through all his teachings Tseng Tzu understood what he meant and interpreted this key remark for the other disciples.

30. References to *Doctrine of the Mean*, ch. 1.

31. This is a conventional expression of humility frequently used when presenting something. The reference is to a well-known tale: although the peasants mistake something very common as a gift fit for a king, their utter sincerity in offering the gift excuses the ignorance and, indeed, is the true value of the gift.

1. Diagram of the Supreme Ultimate

1. The *Diagram of the Supreme Ultimate* (*T'ai chi t'u*), and *Explanation of the Diagram of the Supreme Ultimate* (*T'ai chi t'u shuo*) may be found, together with Chu

Hsi's commentary and a lengthy compilation of further annotation, in the *Hsing-li ta-ch'üan* (hereafter, *HLTC,*) ch. 1. The *Diagram* and *Explanation* have been translated by Derk Bodde in *History of Chinese Philosophy,* by Feng Yu-lan, vol. 2, pp. 435–438. *A Source Book in Chinese Philosophy,* by Wing-tsit Chan, pp. 463–464, contains a translation of the *Explanation.* Both translations are in substantial agreement, and my own owes much to theirs. For a further discussion of the origin and nature of the *Diagram,* see Feng Yu-lan, *ibid.*, pp. 438–442.

2. The *Chin ssu lu,* compiled by Chu Hsi and Lü Tsu-ch'ien, is the earliest compilation of the thought of the early masters and has been extremely influential. It has been translated by Wing-tsit Chan as *Reflections on Things at Hand.* On the *HLTC,* see above, Introduction, n.26.

3. See *HLTC,* 1.lb-3a.

4. *Ch'ien* and *K'un* are the names of the first two hexagrams of the *Book of Changes* (hereafter, *Changes*). *Ch'ien* is entirely composed of yang lines and symbolizes Heaven and the male; *K'un* is composed entirely of yin lines and symbolizes Earth and the female.

5. For a complete elaboration of the correlation of the Five Agents and the constituent principles of human nature as well as the psychological theory developed on this basis, see below, ch. 6.

6. *Changes,* commentary on *Ch'ien* hexagram.

7. *Ibid.*, Remarks on Certain Trigrams, ch. 2.

8. *Ibid.*, Appended Remarks, pt. 1, ch. 4.

9. The *Book of Changes* was an ancient divination text held in high esteem by both Confucians and Taoists. It is based upon eight trigrams which represent the possible combinations of unbroken (yang) lines and broken (yin) lines; these in turn were combined into hexagrams, thus making a total of 64 symbolic graphs representing different combinations of yin and yang. The 8 trigrams were attributed to the legendary sage Fu Hsi, while the hexagrams were held to be the work of King Wen (1171–1122 B.C.); the texts accompanying the hexagrams were attributed to King Wen and the Duke of Chou (d. 1094 B.C.). As important as the text itself were seven commentaries which were incorporated into the work and ascribed to Confucius (551–479 B.C.). Originally a divination text, the *Book of Changes* came to be used as the fundamental source for virtually all Chinese cosmological speculation and was also an important source of ethical teachings. Modern scholars generally hold the commentaries to be the work of diverse authors and composed sometime between the fifth and fourth centuries B.C.

10. *Chu-tzu yü-lei* (hereafter, *YL*), 94.17b-18a.

11. *HLTC,* 1.45b-46a, slightly abridged. T'oegye sees the doctrine of mindfulness as a central theme running throughout his *Ten Diagrams* and deliberately introduces this comment to show how Chu Hsi supplements Chou's more one-sided emphasis on tranquility with the doctrine of mindfulness (see the annotation he appends to ch. 4).

12. The honorific name of Yeh Ts'ai (fl. 1248). Yeh was a disciple of Chu Hsi's pupil, Ch'en Ch'un (1153-1217) and the author of the earliest commentary on the *Chin ssu lu.*

13. *Changes,* Appended Remarks, pt. 1, ch. 11.

14. A slight paraphrase of Yeh's remark as found in *HLTC,* 1.59b-60a.

15. *HLTC,* 1. 596-60a.

16. *Chu-tzu ta ch'üan* (The Complete Works of Chu Hsi, hereafter *CTTC*), 71.4b (*Chi Lien-hsi ch'uan*).

17. The *Elementary Learning (Hsiao hsüeh)* and the *Great Learning* (*Ta hsüeh*) are the subjects of the third and fourth chapters of the *Ten Diagrams.*

18. *Changes,* Remarks on Certain Trigrams, ch. 1.

19. *Changes,* Appended Remarks, pt. 2, ch. 3.

20. *OHN,* 1.1b, B, p. 789; 1.20b, B, p. 798.

21. *OHN,* 1.20b, p. 798.

22. *YL,* 1.2b.

23. There were sharp differences in the orientations underlying the monistic philosophies of Chang and Lo. For an excellent study of Lo's thought that clearly distinguishes him from Chang, see Irene Bloom, "On the 'Abstraction' of Ming Thought: Some Concrete Evidence from the Philosophy of Lo Ch'in-shun," in *Principle and Practicality,* ed. by Wm. Theodore deBary and Irene Bloom, pp. 69–125.

24. The courtesy name of Sŏ Kyŏngdŏk (1489–1546) was Kagu, but in Korea he is best known by his honorific name, Hwadam; he is popularly regarded, along with T'oegye and Yulgok (Yi I), as one of the three outstanding philosophers of the Yi dynasty. He strongly asserted the absolute independence and originality of his ideas, though they bear a close resemblance to the monistic philosophy of *ch'i* developed in China by Chang Tsai, to whom his followers constantly likened him. He refused to take office and lived an impoverished life in retirement devoted to study and teaching. T'oegye had contact with a number of Hwadam's students, and frequently expressed his impatience with what he regarded as their misplaced enthusiasm and exaggerated claims for their master. Hwadam claimed his teaching and insights would endure through the ages, but unfortunately the slim volume of his writing which survived—perhaps his only writing—the *Hwadamjip,* contains only a sketchy exposition of his philosophy, making it impossible, in spite of his high repute, to assess the full range and depth of his ideas.

25. See, for example, his *Pi i ki wi il mul pyŏnjung* (An Evidenced Argument That Li and Ki Are Not One Thing), *TGCS,* A, 41.20b-23a, pp. 920–922, in which he attacks the monism of Lo Chin-shun and Sŏ Kyŏngdŏk.

26. For T'oegye's handling of this question and its ramifications See below, Commentary, "The Supreme Ultimate and Material Force," and chapter 4, Commentary, "Can Principle 'Approach'?"

27. On Chu Hsi's adopting and interpreting Chou's *Diagram,* which was before that relatively unknown, see Wing-tsit Chan, "Chu Hsi's Completion of Neo-Confucianism," pp. 67–72.

28. This remark appears among the passages appended to Chu Hsi's commentary on the *Diagram of the Supreme Ultimate, HLTC,* 1.4a; I have not been able to locate its original source.

29. *CTTC,* 56.33b (Letter to Ch'eng Tzu-shang).

30. *YL*, 1.3a.

31. Mien-tsai was the honorific name of Huang Kan (1152–1221), Chu Hsi's son-in-law and one of his leading disciples. He has generally been considered the orthodox interpreter and transmitter of Chu Hsi's thought.

32. *HLTC*, 1.23b.

33. See above, n. 27.

34. See Yun Sasun, *T'oegyeŭi ch'ŏrhak yŏn'gu* (Research on T'oegye's Philosophy), pp. 59–66, and Chŏn Tuha, "T'oegyeŭi ch'ŏrhagŭi haeksim," (The Heart of T'oegye's Philosophy), pp. 135–170, (esp. pp. 135–145). The two scholars differ insofar as Yun is inclined to emphasize the implicit contradictions in this monistic dualism while Chŏn, who is deeply influenced by Hegel, is inclined to see it in a dialectical framework.

35. On Ki Taesŭng, see above, Introduction, n. 32. He is famous for his role in the Four-Seven Debate with T'oegye, the most famous and important intellectual controversy in the history of Yi Dynasty thought (see below, chapter 6, for a discussion of the debate).

36. The courtesy name of Yi I (1536–1584) was Sukhŏn, but he is universally known in Korea by his honorific name, Yulgok. He rivals T'oegye for the title of the finest thinker of the Yi Dynasty, and the Korean intellectual world became permanently divided into schools which trace their intellectual descent from one or the other. Yulgok had an illustrious official career, holding posts such as Censor General, Inspector General, and Minister of the Board of Personnel, and has a high reputation not only as a philosopher but as a man of practical affairs.

37. Cf. *HLTC*, p.10b.

38. On the differentiation of principle according to the relative purity or turbidity of material force, see below, chapter 3, Commentary, "Material Force and the Difference Between the Sage and the Ordinary Man."

2. Diagram of the Western Inscription

1. On Chang Tsai, see first section of Introduction. The *Western Inscription* was originally ch. 17 of Chang's *Cheng-meng,* and was entitled "Correcting Obstinacy" (*Ting-wan*); Ch'eng I, fearing that this obscure title would cause problems, changed it to "Western Inscription," a reference to the fact that it was inscribed on the western window of Chang's lecture hall. It was included in the second chapter of Chu Hsi's *Chin-ssu lu* (see Wing Tsit Chan's translation, *Reflection of Things at Hand,* pp. 76ff.) and is also presented, along with Chu Hsi's commentary and annotations from other sources, in *HLTC,* chüan 4. T'oegye's careful phrase-by-phrase analysis of its sources and meaning, the *Sŏmyŏng koch'ŭng kangŭi* (Lecture on the Sources of the *Western Inscription*) appears in *TGCS,* A, 7.49a-62a; this lecture was originally presented by him from the Classics Mat before king Sŏnjŏ. His comments indicate that he was using the *HLTC* material. English translations of the *Western Inscription* are to be found in Wing Tsit Chan's *Source Book in Chinese Philosophy,* pp. 497–500, and Derk

Bodde, tr., *History of Chinese Philosophy*, by Feng Yu-lan, vol. 2, pp. 493–495; my own translation is indebted to both.

2. "What fills up all between Heaven and Earth" and "that which directs" are references to *Mencius* 2A: 2, a famous passage which describes man as possessing a "vast, flowing passion nature" (*hao-jan chih ch'i*), which, if nurtured on righteousness, fills up all between Heaven and Earth.

3. Reference to *Mencius*, 4A; 12.

4. Reference to *Mencius*, 1A: 7. T'oegye notes that the pronoun translated by Bodde as "their" should really be understood as "my" and I have followed his interpretation. Cf. *TGCS*, A, 7.53a, p. 220. "My" young and aged would ordinarily refer to one's family members; here my family is extended to include all persons.

5. *Changes*, Commentary on *Ch'ien* hexagram.

6. Reference to *Mencius*, 1A: 5.

7. A combination of references to the *Book of Odes* (hereafter, *Odes*), #272 and 244 respectively.

8. A combination of references to *Changes*, Appended Remarks, pt. 1, ch. 4, and *Tso chuan* (Tso's Commentary on the Spring and Autumn Annals), 1.1.

9. A combination of references to *Analects*, 4.5, and the *Classic of Filial Piety*, ch. 9.

10. A combination of references to *Analects*, 15.9, and *Mencius*, 3B: 9.

11. Reference to *Tso chuan*, 6.18.

12. A combination of references to *Mencius*, 7A: 38, and *Mencius*, 5A: 6.

13. Each half of this sentence combines references to *Changes*, Appended Remarks, pt. 2, ch. 3, and *Doctrine of the Mean*, ch. 19.

14. A combination of references to *Odes*, #256 and # 196.

15. A combination of references to *Mencius*, 7A: 1, and *Classic of Filial Piety*, ch. 4. *Mencius*, 7A: 1 is a key reference point for Neo-Confucians, for it links Heaven and man's nature and, in the phrase here quoted, sums up the essence of self-cultivation.

16. A combination of references to *Mencius*, 4B: 20 and 4B: 30.

17. *Tso chuan*, 1.1. Ying Kao-su, by the example of his own filial piety to his mother, caused Duke Chuang to repent and be reunited with his own mother, whom he had sworn never to see again.

18. *Mencius*, 4A: 28. According to tradition the father of the sage, Shun, was a depraved villain who repeatedly attempted to kill his son; however, he was finally won over by Shun's constant filial piety.

19. *Book of Rites*, T'an kung, pt. 1: 3. Shen Sheng, when falsely accused of attempting to poison his father, Duke Hsien of Chin, committed suicide rather than flee.

20. Tseng Tzu was a disciple of Confucius particularly noted for his filial piety. *Analects* 8.3 tells how on his death bed he called his disciples to view his hands and feet, witnessing that he had fulfilled his filial duty to preserve his body intact. The *Classic of Filial Piety*, though of later origin, was traditionally attributed to him.

21. Po-ch'i was a prince who accepted his father's expulsion of him even

though it was caused by the machinations of a stepmother who wanted him replaced by her own son. Wing Tsit Chan (*Reflections,* p. 78, n. 221) has traced the story to the annotation of the eulogy at the end of *Ch'ien Han shu,* ch. 79, where it is referred to the *Shuo yüan;* he notes that it is not to be found in modern editions of the *Shuo yüan.*

22. Reference to *Odes,* # 253.

23. Ch'eng I applied this *dictum* in answering doubts about the *Western Inscription* expressed by his pupil, Yang Shih. Cf. below, note 27, and Commentary, "Confucian Ethics on a New Foundation." The correspondence between the two on this question may be found in *HLTC,* 4.12a-13b. A translation of Ch'eng's letter appears in Chan, *Source Book,* pp. 550–551.

24. Mo Tzu (fl. 479–438 B.C.) was a philosopher who expounded a doctrine of universal, egalitarian love. His school was one of the chief rivals of the early Confucians, and it was in response to it that Mencius clearly enunciated the Confucian doctrine of graded love. See *Mencius,* 3B: 9. On Mo Tzu and this doctrine, see Chan, *Source Book,* pp. 211-217.

25. Chu Hsi's *Commentary on the Western Inscription, HLTC,* 4.10b–11a.

26. *Ibid.*, 4.21a.

27. Kuei-shan was the honorific name of Yang Shih (1053–1135), a pupil of the Ch'eng brothers who became a leading Neo-Confucian scholar. T'oegye in his "Sim mu ch'e yong pyŏn" (Discourse Against the Theory That the Mind Does Not Have Substance and Function), *TGCS,* I, 41.19b, p. 920, criticizes his inclination for lofty and abstruse theorizing.

28. *Mencius,* 7A: 45. This is the classical *locus* for the Confucian doctrine of "graded love."

29. *HLTC,* 4.11b. "Righteousness" in a Confucian context is not an abstract virtuousness, but the characteristic of acting in a manner appropriate to the given situation, and hence is correlated with the diversity of principle.

30. Shuang-feng was the honorific name of Yao Lu (fl. 1256), and his courtesy name was Chung-yüan. He was a leading disciple of Chu Hsi's son-in-law, Huang Kan. An account of him appears in T'oegye's *Ihak t'ongnok* (Comprehensive Record of Neo-Confucians), 9.40b, *TGCS,* B, p. 501.

31. *HLTC,* 4.24a-b.

32. The honorific name of Ch'eng Fu-hsin (1279–1368); his courtesy name was Tzu-hsien. A Yüan dynasty scholar, he was best known for a book of diagrams, the *Ssu-shu chang t'u* (Diagrams of the Chapters of the Four Books), a work upon which he spent some 13 years, and which T'oegye obtained about 1560. As is clear from comments he makes in chapter 8, T'oegye held Ch'eng in high esteem, and two more of his diagrams appear in chapters 6 and 8. There is an account of him in T'oegye's *Ihak t'ongnok,* 10.31b-32a, *TGCS,* B, p. 519.

33. *I-shu,* 2A, 2a. In the *Chin ssu lu,* Chu Hsi attributes this saying to Ch'eng Hao (see Chan, *Reflections,* p. 79).

34. A paraphrase of *I-shu,* 18.11b, a saying of Ch'eng I.

35. See above, note 23.

36. Commiseration is the active manifestation of the character of *jen*, humanity, which Neo-Confucians view as one of the constitutive qualities of man's nature. This is based upon Mencius' famous discussion of the goodness of human nature in terms of the "Four Beginnings," of which commiseration is the first: "The disposition of commiseration is the beginning of humanity" (*Mencius*, 2A: 6). For a discussion of the Four Beginnings and their relationship to man's nature, see below, chapter 6.

37. Reference to *YL*, 98.12b.

38. In the Confucian tradition, self-understanding could not be ultimately separated from a consideration of the conditions of one's origin and growth as a human being. One originates as an extension of the existence of one's parents and could not have survived without their care. If one understands oneself in this way, there is no place for a self-enclosed conceptualization of one's existence, as in the modern formula, "I have my own life to lead." Rather, filial obedience and service are founded upon a self-identity which includes one's dependence/interdependence on a transpersonal community participating in and transmitting a single life-force. In this view, "my life," rightly understood, cannot be separated from "our life."

39. This will be taken up with the topic of "the investigation of principle" in chapter 4. In general the question of objective vs. subjective emphasis is a critical issue in Neo-Confucian thought. The school of the Ch'eng brothers and Chu Hsi tries to maintain a delicate balance between the two; its chief rival, the school of Wang Yang-ming (Shou-jen, 1472–1529), which picked up and developed the thought of Chu Hsi's contemporary, Lu Hsiang-shan (Chiu-yüan, 1139–1193), emphasized the subjective side and thus moved in a sharply different direction. T'oegye vigorously opposed this development and wrote several essays in which he was harshly critical of Wang Yang-ming (see *TGCS*, A, 41.23a–32b).

3. Diagram of the *Elementary Learning*

1. The Five Relationships are those presented in the diagram under the heading, "clarifying relationships." The *locus classicus* for this formulation is *Mencius*, 3A: 4. The quality appropriate to the relationship of friends is classically and traditionally expressed as "faithfulness"; there is no explanation of which I am aware as to why it has been changed to the noncommittal "intercourse" in the heading of this section of the *Elementary Learning*.

2. This was initiated at the suggestion of Kwŏn Kŭn (1352–1409). Kwŏn was one of the most prominent Neo-Confucian scholars during the transition period between the Koryŏ and Yi dynasties.

3. Hyŏn Sangyun, *Chosŏn yuhak sa* (History of Korean Confucianism), p. 36.

4. The text of this *Introduction* (*Hsiao-hsüeh t'i-tzu*) is to be found in *CTTC*, 76.19a–b; it is identical with the text as presented in the *Ten Diagrams*.

5. The "Four Beginnings" were first described by Mencius in the course of

his argument that human nature is good. Cf. *Mencius*, 2A: 6. The correlation of these with the four characteristics of Heaven is discussed below, Commentary, "The Four Characteristics of Heaven, the Mandate, and Human Nature."

6. *Mencius*, 6A: 6.

7. *Mencius*, 4A: 10 describes those who disregard humanity and righteousness as doing violence to themselves and throwing themselves away.

8. This description refers to *Analects*, 19:12.

9. The "bright Mandate" refers to the Mandate of Heaven. The doctrine of the Mandate of Heaven originally was a legitimation of the king's right to rule, based on his receipt of the Mandate, but the concept was broadened to cover Heaven's ordination with regard to human affairs—Fate, in some contexts, but the moral imperative in the context of moral discourse. The first line of the *Doctrine of the Mean* was of crucial significance for Neo-Confucians, who interpreted human nature in terms of this moral imperative (i.e., principle): "What Heaven mandates is called our nature; to follow our nature is called the Tao."

10. This paragraph sums up the teleology of all learning, elementary or advanced. But it pertains particularly to the *Great Learning* insofar as it more specifically describes the culmination of the process of study and self-cultivation.

11. A reference to the infamous "burning of the books," a literary proscription in which the First Emperor of the Ch'in dynasty at the instigation of the legalist philosopher, Li Ssu, in 213 B.C. ordered the destruction of all philosophical and historical works; only books in the Imperial Library (later destroyed), the history of his own dynasty, and practical works such as those on medicine and divination were to be preserved. Just how much was lost forever in this persecution can never be known, but the most important classical works survived, and the overall impact of this episode upon the literary heritage of China may well be exaggerated. It did, however, mark a definite end of the creative and multifaceted work of the many diverse philosophical schools which flourished in the disorganized society which preceded the Ch'in unification of the Chinese empire.

12. Allusions to *Mencius*, 6A: 11 and 7A: 1, respectively. See the diagram in chapter 8, below, which schematically presents much of the Neo-Confucian terminology relating to self-cultivation. As a glance at the sources of that diagram's phrases will show, the greater part of Neo-Confucian technical terminology on this topic is drawn from *Mencius* and relates to well-known passages in that work.

13. The traditional "six arts" of Chinese education as enumerated in the *Chou li*, ch. 14.

14. This refers to the first sentence of the *Great Learning*. The text is presented by T'oegye in chapter 4 of the *Ten Diagrams*.

15. Chu Hsi was fond of the statement that mindfulness is both the way of making a beginning and achieving the final completion, and repeats it frequently. Here it would appear that it is a quotation; the most likely source for such a saying would be the *ECCS*, but I have been unable to locate a passage worded in this way. Possibly he is referring in a summary way to the teaching of the Ch'engs on mindfulness, which indeed describes it as fundamental to the whole process of learning.

See, for example, the many passages on the topic cited in the *Chin ssu lu,* ch. 4 (Chan tr., *Reflections,* pp. 123–153).

16. *Ta-hsüeh huo-wen,* lb-3a. The passage has been somewhat abbreviated by T'oegye. I have indicated the omitted portions by dots in the text.

17. A key phrase, "*ko wu,*" is interpreted by Chu Hsi as "reach to things," i.e., approach and investigate them—the "investigation of principle" which is essential to his philosophy. Wang interprets it rather as "rectify things," the essential thing for him being not study, but actively applying and practicing what one already knows innately. See his *Ch'uan-hsi lu,* sec. 137 (*Instructions for Practical Living,* Wing-tsit Chan, tr., pp. 102–106).

18. "Honoring the moral nature (*tsun te-hsing*)" is paired in Neo-Confucian parlance with "following the path of inquiry and study" (*tao wen-hsüeh*). The former phrase refers to the practical application to self-cultivation, the latter to the study and investigation of principle; together they express the two aspects of the learning process as conceived by Chu Hsi.

19. "Destroying principle" reflects T'oegye's view of what Wang is actually doing by emphasizing the subjective possession of principle in the mind and disregarding the need to study it externally in things and affairs.

20. For this letter, see *CTTC,* 42.16a-17b. It is an important discussion of the relation between study and practice, and the relationship of the *Elementary Learning* and *Great Learning* is discussed in this context.

21. The personal name of Cho (1501–1572) was Sik, and his courtesy name was Konjung. Nammyŏng was his honorific name. When younger he studied literature, but later came to Neo-Confucian studies and secluded himself for many years, devoting his efforts to cultivating mindfulness. He came to enjoy a high reputation as a scholar and was repeatedly recommended for official posts, though he avoided them to remain in retirement.

22. The personal name of Yi (1541–1596) was Tŏkhong; Koengjung was his courtesy name and Kanjae his honorific name. He was one of T'oegye's leading disciples and in 1578 was honored as fourth among nine men especially selected for office on the basis of outstanding learning. He was noted for his learning on the *Book of Changes,* and wrote commentaries on a number of works, including the *Heart Classic.* An account of him may be found in the *Tosan munhyŏn nok* (Record of T'oegye's Disciples), *TGCS,* B, 3.19a-27a, p. 987–991.

23. See *OHN,* 1.20b, *TGCS,* B, p. 798. T'oegye's own letter in response to Cho (*TGCS,* 10.4b–6a, A, pp. 283–284) treats it entirely as a proposal that T'oegye correct others and purify public life. In his reply T'oegye argues that there are a number of different degrees of culpability; one cannot tar them all with the same brush, and in any case it is not fitting for a scholar to thus set himself up in judgment over others, nor is it practicable to try to purge them from public life. The tone of these remarks contrasts strongly with the rigid moralism that had proved self-destructive to earlier Neo-Confucians in Yi dynasty public life.

25. The courtesy name of Chŏng (1533–1576) was Chajung, and his honorific name was Munbong. He passed the highest civil service examination in 1558

and was highly reputed as both a philosopher and poet, but his writings were lost during the 1592 Japanese invasion. An account of him may be found in the *Tosan munhyŏn nok,* 2.31a-33a, *TGCS,* B, pp. 972–973. During his official career he served as Censor General and Minister of the Board of Personnel.

26. The courtesy name of Kim Su (1537–1615) was Cha'ang, and his honorific name was Mongch'on. He passed the highest civil service examination in 1573 and in his official career served as governor in several provinces and also served as State Councilor and Minister of the Board of Taxation. An account of him appears in the *Tosan munhyŏn nok,* 3.40a-41b, *TGCS,* B, pp. 997–998.

27. See *Mencius,* 2A: 6.

28. The life-force, associated with yang, arises in spring, pervades and makes all things flourish in summer; the benefits are harvested in fall, and winter, "firmness," is the season when this force is stored up in the earth, preparing to begin the cycle anew in the spring.

29. *Myŏng* (Chinese, *ming*), the term here translated as "ordained," is a reference to the Mandate (*myŏng*) of Heaven (see above, note 8).

30. The *Ch'ŏnmyŏng tosŏl* (Diagrammatic Explanation of the Mandate of Heaven) was originally the work of Chŏng Chiun (1509–1561). T'oegye felt the work needed correction and worked with Chŏng on revising it; he made such extensive correction and revision that it is now considered virtually his work. It is a useful exposition of fundamental Neo-Confucian doctrines, but the work's chief claim to fame is that it contains a statement correlating the Four Beginnings and Seven Feelings with principle and material force respectively, a statement which touched off the historic Four-Seven Debate with Ki Taesŭng (see below, chapter 6).

31. The typology of three categories of man has a long tradition; Neo-Confucians were particularly aware of the elaboration of this theme by the Neo-Confucian precursor, Han Yü (768–824), of the T'ang dynasty. Han's description may be found in Wing-tsit Chan's *Sourcebook,* pp. 451–553; on earlier versions of this theme, see Chan's comments, *Sourcebook,* pp. 276 and 453–454.

4. Diagram of the Great Learning

1. For a complete translation of the *Great Learning,* see Wing-tsit Chan, *Sourcebook in Chinese Philosophy,* pp. 85–94, or James Legge, *The Chinese Classics,* vol. 1.

2. The text arranged by Chu Hsi and accompanied by his commentary is entitled *Ta-hsüeh chang-chu* (The Chapters and Sentences of the *Great Learning*). This became the authoritative version, and from 1314 on it was a basic text for the civil service examinations in China. For a discussion of Chu Hsi's role in establishing and forming the *Great Learning,* see Wing-tsit Chan, "Chu Hsi's Completion of Neo-Confucianism," pp. 81–87.

3. The investigation of things (i.e., principle) is the point of central importance in this text; see Commentary, "The Investigation of Principle. On Wang

Yang-ming's handling of the phrase, see above, chapter 3, note 17; on the variety of ways of interpreting this phrase, see Chan, *Sourcebook*, pp. 561–562.

4. An alternative rendition would be, "When [the principle of] things approaches, knowledge is extended." On the argument concerning such an interpretation, See below, Commentary, "Can Principle 'Approach'?"

5. *I-shu*, 15,20a.

6. *Ibid.*, 15.6b.

7. *HLTC*, 46.14b.

8. *HLTC*, 46.15b, paraphrased. The honorific name of Yin T'un (1071–1142) was Ho-ching. A disciple of Ch'eng Yi, he was more noted for his earnestness than brilliance, and was particularly devoted to mindfulness.

9. *Doctrine of the Mean*, ch. 27. On the significance of this phrase, see above, chapter 3, note 18.

10. *Mencius*, 6A: 15. "The greater" refers to the mind, "the lesser" to the senses, which should not be permitted to interfere with the proper function of the mind. Thus this passage is taken to refer to the *Great Learning*'s "make the intention sincere and rectify the mind."

11. *Analects*, 14:42.

12. *Doctrine of the Mean*, ch. 20.

13. *Ta-hsüeh huo wen*, 2b-3a, slightly abbreviated. The portions omitted are indicated by dots in the text.

14. In the remarks with which Chu Hsi introduces the *Great Learning* he quotes Ch'eng I as referring to it with this phrase.

15. On Kwŏn Kŭn, see above, chapter 3, note 2.

16. The diagram comes from Kwŏn's *Iphak tosŏl* (Diagrams and Explanations for Entering Upon Learning). Its categories and presentation of the various elements of the first chapter of the *Great Learning* closely follow Chu Hsi's remarks in the *Ta-hsüeh huo wen*, which is probably the reason T'oegye chose it. The reference to Kwŏn as an official rather than a scholar is consistent with the fact that his name by T'oegye's time was no longer mentioned in the transmission of the Neo-Confucian Tao to Korea. Even though Kwŏn was, arguably, the foremost Neo-Confucian scholar of the Koryŏ-Yi transition period, he fell into disrepute for having served both dynasties, for the Korean Neo-Confucians came to place a great emphasis upon the purity of not serving in questionable circumstances.

17. This line recapitulates the process described in the *Great Learning*, beginning with the investigation of things, moving to personal self-cultivation ("exalting virtue"), and culminating with the expansion of these effects in the family, state; and whole world.

18. The translation, beginning with "constantly mindful" is a free rendition and expansion of a concise but untranslatable phrase which refers to *Analects*, 15.6.

19. Yen-p'ing is the honorific name of Chu Hsi's teacher, Li T'ung (1093–1163). Li was an important influence in turning Chu Hsi back to Confucianism and away from his earlier interest in Buddhism and Taoism. The focus on the affairs of daily life reflected in this passage was one of the most important lessons Chu Hsi learned from him.

20. *Yen-p'ing ta wen* (Li T'ung's Responses to the Questions of Chu Hsi), *fu-lu* (supplement), pp. 22b–23a.

21. The courtesy name of Kim Sŏngil (1538–1593) was Sasun, and his honorific name was Hakbong. He passed the highest civil service examination in 1568. In his official career, he held posts as First Counselor and Assistant Master of the Confucian Academy. He was honored with the posthumous name, Munch'ung. His collected writings are the *Hakbong chip*. An account of him is to be found in the *Tosan munhyŏn nok*, 3.2a-5a.

22. On Yi I, see chapter 1, note 35.

23. On Yi Tŏkhong, see chapter 3, note 22.

24. *Ta-hsüeh huo wen*, discussion of the supplemented fifth chapter of commentary, p. 36b.

25. See above, chapter 3, Commentary, "The Relationship of the *Elementary Learning* and the *Great Learning.*"

26. Some were concerned mainly with principle's transcendence of the categories of inner and outer, while others were concerned to read the passage in a way that fully reflected the total perfection and unified grasp of all principle as described by Chu Hsi in the passage he supplies to supplement for the "lost" fifth chapter of the commentary section of the *Great Learning*, a chapter which should comment on precisely this crucial section of the Text. These positions are described and criticized by T'oegye in a long letter to Chŏng Chajung, *TGCS*, A, 26.34a-39b, pp. 627–630.

27. On Ki Taesŭng, see Introduction, note 33.

28. *YL*, 1.3a.

29. Ijŏng was the courtesy name of Kim Ch'wiryo (1526–?); his honorific name was Chamjae. He was a devoted disciple who traveled long distances to see T'oegye and carried on an extensive written correspondence with him as well. He does not seem to have held office or made any notable scholarly mark, however. An account of him is to be found in *Tosan munhyŏn nok*, 2.9a-11a, B, pp. 961–962.

30. *Ta-hsüeh huo wen*, discussion of the supplemented missing 5th chapter of commentary, p. 36b.

31. *YL*, 18.23a.

32. In his discussion of T'oegye's final position on this matter Yun Sasun notes its continuity with his position on the role of principle in the creation of the universe and his argument in the Four-Seven Debate. See Yun Sasun, *T'oegye Ch'ŏlhakŭi yŏngu* (Research on T'oegye's Philosophy), pp. 30–32. On T'oegye's view of principle as having substance and function, the fundamental premise of all of T'oegye's positions on these matters, see *ibid.*, pp. 55–57.

5. Diagram of Rules of the White Deer Hollow Academy

1. The rules appear in *CTTC*, 74.16b-17a; T'oegye has left out one sentence which distributes the items which belong to the investigation of principle and earnestly practicing, for this distribution is graphically evident in his diagram.

2. These remarks immediately follow the rules, *ibid.*, 74.17a-b.

3. The *CTTC* text employs a different phrase here, but the meaning is essentially the same.

4. A scholar, not to be confused with the famous T'ang poet, Li Po.

5. *Tao-hsüeh* (Kor. *tohak*), literally "the learning of the (true) Tao" is a common designation for the Ch'eng-Chu school of thought. It focuses particularly upon the serious moral concern which was central to this movement, but it also implies a fullness of truth, and its appropriation by this school of thought aroused considerable antagonism during Chu Hsi's lifetime.

6. See above, Address on Presenting the *Ten Diagrams,* p. 00.

7. See, for example, Letter to Kim Ijŏng, *TGCS,* A, 29.10b, p. 681.

8. *Isan wŏngyu* (Rules for the I Mountain Academy), *TGCS,* 41.52a, A, p. 936.

9. The courtesy name of Pak Yŏng (1471–1540) was Chasil, and his honorific name Songdang. He was primarily a military man and came from a military family, but spent the years 1494–1506 (the reign of Yŏnsangŭn) in retirement chiefly studying the *Great Learning.* His collected works are entitled *Songdang chip.*

10. "Integral substance" is the perfect fullness and wholeness of principle; "great function" is the correlated active and perfect responsiveness to all creatures and circumstances. These stand for the ultimate perfection; thus Chu Hsi describes the final perfection of the investigation of principle and the extension of knowledge in these terms in the passage he introduces to supplement for the "lost" fifth chapter of the commentary section of the *Great Learning.*

11. Chu Hsi was largely responsible for the emergence of the Four Books (*Great Learning, Analects, Mencius,* and *Doctrine of the Mean*) as the authoritative core of the classical corpus; he held that these works contained the words of Confucius and Mencius, while the other Classics were to varying degrees further removed and less reliable reflections of the masters' teachings. On Chu Hsi's revision of the classical corpus and its signigicance, see Wing-tsit Chan, "Chu Hsi's Completion of Neo-Confucianism," pp. 81–87.

12. See below, chapter 6, on the Four-Seven Debate, which was centered on these issues as they relate to understanding the relationship of human nature and kinds of feelings. This passage is part of one of the important letters of the debate.

13. On Kija, see Presentation, note 16.

14. On *tohak,* see above, note. 5

15. The sage King Wen (1184?–1135? B.C.) was the founder of the Chou dynasty.

16. This letter, written in 1543, is the earliest indication that T'oegye had resolved to resign and withdraw from public life. The "humiliating remarks" he mentions refers to the fact that in the atmosphere which prevailed any such attempt would be (and was) cynically criticized as a self-serving evasion of public duty.

17. Cf. Introduction, "Rise of the *Sarim* Mentality and the Literati Purges."

18. The early years of the reign of Yŏnsan'gun (r. 1494–1506) are a clear example of this, for he was blocked at every turn by stubborn resistance and criticism from the three powerful official organs of remonstrance, the Office of the Inspector

General, the Office of the Censor General, and the Office of Special Councilors. There ensued the bloodiest and most violent purges of Neo-Confucian officials in Yi dynasty history. See Edward Wagner, *The Literati Purges,* pp. 33–69.

19. See especially his *Kan Kwae sanggu kangŭi* (Lecture on the Uppermost Yang Line of the *Ch'ien* Hexagram), *TGCS,* A, 7.48a-49a, pp. 217–218. This was a theme to which he frequently returned in his talks with King Sŏnjo.

20. See his *Mujin kyŏngyŏn kyech'a i* (Second Exposition of 1568 from the Classics Mat), *TGCS,* A, 7.3a-4b, p. 195, which is devoted entirely to this theme.

21. See Introduction, "Rise of the *Sarim* Mentality and the Literati Purges." T'oegye wrote his biography, which appears in *TGCS,* A, 48.28a-38a, pp. 1061–1066.

22. T'oegye uses it in this way in the letter in which he appeals for official royal sanction of the White Cloud Hollow Academy. See Letter to Sim Pangbaek, *TGCS,* A, 9.4a-8b, pp. 262–264.

23. The courtesy name of Chu Sebong was Kyŏngyu, and his honorific name Sinjae. His subsequent career included posts as Headmaster of the Confucian Academy and Governor of Hwanghae Province, where he established another private academy which in 1555 was honored with a royal bequest of a name plaque and books.

24. On An Hyang, see Introduction, "The Late Koryŏ–Early YI Transition period."

25. Earlier in this letter T'oegye mentions that in founding this academy Chu Sebong had to overcome criticism from those who questioned his action and thought it strange.

26. These figures are taken from a table in Yi Ch'unhŭi, *Yijo sŏwŏn munch'ang ko* (Investigation of the Library Collections of Yi Dynasty Private Academies), p. 17.

27. *Ibid.*, p. 16. The table on p. 17 lists a total of only 650 private academies; there is no indication of where the figure of "over 800" comes from; perhaps it takes into account the fact that the records upon which the table is based are not exhaustive.

28. After the Japanese Invasions (1590–1598) publishing became a common function of the private academies. Their libraries were an important local cultural resource. The core of these libraries was the standard Neo-Confucian collection of the basic works of the Ch'eng-Chu school such as the *Chu Tzu ta-ch'üan, Chu Tzu yü-lei, Hsing-li ta-ch'üan,* etc. Included also were Korean works, but generally an academy would include only works associated with the intellectual lineage of its own faction, so the minds of those educated in this context were already biased regarding the major issues debated in the course of the Yi dynasty. About 80 percent of the publishing activities were devoted to *munjips* (collected writings) and memoirs selected according to factional ties. See *ibid.*, pp. 22–25.

29. These rituals had a formative or educational function insofar as they were occasions for reflecting upon and honoring ideal role models. But even in the earliest (1595) memorials questioning the development of these academies, it is mentioned that many who are so honored in various academies are in fact insignificant personages. *Ibid.*, p. 18.

30. *Ibid.*, pp. 16–18.

31. *Ibid.*, p. 21. Page 19 presents a chart describing 25 restrictive measures the government took against the academies between 1655–1871; 19 of these measures fall in the first 100 years of that period, reflecting their general ineffectiveness until 1741, when harsh sanctions were enacted and 300 academies actually were destroyed.

6. Diagram of the Saying, "The Mind Combines and Governs the Nature and the Feelings"

1. On Ki Taesŭng, see Introduction, note 33. He was only thirty-two years old, twenty-seven years junior to T'oegye, when the debate between them began. The learning, tenacity, and thoroughness of his argumentation against T'oegye were a great contribution to what was attained in the course of the debate. That T'oegye allowed himself to be pressed so hard by one so much his junior reflects a rare intellectual humility and openness on his part, especially in a social context which normally demanded great deference to one's elders.

2. The courtesy name of Sŏng Hon (1535–1598) was Howŏn, and his honorific name was Ugye. He was a close friend of Yulgok, but although he had never studied with T'oegye, he was convinced of T'oegye's position and debated the issue from 1572–1577 in correspondence with Yulgok. This discussion, occurring just two years after T'oegye's death, attracted wide attention.

3. See *Mencius*, 2A:6.

4. The Seven Feelings are listed in the *Book of Rites*, ch. 9. The shorter list of feelings in the first chapter of the *Doctrine of the Mean*, pleasure, anger, sorrow, and joy, are considered likewise to represent the seven, and along with *Mencius*, the *Doctrine of the Mean's* handling of the feelings is a major consideration in discussing this issue.

5. See chapter 2, note 32.

6. *Chang Tzu chüan-shu*, 14.2a. The verb in this sentence, *t'ung*, has a range of meaning which includes both the idea of combining and the associated idea of excercising governance or command. This ambivalance was fruitfully exploited by Neo-Confucians, who refer to the saying both in the context of discussing the mind as the subject which combines the nature and feelings as its substance and function, and in the context of discussing the distinctive role of the mind as presiding over the two; the present chapter is a case in point. The two discussions are intimately related, and whichever aspect of *t'ung* is in the forefront in a given context, its alternative is implicit within it. For this reason, as well as for consistency, I will translate *t'ung* as "combines and governs," whatever the immediate context, except in cases where it is used in a compound which singles out one of its aspects.

7. This description draws heavily on the language of traditional Confucian formulas. The *Book of Rites*, ch. 9, says: "Thus man is [composed of] the virtue of Heaven and Earth, the interaction of yin and yang, the combination of the physical and the spiritual, and the most excellent material force of the Five Agents." The commentary of Kung Ying-ta (fl. c. 620 A.D.) remarks: "Man is stirred by the most

excellent material force of the Five Agents and hence possesses humanity, righteousness, propriety, wisdom, and faithfulness; these are 'the most excellent material force of the Five Agents.' . . . The combination of the physical and the spiritual, and the most excellent material force of the Five Agents constitute man's nature "*Li-chi cheng-i,* 22). While much of the language of this description is preserved by the Neo-Confucians, the introduction of the dualism of principle and material force and the equation of the nature with principle are a new departure that transforms the significance of the traditional description.

8. From the *Book of Changes,* Appended Remarks, pt. I, ch. 10: "*The Changes* is without thought, without action; it is still and unmoving. When acted on, it immediately penetrates all things." Here the characteristics of the mind of a sage are applied to the *Book of Changes;* Neo-Confucians reapply the passage to describe the substance and function of the mind of everyman. Thus it becomes part of a theoretical frmework which will support everymen's cultivation of sagehood.

9. *Mencius,* 6A:8; see also 7A:21.

10. *Ibid.*, 2A:6.

11. This paragraph is based on the *Doctrine of the Mean,* ch. 1. See discussion below, Commentary, "The Two States of the Mind."

12. *I-ch'uan wen-chi,* 4.1a. Yen Hui was the foremost of Confucius' disciples, and was especially praised by the Master for his love of learning.

13. In speaking with King Sŏnjo, T'oegye says, "The first diagram was made by Ch'eng Lin-yin, but in his distinguishing principle and material force there were many inexact points. Thus I removed them and made the second and third diagrams distinguishing the original nature and the physical nature as they are discussed by Mencius, the Ch'eng brothers, and Master Chu" (*OHN,* 3.27a, B, p. 832). The *T'oegye sŏnsaeng munjip kojŭng,* a book of annotations to T'oegye's *Collected Works* compiled by the eighteenth century Korean scholar, Yu Towŏn, gives further details: "In Ch'eng's original diagram, "mind" was in the center of the circle with "combines and governs the nature" and "combines and governs the feelings" arranged to the right and left. Beneath the word "principle," "called humanity" etc., was absent," in *TGCS* (B, 3.32b-33a, pp. 1119–120). When we put these passages together, it seems likely that T'oegye felt that Ch'eng's arrangement of words within the circle suggested a division of nature and feelings according to principle and material force, an oversimplification which he is careful to correct with his own two additional diagrams.

14. *Doctrine of the Mean,* ch. 1. This work was traditionally attributed to Tzu Ssu, the grandson of Confucius.

15. *Mencius,* 6A:6.

16. *I-shu,* 22A:11a.

17. *Cheng meng,* ch. 6.

18. *Doctrine of the Mean,* ch. 1.

19. *Mencius,* 2A:6.

20. *Ts'ui yen,* 2.25a.

21. *Yü-lei* 4.10b.

22. *Analects*, 17.2.

23. *I-shu*, 1.7b.

24. *Cheng meng*, ch. 6: "After assuming concrete form there is the physical nature; if one is good at returning it [to its original condition] then the nature of Heaven and Earth is preserved in one. Therefore, with regard to the physical nature, there is that which the superior man denies to be his nature." This passage was of great importance, for in it Chang Tsai ennunciates for the first time the key doctrine of a "physical nature," and points the way to the distinction of what comes to be called the "original nature."

25. *Yü-lei*, 4.10b.

26. That is, material force may by its turbidity distort the feelings, which would be purely good if their issuance depended solely upon principle.

27. This twofold formula is famous as T'oegye's culminating expression of the relationship of the Four Beginnings and Seven Feelings. The "principle mounting material force" description of the Seven Feelings is borrowed from a horse and rider image Chu Hsi occasionally used to express the basic relationship of principle and material force. However, he used it only in a cosmic context. It is notable that T'oegye uses it for only one set of feelings; Yulgok argues strongly that this single formula must be used for both sets of feelings, there being only one way in which principle and material force relate, whether at the cosmic or the human level (See *Yulgok chŏnsŏ*, 10.15b-16a).

28. *I-shu*, 6.2a.

29. *Book of Documents*, II.2.15. This passage is the classical locus for the contrasting concepts, "the human mind" and "the mind of the Tao," making it an essential reference point for Neo-Confucians. For further discussion, see below, chapter 8.

30. This separation led to a dispute among T'oegye's contemporaries regarding whether the nature could be regarded as acting prior to the mind. See Letter to Kim Ijŏng, *TGCS*, A, 30.17a-19b, pp. 685–686.

31. *Pal* (Chinese, *fa*), the term here translated as "aroused," I have translated as "issues," "issuance," etc., in discussing the relationship of the nature and the feelings in order to avoid the implication that feelings are something separate from the nature that the nature acts upon and arouses. This is usually done by translating *pal* as "manifests," but this conventional rendition is inadequate for the context of the Four-Seven Debate, where the focus of the issue is the causal activation or issuance of the feelings by principle and material force.

32. "Cautious and fearful" not in the sense of being anxious and watchful, which would be active, but in the sense of the profound reverence and carefulness evoked by the presence of the sacred, an attitude fully in keeping with a quiescent state of mind.

33. T'oegye first used this formula in 1553 in emending a basically similar expression in the *Ch'ŏnmyŏng to* (Diagram of the Heavenly Mandate), a work of his contemporary, Chŏng Chi-un (1509–1561). On the *Ch'ŏnmyŏng to*, see chapter 3,

note 30. For the original and emended diagrams, and T'oegye's long preface, see *TGCS*, A, 41.1a-11a, pp. 911–916. For the chapters of explanation, see *TGCS*, B, 8.12b-20b, pp. 140–144.

34. *TGCS*, A, 16.lb, p. 402.

35. *TGCS*, A, 16.12b-14a, pp. 407–408.

36. *TGCS*, A, 16.8a-12b, pp. 405–407.

37. *Yü-lei*, 53.17b. This brief statement seems to be the only expression of this doctrine in Chu Hsi's works; since Chu Hsi did not devote explicit attention to this issue, it could not be finally settled on his authority.

38. *Sa chil li ki wangbok sŏ* (The Correspondence Exchanged in the Four-Seven, Principle and Material Force Debate), 1.6b-28b, in *Kobong chŏnsŏ* (The Complete Works of Ki Taesŭng), pp. 249–260. This work contains the complete correspondence of both T'oegye and Ki Taesŭng relating to the debate; it was published and circulated separately, and was also incorporated into the *Kobong chŏnsŏ*.

39. *TGCS*, A, 16.19a-45a, pp. 411–424.

40. *TGCS*, A, 16.25a-28a, pp. 414–415.

41. *Sa chil li ki wangbok sŏ*, 2.1a-22b, *Kobong chŏnsŏ*, pp. 273–283.

42. *TGCS*, A, 17.2b-3a, pp. 428–429. Although he never sent a reply to Ki's second long response, he did evidently jot some notes in response to various sections of it. These have been edited and put together with the sections of Ki's original letter to which they are addressed, and treated as if it were a letter to Ki. This work appears only in *TGCS*, A, 17,3a-6b, pp. 429–430.

43. *Sa chil li ki wangbok sŏ*, 2.25a-27a, *Kobong chŏnsŏ*, pp. 285–286.

44. To this point the passage is a paraphrase of T'oegye's position presented in *TGCS*, A, 16,9a-10a, p. 406. Emphasis is mine.

45. Ki and T'oegye are both aware that T'oegye's insistence on a causal differentiation underlying the verbal distinctions made in the authoritative sources is an interpretive move that goes beyond what is explicitly said by Chu Hsi on this matter, although T'oegye is convinced he is being loyal to Chu Hsi's intent.

46. *Sa chil li ki wangbok sŏ*, 1.9a-10a, *Kobong chŏnsŏ*, p. 259.

47. Cf. *TGCS*, A, 16.27a-28a, p. 415.

48. *Sa chil li ki wangbok sŏ*, 1.25b, *Kobong chŏnsŏ*, p. 259.

49. *Mencius*, 2A:6.

50. The language of principle mounting material force was applied by Ki Taesŭng to the Four Beginnings; T'oegye here concedes the usage insofar as it expresses the interdependence of principle and material force. In his own final formulation, however, he abandons this image in describing the Four Beginnings, because it cannot bring out the priority of principle which is his point.

51. The discussion at this point has touched on the *Great Learning*, commentary section, ch. 7, which discusses these four feelings in negative terms. T'oegye views these four, and the remarks made about them, to pertain generically to the Seven Feelings.

52. For a discussion of the differences between the development of Chu Hsi's

thought in China and the issues which become paramount in Korea with T'oegye's thought, see Tu Wei-ming, "T'oegye's Creative Interpretation of Chu Hsi's Philosophy of Principle."

7. Diagram of the Explanation of Humanity

1. *Analects,* 12:22.

2. *Mencius,* 2A:6.

3. The "Treatise" *(Jen shuo)* is to be found in *ChuTzu ta-ch'üan,* 67.20b-21b. For an English translation, see Wing-tsit Chan, *Sourcebook,* pp. 593–597.

4. The "Diagram" appears in *Yü-lei,* 105.71a. The "Treatise" and the "Diagram" appear together in *HLTC* 35.6a-8b.

5. Wing-tsit Chan notes that this formulation is central in Chu Hsi's treatment of *jen,* and appears in over ten places in his notes on the *Analects* and *Mencius,* including *Analects* 1:2 and *Mencius* 1A:1. See Wing-tsit Chan (Chen Jung-chieh), "Lün Chu-tzu chih jen-shuo" (Discussion of Chu Hsi's Treatise on *Jen*).

6. See *ibid.*, p. 391, where Chan discusses the "Diagram".

7. A saying of Ch'eng I: *Wai-shu,* 3.1a. *Sheng,* here rendered "produce and give life," means life, the generation of life, or production. The idea of the universe here is one of a dynamic, vital organism which continually produces new life and also functions to support and foster it through the whole process of growth and fruition, a concept that becomes central in the Neo-Confucian interpretation of *jen.* See discussion below, Commentary, "*Jen* as the Generative Life-Force."

8. From Ch'eng I's comparison of the mind with a seed, and *jen* as its nature to grow: *I-shu,* 18.2a. See discussion below, Commentary, "*Jen* as the Generative Life-Force."

9. *Analects,* 12.1. Chou Tun-i attempted to equate *jen* with impartiality, but while the two are closely connected, impartiality is only a state of consciousness and does not do justice to the social, relational nature of *jen*; thus Chu Hsi here connects them but avoids equating them. See Wing-tsit Chan, "The Evolution of the Neo-Confucian Concept of *Jen,*" pp. 311–312.

10. This follows Ch'eng I's description of the relationship of filial piety, respectfulness, and altruism to *jen*: *I-shu,* 18.1b and 15.8b. One sees here how the Neo-Confucian categories of substance and function serve to give a systematic order to the many ideas that were traditionally closely associated with or equated with *jen.*

11. T'oegye's text has *chih* ("know") instead of the very similar character, *chih* ("wisdom") which appears in both the *HLTC* and the *Chu Tzu ta-ch'üan.* I have followed the latter meaning. The variant reading would not alter the point of the comment, which is a critique of Hsieh Liang-tso's attempt to interpret *jen* as consciousness (see discussion below, Commentary, "*Jen* as consciousness. Chu Hsi says that consciousness is the function of wisdom, and related to *jen* insofar as *jen* encompasses the other virtues of the natures, including wisdom; hence it is a distortion to use it as a direct manifestation of *jen* (see *CTTC,* 42.19a-b, Letter to Wu Hui-shu).

12. T'oegye has shortened the original text of the *Treatise* by 301 characters (the original text totals 824 characters). What he has omitted is either already clear in the *Diagram*, or an embellishment rather than a main idea, or, in the case of the final paragraph which he omitted, an expansion on the difficulties which attend the interpretations of Hsieh Liang-tso and Yang Shih. His intention to shorten the text is clear from the manner in which he omits even inessential pronouns and short phrases that do not alter the basic meaning or coherence of the text. His need to do this undoubtedly stemmed from his intention to produce a text each chapter of which could be mounted on a single panel of a ten-panel screen. The text of this chapter, in its shortened form, can just be fit into such a format. The same considerations are also probably the reason for the very abbreviated nature of T'oegye's own remarks in this chapter.

13. *Changes*, Hexagram number 1, *Ch'ien* (Heaven).

14. *Analects*, 12:1.

15. *Analects*, 13:19.

16. Both of these sayings come from the *Classic of Filial Piety*, ch. 14.

17. A paraphrase of *I-shu*, 11.5b.

18. *I-shu*, 18.1a.

19. Instead of "said," (*wei*), the text in *Chu Tzu ta-ch'üan* reads "criticized" (*he*); the text in *HLTC*, however, like T'oegye, has *wei*.

20. This refers to the doctrine of Yang Shih. See discussion, Commentary, "The Universe as a Single Body."

21. This refers to Hsieh Liang-tso. See discussion, below, Commentary, "*Jen* as Consciousness."

22. *Analects*, 6:30.

23. *I-shu*, 24.3a.

24. *Great Learning*, commentary section, ch. 3.

25. *I-shu*, 2A.2a.

26. *HLTC*, 35.7b, annotation to text of *Treatise*.

27. Wing-tsit Chan tr., *Sourcebook*, p. 596.

28. Chan, "*Lŭn Chu-tzu jen-shuo*," p. 391.

29. The courtesy name of Chang Shih (1133–1180) was Ch'in-fu (or Ching-fu), and his honorific name was Nan-hsien. He was an illustrious scholar and a close friend of Chu Hsi. Chi Hsi formulated his "Treatise" in the context of an ongoing discussion and debate on the issues with Chang. The most important letters dealing directly with the "Treatise" are to be found in *CTTC*, 32.16b-21b.

30. *CTTC*, 32.19a, Letter to Chang Ch'in-fu).

31. *CTTC*, 32.21a.

32. *Analects*, 12:1.

33. *Changes*, Appended Remarks, pt. 2, ch. 1.

34. *Changes*, Hexagram no. 24, *fu* (return).

35. *Yü-lei*, 95.8b-9a.

36. These two phrases are the essence of Chu Hsi's analysis of *jen*. See above, note 5.

37. *I-shu,* 18.2a.

38. *Yü-lei,* 95.9a; this is a continuation of the passage in which he also elaborated Ch'eng Hao's paralysis image (see above, note 31).

39. *CTTC,* 74.19a.

40. Chan, "The Evolution of the Neo-Confucian Concept of *Jen,*" p. 316.

41. The courtesy name of Hsieh Liang-tso (1059–1103) was Hsien-tao, and his honorific name was Shang-ts'ai. He was one of the most distinguished pupils of the Ch'eng brothers.

42. *HLTC,* 35.7b, annotation to text of "Treatise."

43. See *Yü-lei,* 6.16b.

44. See *Yü-lei,* 6.17a.

45. *CTTC,* 32.20a-b, Letter to Chang Ch'in-fu.

46. It is possible that in scanning T'oegye's correspondence some relevant passages may have been missed, but those I have found are as follows: The longest passage (37.11b-13b) discusses *Analects* 6:23, which relates *jen* and wisdom to mountains and water respectively. Two passages (21.22a-b; 35.36b-37a) discuss the substance-function relationship of *jen* and wisdom mentioned by Chu Hsi in his commentary on the Diagram of the Supreme Ultimate." Another passage explains sayings of Ch'eng I that link *jen* to the pulse and to the sight of a baby chick (21.13a-b). There are two passing references to *jen* in terms directly connected with the "Treatise" and "Diagram" (25.36a; 37.26a). One letter explicates a passage in which Ch'eng I discusses commiseration in terms of life or vitality and briefly reaffirms the relationship of consciousness with knowing and wisdom (24.6b-7a); another discusses *jen* and commiseration in the course of considering the transcendent unity of principle and the mind's similar transcending of the distinction of interior and exterior (19.37b-38a).

47. See *Chu sŏ chŏryo* (The Essentials of Chu Hsi's Letters), 3.21a-22a; 28b-29a; 39b-41a (selections from letters to Chang Ch'in-fu [Chang Shih), and 9.11b-12a (Letter to Wu Hui-shu).

48. *TGCS,* A, 24.7a, p. 579, Letter to Chŏng Chajung.

49. See above, note 29.

8. Diagram of the Study of the Mind

1. On the *Classic of the Mind-and-Heart,* see above, Introduction, "T'oegye's Learning."

2. An early Ming dynasty scholar, Ch'eng Min-cheng (1445–1499+), produced the *Hsin-ching fu-chu.* His honorific name was Huang-tun. For a long time T'oegye had no information on his life, but finally became aware of an account which indicated certain flaws in his character, a revelation which was a heavy blow for T'oegye, as he recounts in his postscript to the *Classic* (*Simgyŏng huron,* TGCS, A, 41.12a-13a). Ch'eng's greatly expanded edition adds extensive quotes from Chu Hsi and Ch'eng I dealing with every aspect of mindfulness, making it rather prolix and

repetitious. But T'oegye defended it when some of his pupils suggested that it should be reedited, saying that it already possessed a near classic status and was not to be tampered with (A, 23.30a-b, p. 562, Letter to Cho Sagyŏng).

3. On Ch'eng Fu-hsin, see above, chapter 2, note 32.

4. *Hsin-ching fu-chu,* table of contents, p. 5b.

5. A, 14.36b, p. 378, Letter to Yi Sukhŏn.

6. On the development of the study of the mind-and-heart in the Yüan dynasty, see Wm. Theodore deBary, *Neo-Confucian Orthodoxy and the Learning of the Mind-and-Heart,* pp. 67–185; pp. 73–82 deal particularly with Chen's *Classic of the Mind-and Heart.*

7. This text appears in *Hsin-ching fu-chu,* table of contents, pp. 5a-b.

8. *Mencius,* 4B:12: "The Great Man is he who does not lose his mind of the infant."

9. *Mencius,* 6A:8. After describing how a mountain is deforested not because it is naturally barren but because of the constant violence cutting timber and pasturing animals have done its vegetation, he says: "As for man, how could he but have a mind of humanity and righteousness! The way he loses his naturally good mind is similar to the way the bills and axes [destroyed] the trees."

10. *Book of Documents,* pt. 2, 2.15. See below, Commentary, "The Human Mind and the Mind of the Tao."

11. See above, note 7.

12. *Mencius,* 6A:10.

13. See above, note 10.

14. *Book of Documents,* pt. 2, 2.15, and *Doctrine of the Mean,* ch. 20, respectively.

15. *Doctrine of the Mean,* ch. 1: "There is nothing more visible than what is hidden, nothing more manifest than what is subtle; therefore the superior man is watchful over himself when alone." As for the other items on this side, "overcome and return" is from *Analects,* 12:1: "To overcome oneself and return to propriety constitutes humanity." "The mind is present" refers to *Great Learning,* commentary section, ch. 7: "When the mind is not present, we look but do not see, listen but do not hear, eat, but do not know the taste. This is what is meant by saying that the cultivation of one's person consists of the rectification of one's mind." "Recovering the errant mind," comes from *Mencius,* 6A:11: "How lamentable it is to neglect the path and not pursue it, to lose one's [innately good] mind and not know to seek it! . . . The tao of learning is nothing other than seeking the errant mind, and that is all." "The mind is rectified" refers to the *Great Learning,* ch. 1: "Those who wished to cultivate their persons would first rectify their minds."

16. *Mencius,* 2A:2, in which Mencius says of himself, "At forty my mind was not moved [by high position, power, and the like]."

17. *Mencius,* 3B:2. This is from his description of "the great man."

18. *Doctrine of the Mean,* ch. 1: "The Tao cannot be separated from us for a moment; what can be separated from us is not the Tao. Therefore the superior man is cautious about what he does not see and apprehensive about what he does not

hear." As for the other items on this side, "grasp and preserve" comes from *Mencius*, 6A:8: "Confucius said, "If you grasp it, it will be preserved; if you let it go, it will be lost . . . ' This is the characterization of the mind." "The mind exercises thought" refers to *Mencius*, 6A:15: "The office of the mind is thought. If it exercises thought, it attains [what is proper]; if it does not exercise thought, it does not attain it." "Nurturing the mind" refers to *Mencius*, 7B:35: "To nurture the mind, there is nothing as good as making the desires few." "Exhaustively realized" comes from *Mencius*, 7A:1: "He who has exhaustively realized his mind will know his nature; he who knows his nature knows Heaven. Preserving the mind and nurturing one's nature are the ways to serve Heaven."

19. *Analects*, 2:2, where Confucius says of himself, "At seventy, I could follow the inclinations of my heart and mind without transgressing what was right."

20. *Doctrine of the Mean*, ch. 20; this describes the qualities of a sage.

21. *I-shu*, 15.20a.

22. *I-shu*, 15.6b.

23. A saying of Hsieh Liang-tso, *HLTC*, 46.14b. These three sayings are among the most important early descriptions of mindfulness.

24. See *Great Learning*, ch. 1.

25. This was actually T'oegye's own major reservation about this diagram until he hit upon this solution. See A, 23, 27b-29b, pp. 561–562, Letter to Cho Sagyong.

26. *Mencius*, 6A:11.

27. *Great Learning*, commentary section, ch. 7.

28. *Analects*, 6:7.

29. See *Changes*, Appended Remarks, pt. 2, ch. 4.

30. T'oegye especially praises Ch'eng Fu-hsin for his reluctance to serve a ruler whose proper claim to the throne was questionable (this was a Mongol dynasty), a quality highly emphasized by Korean Neo-Confucians (see Introduction on the "*sarim* mentality"), and also for his devotion to the pursuit of learning during long years of retirement, which T'oegye himself esteemed highly and sought with an urgency that approached almost desperation.

31. On these phrases, see above, notes 8–13.

32. *Book of Documents*, pt. 2, 2.15.

33. The "emptiness" of the mind refers to its being empty of any definite object, including the self (no innate self-centeredness) or any other object; hence it is universal in scope, able to respond to anything appropriately. T'oegye is thus inclined to attribute emptiness particularly to the "principle" aspect of mind in view of the transcendent all-inclusiveness and nonspecificity of principle. "Spirituality" (*yŏng, ling*) has to do with the mysterious, nonphysical mode of the mind's activity, which T'oegye attributes to the purity of subtlety (*yŏng, ling*) of the material force aspect of the mind's constitution. See *Chŏnmyŏng tosŏl*, ch. 6, B, 8.17a-b, p. 143. See also his lengthy defense of this position, especially with reference to relating principle and emptiness, which Ki Taesŭng critized: A, 16.40a-42a, pp. 421–422, Letter to Ki Myŏngŏn.

34. *Hsin-ching fu-chu,* 1.1a-b.

35. Wm. Theodore deBary, *Neo-Confucian Orthodoxy and the Learning of the Mind-and-Heart,* pp. 81–82.

36. A, 23.23b-24a, p. 559, Letter to Cho Sagyŏng.

37. A, 25.19a-b, p. 600, Letter to Chŏng Chajung.

38. From the beginning of the Four-Seven Debate T'oegye saw the distinction between the Four Beginnings and Seven Feelings as paralleling the mind of the Tao and human mind, and one notes a similarity between his careful qualification of the human mind as initially 'correct' and the recognition, forced upon him by Ki Taesŭng's criticism, that the Seven Feelings are originally "nothing but good." (See his comments in chapter 6 on the third diagram.)

39. deBary, *Neo-Confucian Orthodoxy and the Learning of the Mind-and-Heart,* pp. 81–82.

40. A, 14.40b, p. 380, Letter to Yi Sukhŏn.

41. On this development, see deBary, *Neo-Confucian Orthodoxy and the Learning of the Mind-and-Heart,* pp. 78–82. Ki Taesŭng's strong defense of the Seven Feelings in the Four-Seven Debate originated from his opposition to a current tendency in Korea that gave them no connection with man's original nature, a manifestation of a similar sort of excessive rigorism and negativity regarding the place of these feelings. See *Sa chil i ki wangbok sŏ,* 2.18b, in *Kobong chŏnjip,* p. 281.

9. Diagram of the *Admonition for Mindfulness Studio*

1. *OHN,* 1.20b, *TGCS,* B, p. 798.

2. See below, note 9.

3. Reference to *I-shu,* 18.3a.

4. Reference to *I-shu,* 11.2a, a paraphrase of *Odes,* #266.

5. According to Chu Hsi's explanation, *YL,* 105.8a, these are not the familiar small anthills, but hillocks or towers of mud which are found in north China; they are close together, the path between them being like narrow, twisting alleys.

6. *Analects,* 12:2.

7. *Odes,* #195, also quoted in *Analects,* 8:3, and *Classic of Filial Piety,* ch. 3: "Always cautious and fearful, as if overlooking a deep gulf, as if treading on thin ice."

8. *Book of Rites,* ch. 24, On What is Proper in Ancestor Sacrifices (*Li chi cheng-i,* chŭan 47, in *Shih-san ching chu-shu,* p. 1593): "How reverent! How sincere! As if [fearing] not to succeed, as if about to lose it; their filial and reverent dispositions are indeed perfect!"

9. The versions of the *Admonition* found in *Chu Tzu ta-ch'ŭan,* 85.6a, and *Hsing-li ta-ch'ŭan,* 70.24a have *ching* ("discerning, refined") instead of *hsin* ("heart, mind") in this phrase, a reading which would make it a quote of the *Book of Documents,* pt. 2, 2.15; "The human mind is insecure, the mind of the Tao is subtle; be discerning, be undivided. Hold fast the Mean!" The text as it appears in the annotated and

supplemented version of the *Classic of the Mind-and-Heart* (*Hsin-ching fu-chu,* 4.21a) has the reading followed by T'oegye.

10. A paraphrase of *I-shu,* 15.9a.

11. Paraphrasing *Chuang Tzu,* ch. 11, which says of man's mind-and-heart: "Its heat is that of burning fire, its cold that of solid ice," a reference to the feelings of anger and fear, respectively.

12. Ssu-ma Ch'ien's preface to the *Shih chi* (*Shih chi,* chŭan 130): "Miss it by a hair's breadth and it becomes a discrepancy of a thousand *li.*" He ascribes the saying to the *Book of Changes,* but it is no longer to be found there. The saying became a commonplace of which Neo-Confucians were particularly fond. It applies both to dealing with affairs, and even more to the world of the intellect, where it was felt slight inaccuracies might ramify into a serious departure from the true Tao—especially slipping into Buddhism.

13. The "Three Guidelines" are the bonds between ruler and minister, father and son, and husband and wife, the former providing the standard for the latter in each of these relationships. The "Nine Laws" refers to the nine sections of the Grand Plan (Legge, *Book of Documents,* V.4), which constitute a virtual charter for civilization.

14. *YL,* 105.8a, abbreviated.

15. *YL,* 105.8a.

16. *YL,* 105.82.

17. Quoted in *Hsin-ching fu-chu,* 4.21b.

18. Lin-ch'uan was the honorific name of Wu Ch'eng (1249–1333); his courtesy name was Yu-ch'ing, and he is also known by another honorific name, Tsao-lu. He was a leading Yüan dynasty exponent of the Ch'eng-Chu school of thought. An account of him appears in the *Ihak t'ongnok,* 10.8a-11b, *TGCS,* B, pp. 507–509.

19. Quoted in *Hsin-ching fu-chu,* 4.22b.

20. On Chen, see Introduction, note 23.

21. *Hsin-ching fu-chu,* 4.22b.

22. On Chang Shih, see chapter 7, note 29.

23. *Chu-tzu ta-ch'üan,* 85.5b.

24. *YL,* 105.7b.

25. The courtesy name of Wang Po (1197–1274) was Hui-chih, and Lu-chai was his honorific name. He was a leading scholar who studied with He Chi, a disciple of Chu Hsi's son-in-law and chief doctrinal heir, Huang Kan. The doctrine of mindfulness was one of his chief concerns, and this diagram arose through his own attempt to make Chu Hsi's *Admonition* the norm and guide of his daily life. For an account of him, see *Sung-Yüan hsüeh-an,* chüan 75.

26. Paraphrase of *YL,* 12.7b.

27. *Mencius* 6A:11.

28. *Ibid.,* 7A:1.

29. *I-shu,* 15.1a.

30. *Doctrine of the Mean,* ch. 1.

31. *Analects,* 1:4: "Tseng Tzu said: 'Everyday I examine myself on three

points: In acting on behalf of others, have I been loyal; in my intercourse with friends, have I been faithful to my word; regarding [the instruction] that has been passed on to me, have I versed myself in it."

32. *Analects,* 8:4: "With regard to the Tao, the gentleman especially values three things: that in his deportment and manner he keep far from violence and heedlessness; that in regulating his countenance he keep near to good faith; that in his words and tones he keep far from lowness and impropriety."

33. *Analects,* 12:1: "Yen Yüan said: "I beg to ask the items [involved in overcoming oneself and returning to propriety].' The Master said: "Do not look at what is contrary to propriety, do not listen to what is contrary to propriety, do not say what is contrary to propriety, make no movement which is contrary to propriety' "

34. Confucius' two foremost disciples.

35. This is a slightly abridged quote from a letter of Chu Hsi to He Shu-ching which T'oegye cites in his account of He Shu-ching (*Ihak T'ongnok,* 3.7a, *TGCS,* B, p. 311). However the passage does not appear in any of Chu Hsi's 32 letters to He which appear in *Chu Tzu ta-ch'üan,* chüan 40, nor is it included in T'oegye's abridged edition of Chu Hsi's letters, the *Chusŏ chŏryo.*

36. *I-shu,* 15.6b.

37. *I-shu,* 15.6b.

38. *I-shu,* 15.1a.

39. A saying of Ch'eng I's disciple, Yin T'un. On Yin, see above, chapter 4, number 8.

40. This is Hsieh Liang-tso's expression of what constitutes mindfulness. See *HLTC,* 46.14b. On Hsieh, see above, chapter 7, number 41.

41. *Mencius* 2A:2.

42. On Yi Tŏkhong, see above, chapter 3, nunber 22.

43. On these sayings, see above, numbers 40 and 39 respectively.

44. *Mencius,* 2A:2.

45. Ch'eng I's description, *I-shu,* 15.6b.

46. Paraphrase of *Doctrine of the Mean,* ch. 1.

47. Reference to *Mencius,* 6A:11.

48. See above, notes 40, 39, 38 respectively.

49. The original letter from Yi I appears in *Yulgok chŏnsŏ* (The Complete Works of Yi I), 9.2b-3a. I have not been able to locate the original source of either of these quotations. According to the annotation in *T'oegye munjip koch'ung,* 4.30b (*TGCS,* B, p. 1141) the "Mister Fang" referred to is Fang Feng-ch'en (fl. c. 1250), a Sung dynasty scholar. His courtesy name was Chün-hsi, and his honorific name was Chiao-feng.

50. *Odes,* #288.

51. *Odes,* #272.

52. *Mencius,* 7A:1.

53. *Hsin-ching fu-chu,* 1.4b; the passages quote *Odes* #236 and #300 respectively.

54. *Hsin-ching fu-chu,* 1.5a. T'oegye (Reply to Cho Sagyŏng, A, 23.31b-

32a, p. 563) notes that there is some doubt about the ascription of this passage to Chu Hsi, since it cannot be found in his commentary on the *Odes,* but he nonetheless feels it is possible the passage comes from somewhere else in Chu's works and is not inclined to ascribe it to the pen of Chen Te-hsiu.

55. Reply to Kim Tonsŏ, A, 28.22b, p. 662.

10. Diagram of the *Admonition on "Rising Early and Retiring Late"*

1. The title is a reference to a passage in *Book of Odes,* #256. The author of the *Admonition* is Ch'en Po, a Sung dynasty scholar. His courtesy name was Mao-ch'ing and his honorific name was Nan-t'ang. There is no mention of him in the *Sung-Yüan hsüeh-an* or other standard biographical sources.

2. A, 10.14a, p. 288, Letter to No Susin.

3. Yen Hui and Tseng Tzu were two of Confucius' foremost disciples.

4. Ref. to *Mencius,* 6A:8, which describes how the atmosphere of the night tends to restore human nature to its proper condition and repair the violence done to it during the day.

5. *Changes;* the *Ch'ien* (Heaven) hexagram mentions four characteristics of Heaven. These were commonly matched with the four seasons, with steadfastness and origination belonging to winter and spring, respectively.

6. See above, number 1.

7. See chapter 9, number 25.

8. *Doctrine of the Mean,* ch. 1.

9. *Ibid.*, ch. 1.

10. Reference to the final passages of Chu Hsi's *Admonition for Mindfulness Studio,* which appears above, chapter 9.

11. Mencius, 6A:15.

12. *Ibid.*, 2A:2.

13. *Ibid.*, 2A:2.

14. *Analects,* 9:11. In admiration on Confucius' teaching, Yen Hui says, "The more I try to bore into it, the harder it becomes."

15. *Ibid.*, 1:8.

Glossary

An Hyang 安珦
Chan Wing-tsit, Chen Jung-chieh 陳榮捷
Chang Chiu-ling 張九齡
Chang Shih, Ch'in-fu, Ching-fu, Nan-hsien 張栻, 欽夫, 敬夫, 南軒
Chang Tsai, Heng-ch'ü 張載, 橫渠
Chang Tzu ch'üan shu 張子全書
Chasŏngnok 自省錄
Ch'e-hsüeh yü wen-hua 哲學與文化
Ch'en Ch'un 陳淳
Ch'en Hsien-chang, Po-sha 陳獻章, 白沙
Ch'en Po, Mao-ch'ing, Nan-t'ang 陳柏, 茂卿, 南塘
Chen Te-hsiu 眞德秀
Ch'eng-Chu 程朱
Ch'eng Fu-hsin, Tzu-hsien, Lin-yin 程復心, 子見, 林隱
Ch'eng Hao, Ming-tao 程顥, 明道
Ch'eng I, I-ch'uan 程頤, 伊川
Cheng meng 正蒙
Ch'eng Min-cheng 程敏政
Ch'eng Tzu-shang 程子上
Chi Lien-hsi ch'uan 記濂溪傳
Chia-li 家禮
Ch'ien 乾
Ch'ien Han shu 前漢書
chih (know) 知
chih (wisdom) 智
chil, chih 質
Ch'in (dynasty) 秦

Chin-hua 金華
Chin-ssu lu 近思錄
chipdaesŏngja 集大成子
Cho Kibaek 趙起伯
Cho Kwangjo 趙光祖
Cho Sik, Kŏnjung, Nammyŏng 曹植, 楗仲, 南冥
Cho Sagyŏng 趙士敬
Chosŏn Yuhak sa 朝鮮儒學史
Chou (dynasty) 周
Chou li 周禮
Chou-i pen-i 周易本義
Chou Tun-i, Lien-hsi 周敦頤, 濂溪
Chŏn Tuha 全斗河
Chŏng Chiun 鄭之雲
chŏngjwa, ching tso 靜坐
Chŏng Mongju, Talga, P'oŭn 鄭夢周, 達可, 圃隱
Chŏng Sasŏng 鄭士誠
Chŏng Tojŏn, Chongji, Sambong 鄭道傳, 宗之, 三峰
Chŏng Yuil, Chajung, Munbong 鄭惟一, 子中, 文峯
Ch'ŏnmyŏng to 天命圖
Ch'ŏnmyŏng tosŏl 天命圖說
Chŏnsŭmnok nonbyŏn 傳習錄論辯
Ch'u (state) 楚
Chu Hsi 朱熹
Chu Sebong, Kyŏngyu, Sinjae 周世鵬, 景游, 愼齋
Chu sŏ chŏryo 朱書節要
Chu Tzu yü-lei 朱子語類
Ch'uan-hsi lu 傳習錄
Chuang (duke) 莊
Chuang Tzu 莊子
Chung-yung chang-chü 中庸章句
Erh Ch'eng ch'üan-shu 二程全書
Fang Feng-ch'en, Chun-hsi, Chiao-feng 方逢辰, 君錫, 蛟峯
Feng Yu-lan 馮友蘭
fu 復
Fu Hsi 伏羲
Hakbong chip 鶴峯集
Han (dynasty) 漢
hao-jan chih ch'i 浩然之氣

he 訶
He Chi 何基
He Shu-ching 何叔京
hobal, hu-fa 互發
Hongmungwan 弘文館
hŏ, hsü 虛
Hsiang-chün po-shih 鄉郡博士
Hsiao-hsüeh 小學
Hsiao-hsüeh t'i-tzu 小學題辭
Hsieh Liang-tso, Hsien-tao, Shang-ts'ai 謝良佐, 顯道, 上蔡
Hsien (duke) 獻
Hsin-an 新安
hsin-hsüeh 心學
Hsing-li ta-ch'üan 性理大全
Huang Kan, Mien-tsai 黃幹, 勉齋
Hwadamjip 花潭集
Hwang Chunggŏ 黃仲擧
hyangyak, hsiang-yüeh 鄉約
Hyŏn Sangyun 玄相允
i, li 理
Ihak t'ongnok 理學通錄
I-hsüeh ch'i-meng 易學啓蒙
Injong 仁宗
Iphak tosŏl 入學圖說
Isan sŏwŏn 伊山書院
Isan wŏngyu 伊山院規
jen 仁
Jen-shuo 仁說
Jen Tsung 仁宗
Kan kwae sanggu kangŭi 乾卦上九講義
kang 綱
ki, ch'i (material force) 氣
ki, chi 幾
Kija, Chi Tzu 箕子
Ki Taesŭng, Myŏngŏn, Kobong 奇大升, 明彥, 高峰
Kim Allo 金安老
Kim Ch'wiryo, Ijŏng, Chamjae 金就礪, 而精, 潛齋
Kim Koengp'il 金宏弼
Kim Kuyong 金九容

Kim Sŏngil, Sasun, Hakbong 金誠一, 士純, 鶴峯
Kim Su, Cha'ang, Mongch'on 金晬, 子昂, 夢村
Kim Tonsŏ 金惇叙
ko wu 格物
Kobong chŏnsŏ 高峰全書
Kongmin 恭愍
Koryŏ 高麗
K'uang-lu 匡盧
K'un 坤
Kung Ying-ta 孔穎達
Kuo-hsiang 國庠
Kuo-yü 國語
kwanhakp'a 官學派
kwŏn, chüan 卷
Kwŏn Kŭn, Kawŏn, Yangch'on 權近, 可遠, 陽村
Kyemong chŏnŭi 啓蒙傳疑
kyŏng, ching 敬
Kyŏngsang 慶尙
kyŏngyŏn 經筵
Lao Tzu 老子
li (principle) 理
Li chi cheng-i 禮記正義
Li Po 李渤
Li Ssu 李斯
Li Te-yü 李德裕
Li T'ung, Yen-p'ing 李侗, 延平
Liu Ch'ing-chih 劉淸之
Lo Ch'in-shun 羅欽順
Lu Chiu-yüan, Hsiang-shan 陸九淵, 象山
Lu-Wang 陸王
Lun Chu Tzu chih jen-shuo 論朱子之仁說
Lun-yü chi-chu 論語集註
Lü Ta-chün 呂大鈞
Lü Tzu-ch'ien 呂祖謙
Meng Tzu chi-chu 孟子集註
Ming (dynasty) 明
Mo Tzu 墨子
Mujin kyŏngyŏn kangŭi kyech'a 戊辰經筵講義啓箚
myŏng, ming 命

Myŏngjong 明宗
naejip 內集
Nan-k'ang 南康
No Susin 盧守愼
Ŏnhaengnok 言行錄
Paegundong sŏwŏn 白雲洞書院
Paek Ijŏng 白頤正
Paeksa sigyo chŏnsŭmnok ch'ojŏn insŏ kihu 白沙詩教傳習錄抄傳因書其後
Pak Sangch'ung 朴尚衷
Pak Sun 朴淳
Pak Yŏng, Chasil, Songdang 朴英, 子實, 松堂
pal, fa 發
P'anjungch'ubusa 判中樞府事
Pi i ki wi il mul pyŏnjŭng 非理氣爲一物辯證
Pin-feng ch'i-yüeh t'u 豳風七月圖
Po Ch'i 伯奇
ponyŏn, pen-jan 本然
ponyu, pen-yu 本有
pu-jen 不仁
P'ulssi chappyŏn 佛氏雜辨
P'unggi 豐基
pyŏljip 別集
sa 私
Sa ch'il i ki wangbok sŏ 四七理氣往復書
saeng, sheng 生
Saganwŏn 司諫院
Sahŏnbu 司憲府
sarim 士林
Shang-ts'ai 上蔡
Shen-sheng 申生
Shih-chi 史記
Shih-san ching chu-shu 十三經註疏
Shun 舜
Shuo yüan 說苑
Sillok 實錄
Sim ki i p'yŏn 心氣理篇
Sim mu ch'e yong pyŏn 心無體用辯
Sim Pangbaek 沈方伯
simbŏp, hsin-fa 心法

Simgyŏng, hsin-ching 心經
Simgyŏng, huron 心經後論
so chu 所主
sokjip 續集
Songdang chip 松堂集
Songgye Wŏn Myŏng ihak t'ongnok 宋季元明理學通錄
Sŏng Hon, Howŏn, Ugye 成渾, 浩原, 牛溪
Sŏ Kyŏngdŏk, Kagu, Hwadam 徐敬德, 可久, 花潭
Sŏmyŏng kojŭng kangŭi 西銘考證講義
Sŏnghak sipto 聖學十圖
Sŏnggyun'gwan 成均館
Sŏnjo 宣祖
sŏwŏn, shu-yüan 書院
Ssu-shu chang t'u 四書章圖
Ssu-shu wu-ching ta ch'üan 四書五經大全
Ssu-ma Ch'ien 司馬遷
Sukjong 肅宗
Sung (dynasty) 宋
Sung Ching 宋璟
Sung Yüan hsüeh-an 宋元學案
Ta-hsüeh 大學
Ta-hsüeh chang-chü 大學章句
Ta-hsüeh huo-wen 大學或問
Ta Tai li chi 大載禮記
T'ai-chi-t'u 太極圖
T'ai-chi-t'u shuo 太極圖說
T'ai-chou 台州
T'ai Tsung 太宗
Tan-i liu-chen 丹扆六箴
T'an kung 檀弓
T'ang (dynasty) 唐
Tanyang 丹陽
tao wen-hsüeh 道問學
T'ao Yüan-ming 陶淵明
te 德
T'ien-ch'iu chin-chien lu 千秋金鑑錄
Ting-wan 訂頑
T'oegye 退溪
T'oegye chŏnsŏ 退溪全書

T'oegye hakbo 退溪學報
T'oegye sŏnsaeng munjip kojŭng 退溪先生文集考證
T'oegye sŏnsaeng ŏnhaengnok 退溪先生言行錄
T'oegye sŏnsaeng ŏnhaeng t'ongnok 退溪先生言行通錄
T'oegyeŭi ch'ŏrhagŭi haeksim 退溪의哲學의核心
T'ogye 兎溪
tohak, tao-hsüeh 道學
t'ong, t'ung 統
Tosan 陶山
Tosan munhyŏn nok 陶山門賢錄
Tseng Tzu, T'san 曾子, 參
Tso-chuan 左傳
T'sui-yen 粹言
tsun te-hsing 尊德性
Tu Wei-ming 杜維明
T'ung-shu 通書
Tzu Ssu 子思
U Kyŏngsŏn 禹景善
waejip 外集
Wang Po, Hui-chih, Lu-chai 王柏, 會之, 魯齋
Wang Shou-jen, Yang-ming 王守仁
wei 謂
Wen 文
Wu 武
Wu Ch'eng, Tsao-lu, Lin-ch'uan 吳澄, 草廬, 臨川
Wu Huei-shu 吳晦叔
Wu-i t'u 無逸圖
wu ko 物格
Wu-wang chien tsu 武王踐阼
Yamasaki Ansai 山崎闇齋
yang 陽
Yang Shih, Kuei-shan 楊時, 龜山
yangban 兩班
Yao 堯
Yao Lu, Shuang-feng 饒魯, 雙峯
Yeh T'sai, Ping-yen 葉采, 平巖
Yen-p'ing ta wen 延平答問
Yen Yüan, Hui 顔淵, 回
Yi (dynasty) 李

Yi Ch'unhŭi 李春熙
Yi Hae 李瀣
Yi Hwang, T'oegye 李滉, 退溪
Yi I, Yulgok 李珥, 栗谷
Yi Kongho 李公浩
Yi P'yŏngsuk 李平叔
Yi Saek, Yŏngsuk, Mogŭn 李穡, 穎叔, 牧隱
Yi Sŏnggye 李成桂
Yi Sukhon 李叔獻
Yi Sungin 李崇仁
Yi T'aejo 李太祖
Yi Tŏkhong, Koengjung, Kanjae 李德弘, 宏仲, 艮齋
Yi U 李堣
Yi Yonggyo 李寗寙
Yijo sŏwŏn munch'ang ko 李朝書院文庫考
yin 陰
Yin T'un 尹焞
Ying Kao-su 穎考叔
yŏnbo, nien-fu 年譜
yŏng, ling 靈
Yŏngjo 英祖
Yŏnsan'gun 燕山君
Yun Pyŏngt'ae 尹炳泰
Yun Sasun 尹絲淳
Yun Wŏnhyŏng 尹元衡
Yü 禹
Yu Towŏn 柳道源
Yüan (dynasty) 元
yüan, heng, li, chen 元, 亨, 利, 貞

Selected Bibliography

Chan, Wing-tsit. "Chu Hsi's Completion of Neo-Confucianism." *Études Song: In Memoriam Étienne Balazas,* Francoise Aubin, ed. Ser. II, no. 1, 1973, pp. 59–90.

——"The Evolution of the Neo-Confucian Concept of *Jen.*" *Philosophy East and West* (1955), no. 4, pp. 295–319.

——(Chen Jung-chieh). "Lün Chu-tzu chih jen-shuo." *Ch'e-hsüeh yü wen-hua* (Eng. title: *Universitas: Monthly Review of Philosophy and Culture*) (June 1981), 8(b): 383–396.

——*A Source Book in Chinese Philosophy.* Princeton: Princeton University Press, 1963.

Chang Tsai. *Chang Tzu ch'üan-shu* (The Complete Works of Chang Tsai), Ssu-pu pei-yao ed.

——*Cheng meng* (Correct Discipline for Beginners). In *Hsing-li ta-ch'üan.*

——*Hsi-ming* (The Western Inscription). In *Hsing-li ta-ch'üan.*

Chen Te-hsiu. *Hsin ching* (Classic of the Mind-and-Heart), *see* Ch'eng Min-cheng, *Hsin ching fu-chu.*

Ch'eng Hao and Ch'eng I. *Erh Ch'eng ch'üan-shu* (The Complete Works of the Two Ch'engs). Ssu-pu pei-yao ed.

——*I-shu* (Surviving Works). In the *Erh Ch'eng ch'üan-shu.*

——*Ts'ui-yen* (Pure Words). In the *Erh Ch'eng ch'üan-shu.*

——*Wai-shu* (Additional Works). In the *Erh Ch'eng ch'üan-shu.*

Ch'eng I. *I-ch'üan wen-chi* (The Collected Literary Works of Ch'eng I). In the *Erh Ch'eng ch'üan-shu.*

Ch'eng Min-cheng. *Hsin ching fu-chu* (Supplemented and Annotated *Classic of the Mind-and-Heart).* 1794 Korean ed.

Ch'ien Mu. "Chu Tzu hsüeh liu-yen Han-kuo kao" (An Examination of the Spread of Chu Hsi Study to Korea). Chinese text with Korean tr. by Yi Sangŭn, *T'oegye hakbo* (1975), no. 5.6, pp. 44–45.

Chŏn Tuha. *T'oegye sasang yŏn'gu* (Research on T'oegye's thought). Seoul: Tonga Ch'ulp'ansa, 1974.

——"T'oegyeŭi ch'ŏrhagŭi haeksim" (The Heart of T'oegye's Philosophy). *T'oegye hakbo* (1978), no. 19, pp. 135–170.

——"Yi T'oegeyŭi chonyang sŏngch'allon" (Yi T'oegye's theory of possessing and nurturing [the mind] and exercising reflection and discrimination). *T'oegye hakbo* (1979), no. 22, pp. 15–25.

Chou Tun-i. *T'ai chi t'u* (Diagram of the Supreme Ultimate). In *Hsing-li ta-ch'üan.*

——*T'ai chi t'u shuo* (Explanation of the Diagram of the Supreme Ultimate). In *Hsing-li ta-ch'üan.*

——*T'ung-shu* (Explanatory Text on the *Book of Changes*). In *Hsing-li ta-ch'üan.*

Chu Hsi. *Chu Tzu ta-ch'üan* (The Complete Works of Master Chu). Taiwan: Chung-hua Shu-chü, 1970. Photo reprint of Ssu-pu pei-yao ed.

——*Chu Tzu yü-lei* (Classified Conversations of Master Chu), comp. by Li Ching-te. Taiwan: Cheng-chung Shu-chü, 1962. Photo reprint of 1473 ed.

——*Chung-yung chang-chü* (Commentary on the *Doctrine of the Mean*). In *Ssu-shu wu-ching.*

——*Chung-yung huo-wen* (Questions and Answers on the *Doctrine of the Mean*). Seoul: Kyŏngmunsa, 1977. Photo reprint, n.d.

——*Meng Tzu chi-chu* (Commentary on the *Mencius*). In *Ssu-shu wu ching.*

——*Ta hsüeh chang-chü* (Commentary on the *Great Learning*). In *Ssu-shu wu-ching.*

——*Ta hsüeh huo-wen* (Questions and Answers on the *Great Learning*). Seoul: Kyŏngmunsa, 1977. Photo reprint, n.d.

Chu Hsi, comp. *Yen-p'ing ta-wen* (Li T'ung's Answers to Chu Hsi's Questions). In *Ilbon kakp'an Yi T'oegye chŏnjip* (Japanese edition of the works of Yi T'oegye).

Chu Hsi and Lü Tsu-ch'ien, comp. *Reflections on Things at Hand* (*Chin ssu lu*), tr. and annotated by Wing-tsit Chan. New York and London: Columbia University Press, 1967.

DeBary, Wm. Theodore. *Neo-Confucian Orthodoxy and the Learning of the Mind-and-Heart.* New York: Columbia University Press, 1981.

Deuchler, Martina. "Neo-Confucianism: The Impulse for Social Action in Early Yi Korea." *Journal of Korean Studies* (1980), 2:71–111.

Feng Yu-lan. *A History of Chinese Philosophy,* tr. by Derk Bodde. 2 vols. Princeton: Princeton University Press, 1952 and 1953.

Hu Kuang et al. *Hsing-li ta-ch'üan* (The Great Compendium of Neo-Confucianism). Seoul: Kwangsŏng Munhwasa, 1975. Photo reprint, n.d. on ed.

Hyŏn Sangyun. *Chosŏn yuhak sa* (History of Korean Confucianism). Seoul: Minjung Sŏgwan, 1948.

I-shu, see under Ch'eng Hao and Ch'eng I.

Ki Taesŭng, *Kobong chŏnsŏ.*

Kung Ying-ta. *Li-chi cheng-i* (Commentary on the *Book of Rites*). Contained in *Shih-san ching chu-shu.*

Kwŏn Kŭn. *Iphak tosŏl* (Diagrammatic Explanations for Beginning Study), tr. by Kwŏn Tŏkju. Seoul: Ŭlyu Munhwasa, 1974.

Legge, James. *The Chinese Classics.* 5 vols. Taiwan: Chin Hsüeh Shu-chü, 1958. Photo reprint of Oxford University Press ed.

Pae Chongho. *Hanguk yuhak sa* (History of Korean Confucianism). Seoul: Yŏnse Taehakkyo Ch'ulp'anbu, 1974.

Pak Chonghŭng et al., eds. *T'oegyehak yŏn'gu* (Research in T'oegye Studies). Seoul: Seoul Taehakkyo Ch'ulp'anbu, 1972.

Shih-san ching chu-shu (The Thirteen Classics with Notes and Commentary). Shanghai: Shih-chieh Shu-chü, 1935. Photolithographic reprint of 1815 ed.

Ssu shu wu ching (The Four Books and Five Classics). Shanghai: Shih-chieh Shu-chü, 1936.

Sung-Yüan hsüeh-an (Anthology and Critical Accounts of Neo-Confucians of the Sung and Yüan dynasty), comp. by Huang Tsung-hsi et al., re-ed. by Ch'en Shu-ching and Li Hsin-chuang. Taiwan: Cheng-chung Shu-chü, 1963.

T'sui Yen, see under Ch'eng Hao and Ch'eng I.

Tu Wei-ming, "T'oegye's Creative Interpretation of Chu Hsi's Philosophy of Principle." *T'oegye hakbo* (1982), no. 35, pp. 35–37.

Wagner, Edward W. *The Literati Purges: Political Conflict in Early Yi Korea.* Cambridge: East Asian Research Center, Harvard University, 1974.

Wai-shu, see under Ch'eng Hao and Ch'eng I.

Wang Yang-ming. *Instructions for Practical Living* (Ch'uan-hsi lu), tr. by Wing-tsit Chan. New York: Columbia University Press, 1963.

Yi Ch'unhŭi. *Yijo sŏwŏn munch'ang ko* (Investigation of the Library Collections of Yi Dynasty Private Academies). Seoul: Taehanmin'guk Kukhoe Tosŏgwan, 1969.

Yi Hwang. *Chu sŏ chŏryo* (The Essentials of Chu Hsi's Letters). In *Ilbon kakp'an Yi T'oegye chŏnjip* (Japanese edition of the works of Yi T'oegye), comp. by Abe Yoshio. 2 vols. Seoul: Taeil Chongp'ansa, 1975.

——*Kugyŏk T'oegye chip* (Collected Works of T'oegye in Korean Translation), comp. and tr. by Kim Yun'gyŏng et al. 2 vols. Seoul: Minjok munhwa ch'ujin Hoe, 1968.

——*T'oegye chŏnsŏ* (The Complete Works of Yi Hwang). 2 vols. Seoul: Sŏnggyun'gwan Taehakkyo Taedong Munhwa Yŏn'guwŏn, 1958. Photo reprint.

Yi I. *Yulgok chŏnsŏ* (The Complete Works of Yi I). Seoul: Sŏnggyun'gwan Taehakkyo Taedong Munhwa Yŏn'guwŏn, 1958. Photo reprint.

Yi Sangŭn. *T'oegyeŭi saengaewa hangmun* (T'eogye's Life and Learning). Seoul: Seomoon Moongo, 1973.

Yi Wŏnjae. "I ki obal sŏrŭi yuga chŏnt'ong sasangjŏk somyŏng" (A Clarification of the Mutual Issuance Theory of Principle and Material Force in the Light of Traditional Confucian Thought). *T'oegye hakbo* (1978), no. 19, pp. 191–199.

Yi Sŭngguk. "T'oegye ch'ŏrhakŭi kŭnbon munje" (The Fundamental Problem in T'oegye's Philosophy). *T'oegye hakbo* (1978), no. 19, pp. 51–58.

Yu Towŏn. *T'oegye sŏnsaeng munjip kojung* (Annotations on T'oegye's Collected Works). In *T'oegye chŏnsŏ.*

Yun Pyŏngt'ae. "Simgyŏng puju yuhuron ponŭi kanbon" (The Publication of Editions of the *Hsin ching fu-chu* with T'oegye Epilogue). *T'oegyehak yŏn'gu* (December 1979), no. 6, pp. 83–113.

——"T'oegye sŏjiŭi yŏn'gu" (Bibliographic Research on T'oegye). *Han'gugŭi ch'ŏrhak* (March 1977), no. 5, pp. 87–152.

——"T'oegyewa Simgyŏng puju" (T'oegye and the *Hsin-ching fu-chu*). *Han'gugŭi ch'ŏrhak* (December 1979), no. 8 pp. 67–81.

Yun Sasun. *Han'guk yuhak non'gu* (Studies in Korean Confucianism). Seoul: Hyŏnam Sa, 1980.

——*T'oegyeŭi ch'ŏrhak yŏn'gu* (Research on T'oegye's Philosophy). Seoul: Koryŏ Taehakyo Ch'ulp'ansa, 1980.

Index